2006

BETWEEN THE LINES

A Boy's Survival in the Combat Zone: 1939 - 1945

Walter Beller

*To Peter
with warm wishes
W. H. Beller*

Bardolf & Company   Sarasota   2006

Published by Bardolf & Company

Between the Lines

Catalog-in-Publication Data is on file with the Library of Congress
ISBN 0-9778199-0-6

For information, write

Bardolf & Company
5430 Colewood Pl
Sarasota, FL 34232
941-232-0113

Printed in the United States of America.

Cover Design by Shaw Creative
Maps by Dawn M. Klee

To my wife Cheryl
and
my daughter Bettina

for their constant support
and encouragement

Contents

Picture pages 145-152

MAPS

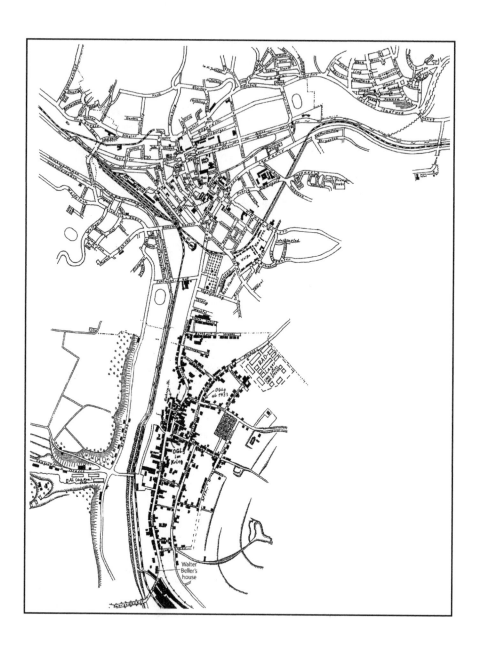

The southern part of Zweibruecken and the suburb of Ixheim. Walter Beller's house is at the bottom with his father's factory, the nailworks, below

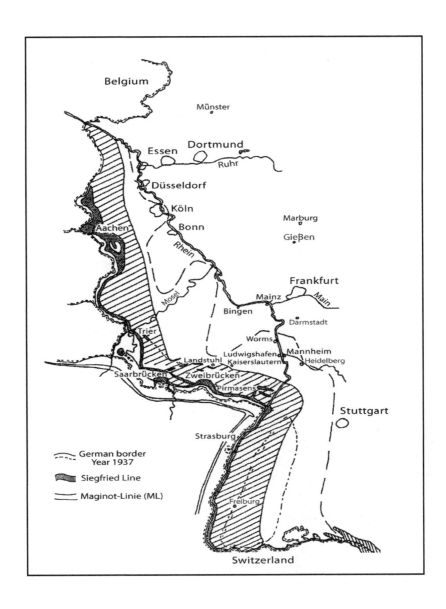

The western border of Germany prior to World War II
with Siegfried and Maginot Lines

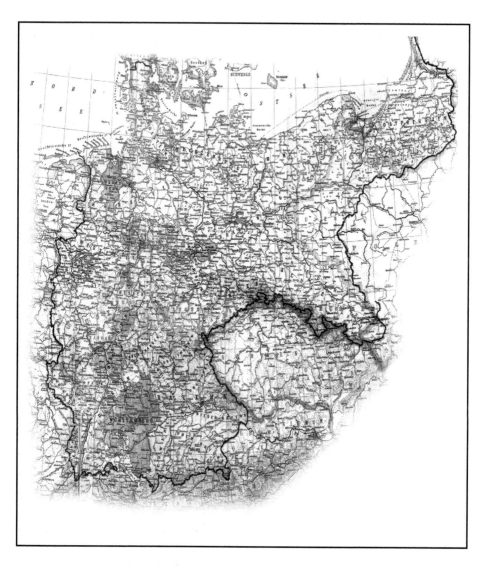

German borders prior to World War I

Germany today, since reunification

Introduction

If you look for an explanation of how World War II started, you will notice many versions, but two are of particular interest to me. One is well documented in the history books and social consciousness of my adopted country, the United States of America. The other, less well known, represents the experience of Germans who, like me, lived through these difficult times. Indeed, it is the latter version that profoundly affected my formative years, and in all honesty, informs most of the decisions I make today.

It is commonly held by the German people, especially those in eastern portions of the country, that Germany was forced to sign the Treaty of Versailles to end World War I in 1919, and in doing so, to forfeit territory in the east to Poland. At the time, it would have been impossible to reject the treaty due to the widespread poverty and helplessness of the German people. Sadly, nothing improved in the years immediately following the treaty. Famine spread throughout Europe, and inflation and unemployment made difficult living conditions downright harsh. In retrospect, those conditions laid the foundation for the National Socialist Party's rise to power and the emergence of its now notorious leader, Adolf Hitler.

School children studying World War II often question Hitler's popularity. Why did so many Germans accept and elect Hitler and his party? The answer to this question is complex, but from the German perspective, Poland and poverty were primarily to blame.

Bickering over the terms of the Treaty of Versailles had continued among members of the League of Nations (in German, *Völkerbund*), founded in 1919 under the leadership of the U.S. president, Woodrow Wilson. At issue were land treaties between Germany and Poland. Citing stubbornness on the part of members England and France, Germany resigned from the organization in protest in October 1933. By 1935, Hitler and the Nazi party had reinstated the German draft, and shortly thereafter undertook massive defense construction projects to restore Germany's infrastructure and rebuild its military capability. After annexing Austria, despite efforts by British Prime Minister Neville Chamberlain to negotiate a peaceful resolution to the dispute, Hitler ultimately ordered the invasion of Poland and World War II began.

There is no doubt that the buildup of German defenses threatened the rest of the world. But to the citizens of Germany, it was the light at the end of what had been a long and impassable tunnel. Increased military activity, coupled with the construction of roads, factories, dams and eventually lines of defense, meant jobs to a nation of people who had survived many years of hunger, recession, and unwanted foreign occupation. Unemployment statistics from my hometown of Zweibruecken, for example, may prove instructive. In January 1939, Zweibruecken's Bureau of Unemployment registered only nine unemployed people in a city of 30,000 inhabitants. By then, Germany's economy had rebounded and many of its citizens were even vacationing again. So jealous of this development was England that it closed its ports to German cruise ships. How could England explain German workers taking vacations when its own workers could not?

Before you put down this book in protest or disbelief, assuming that it contains pro-war rhetoric sprinkled with modern-day Nazi sympathy, please be advised that you are about to experience nothing of the sort. Atrocities committed at the hands of the Nazi party and in the name of Germany during World War II were unforgivable. But it is important to note that while millions of innocent Jewish people suffered and died at the hands of the Nazi regime, Germans were either tricked or intimidated into believing – or pretended to believe – that the prosperity Germany had achieved in the years leading up to the war would continue if they resisted the Allies. In effect, German citizens were victimized by their own regime, and war casualties would ultimately reach ten percent of the population.

The story that follows, though, originally was not intended to offer a fresh perspective on World War II. I was born in the beautiful and historic town of Zweibruecken, nestled on the west side of the Rhine River valley in the part of Germany know as *die Rheinpfalz*, or the Palatinate. The area, a buffer zone against France, was sandwiched between two powerful defensive systems, the Maginot and Siegfried Lines. In essence, my hometown, my family and I were trapped between two enemies and their extensive military fortifications, trapped "between the lines." During the Second World War, that area became a bloody battlefield, where fierce political and military combatants fought without concern for the local inhabitants. The oppression of the German people by the Nazi megalomaniacs on the one hand, and the unrelenting allied bombardments on the other, exposed me at an early age to things unfit for any human eyes, much less those of an innocent but insightful child. In retrospect and given the circumstances, my survival is extraordinary. At the time, though, I was just trying to find my way in the world.

PART I

1

Before the War: My Peaceful Life

Bedded in the foothills of two scenic and beautiful valleys, one leading westerly and the other southwesterly to France, was the suburb of Ixheim and my father's factory. This area of manufacturing plants, offices and company housing on the outskirts of the city of Zweibruecken was known to everyone as *am Nagelwerk* (by the nailworks), so named because of the most important factory in the area. Originally a flour mill in the mid-1750s, the plant had served for many years as a mill to grind large animal bones into meal for Duke Karl August's 100 dogs. By the mid 1800s, it had been converted into a nail factory, and in wartime it produced chains and barbed wire.

There could not have been a more exciting place for a boy to grow up.

Before the war, everybody in my family was living at home, and we had a very nice but regulated family life. We played games in the evening and listened to plays on the radio. There was no television, which was probably very good for family togetherness. Everybody had to be at the dinner table on time, and only after my father finished eating and got up were we boys permitted to excuse ourselves from the table. My brother Emil normally helped my mother with the dishes. Since I was twelve years younger than the last of my three brothers, every one of them played a mothering role in my life. Edi, for example, cut my hair until I was nine years old. I hated it. Emil watched very carefully when I entered the house for dinner after playing outside. I could not just quickly wash my hands. Every single finger had to be washed with soap and water, then dried carefully to prevent the development of cracks in the skin. Albert and Emil watched my homework and grades, and they practiced reading and writing with me. My brothers always wore jackets and ties when leaving the house. Most of the time they wore bow ties.I was very close to my mother, but I admired my father in everything he did, and I liked everything he liked. He told me of a month during his World War I military service when he had eaten barley almost every day. As a result, he had lost his taste for barley, and therefore I disliked it, too. My mother cooked fresh meals every day. My favorite meal was potato pancakes with applesauce. Meat or sausage was served only twice a week, and my father was always given the first and largest piece. I enjoyed eating meats and sausages, but preferred fresh vegetables, potatoes and homemade noodles. Nearly every Sunday we had homemade cake for breakfast and at the 4 p.m.. coffee hour.

My father came from a very religious Catholic family in Bavaria. He told us his mother went to church at 6 o'clock every morning in the spring, summer and fall, after she cut grass for the animals. But superstition was also common in Bavaria, and my father said that on stormy days his mother fed the wind with flour to keep away harm. Since my father married a Lutheran, he had to promise his parents to have all his children baptized Catholic. To marry a protestant was a sin at this time for Bavarian Catholics. I, like all my brothers, was baptized as a Catholic, participated in First Communion, and was confirmed as a Catholic. Most Sundays, I went to church with my father. My mother went to her church, although less frequently. To my father's dismay, I acted as an altar boy only a few times. I did not like it.

The one-story, three-bedroom house in which my middle-class family resided was company-owned, and living there was part of my father's employment contract. It was located just 300 yards east of the factory. During the night shift, the nail-making machines were astoundingly loud. Surprisingly, the noise didn't bother any-one in our house; it was only when the machines stopped during the night that we woke up.

Our house was built of huge sandstone walls with a cellar on the right side. The family's gathering spot was the large kitchen, in the middle of which sat a sizeable, solid-oak oval dining table with two chairs on each side and one at each end. My father took his place at the head of the table, while my mother and brothers occupied the chairs on either side and I sat opposite my father. My parents used the wood- and coal-fired stove in the kitchen for both cooking and heating. My father would start the stove very early in the morning, so that when my mother, my three brothers and I got up, the kitchen was already cozy. My brothers and I dutifully brought wood or coal into the house each day for this purpose.

The only other source of heat in the house was a small heating oven in the living room. Since we were only permitted in the living room on Sundays, for birthdays or for special family gatherings, that heater saw much less action than its larger counterpart in the kitchen. The rooms of the house had ten-foot-high ceilings, and the windows were tall but relatively narrow. In the bedrooms there were no heaters at all, so they were very cold in winter. To make sleeping more comfortable in winter, we covered ourselves with thick blankets, on top of which were placed 10-inch thick comforters filled with down. Mother warmed bricks in the kitchen stove, wrapped them in fabric, and placed them in our beds about 30 minutes before bedtime. As we crawled into bed, the bricks were moved to the foot of the bed, where they stayed warm late into the night. Occasionally, they would still be lukewarm in the morning.

My bedroom had a second door to the living room. Until I was 10 years old, I had to go to bed before 10 p.m. Quite often, when my relatives – especially my uncles – visited, I would keep the door slightly ajar to eavesdrop on their conversations with my father. The most interesting conversations included stories from my father's birthplace, the city of Loham, on the Danube River in Bavaria. Because Bavarians were notoriously superstitious, many of those stories were actually morality tales. Since his parents had not been married when he was born, my father was often seen as the so-called victim of God's retribution.

One day when he was a young adult, my father was guiding his horse-drawn delivery carriage down an unpaved street, onto which had spilled the branches of overgrown trees. Little did my father know that on one of those low-hanging branches sat a poisonous snake, a *Kreuzotter*. It bit his right cheek as he attended to his horses, causing my father's cheek to turn red and swell for nearly six months. The villagers cited the bite and its results as a penalty from God for my father's extramarital birth.

My father was an avid cyclist in his youth, and he often competed in bicycle races. He had a very light bicycle with wooden rims and air-filled rubber tires. During one race through several Bavarian cities, including Loham, the two-year-old child of a twenty-year-old single mother ran into his path. My father did not see the child until his bicycle and the child collided, leaving my father seriously injured and ending the toddler's life. It was said that God took the child from his mother as punishment for her having given birth out of wedlock.

After the accident and my father's recovery, the young mother, her parents, and even my father's parents encouraged my father to marry the young woman to make up for the tragic accident, in effect to do penance. He resisted and left Bavaria six months later to pursue work in the Palatinate. Interestingly, the woman never married but wrote two letters to my father every year for sixty years, despite the fact that my father was happily married with four sons of his own.

One of my uncles owned a financial rating service and a private investigation company, so I also delighted in the stories I overheard about his cases, mostly related to arson. (*At the time I had no idea that I would be working for this uncle in the future as an investigator to earn money for my higher education.*) One evening, he described the burned-out home of a miner that he had been investigating for four weeks. While combing through the rubble, he detected a very foul odor. Upon calling for reinforcements, he and the crew entered the basement and discovered, to their horror, the badly burned and decomposed bodies of two children. While no official reports ever mentioned the children, it was widely believed that they had been murdered.

Interestingly, there were no meters for electricity, gas or water in our company-owned home. We always had the brightest light bulbs, and we used a lot of electricity in the house. No one ever worried about turning lights off to conserve power.

Middle-class homes, including ours, did not have in-house toilets or bathrooms at this time. There was one outhouse at the end of our large garden, and I hated to go out there, especially when it was rainy and cold, because I had to walk to it along a narrow path bordered by wet currant and gooseberry bushes. My family was luckier than most of our neighbors, because we could use the toilets and bathrooms of the company-owned *Gemeinschaftshaus* (the community lodge), a large building which was used for assembling all workers and which the workers used for showering and dressing. We were the only family with a key for this place, and sometimes on weekends I sneaked in with some friends and let them take showers. We were very please when a toilet and bathroom were added to our house in 1941.

Speaking of keys, the keys to the front and back doors of our home were the size of a church key. We could not take the keys away from home, because they were too big and heavy. They were always hidden in a special place in the bushes when nobody was at home.

The large stable and barn on our property had been the parking area for all the company horses, before the company had trucks and other vehicles. My father was hired as the head of horse and vehicle transportation and later was the only quality control person in the company. He had only an elementary school education, but he did all the quality control work for many years. At the beginning of World War II, we raised goats, pigs, chickens and geese in the stable, so as to be self-sufficient. Although I was grateful that my family had food to eat, I hated when one of our animals was killed and served on a dinner plate.

Our house had large stairs in front, the top one made of cast iron. Every evening in spring, summer and fall – weather permitting – every available spot on the stairs was filled with neighbors and friends. Journalists from the local Zweibruecken newspaper later wrote articles about *"Beller's Trepp"* (the stoop in front of our house). In some of the articles, not only was my family's name mentioned, but particularly that of my mother.

My mother routinely fed sandwiches to me and my friends while we played outside. She specifically fed poor children from the families of blue collar workers from my father's factory. Many of those children lived a few blocks away from the factory in a very poor neighborhood, and some of the families that lived there had upwards of 10 children.

Twice a week, four men from this poor neighborhood, all wounded war veterans, walked past our house en route to a little *Gasthaus* (inn) in the Forest Birkhausen to play cards. One of the men had a silver plate covering a head injury from World War I. He obviously could not handle much alcohol, and after the card game, when he and his friends walked back home past our stairs, one could see that he was drunk. I always had to lead him into the company facility so he could do some private business, after which he would give me money for my trouble. He got very angry when I tried to refuse the money, so I decided to take it. If my father discovered that I had taken the money, he made me return it to the man or his wife the next day. I could have, in those days, bought a 10 days' supply of ice cream with that money.

Two valley roads from France merged near our house to form the wide *Bitcher Strasse* – Bitche is a small town in France – which continued all the way to downtown Zweibruecken. This wide cobblestone street was very hard on bicycles and vehicles, and it was especially hard on our feet. Since we walked downtown most of the time, our feet often hurt when we returned home.

Across from the company and my parents' house was a very large open field that we used as a playground and a soccer field, although many times we also played soccer in the road right in front of our house (since it was wider there). During a typical pre-war day, only one or two cars passed by on the roads that were mainly used by farmers on horseback or oxen-drawn wagons and people riding bicycles or walking.

Most of the 350 workers in my father's factory came from surrounding villages, where they farmed in the evening after a hard day's work. Quite a few of them walked to work. I remember my father saying that some walked 10 miles round-trip, six days a week. The company had a large bicycle rack, and checking out the different bicycles – new, old, and some assembled from spare parts – was often one of our boyhood routines. Quite a few still had old *Karbid* lamps, fueled by carbide and water, for riding after dark. The mixture developed gas, which was ignited at a nozzle on top of the lamp. Some bicycles had small, more modern generators, called *Fahrad Dynamos*, which were attached to the frame and powered by the turning of the front wheel. Although it was forbidden to go to the bicycle rack, we sneaked in to look at them through holes in the fence that surrounded the whole building nonetheless.

The Bickenalb River, which carved the westernmost of the two French valleys that converged near my home, was small and shallow, and its water was always 5 to 10 degrees colder than that of the River Hornbach. As a result, we did not use it for swimming. The Bickenalb was better suited for trout fishing.

The River Hornbach, with its winding bed between large and small willow trees and its great depth at some places, had a dam and a channel that kept water flowing through the factory. The dam was a dangerous and exciting place, especially during the two or three times each year when the entire valley was flooded. In summer, the section of the Hornbach near the dam was our only swimming place, even though it was strictly forbidden to swim and dive there. Many times we were chased away, but we always returned. The dam area was also a great place to fish, and we fished there without licenses.

In the winter, the River Hornbach froze in the slow-flowing areas, and we young, adventurous boys never missed an opportunity to use the river for ice-skating. This could be quite dangerous. Tree branches dipped into the river at the slow-flowing places, and the ice that formed around them was full of air bubbles and never froze to the same safe-for-skating degree as the rest of the river. One time I skated too near to one of those slow-flowing areas, broke through the ice, and found myself in wickedly frigid water up to my belt. I somehow managed to climb out of the river and back onto terra firma, but the stiff-legged jog home was not the kind of adventure I had bargained for when my skating escapade had begun.

A beautiful forest called Birkhausen, home to the city-owned horse breeding farm, was situated half a mile from my parents' house. The city of Zweibruecken had its own breed of horse called the *Zweibrücker*, a medium-sized animal used mainly for farming. For obvious reasons, of tremendous appeal to my friends and me was the breeding process. Farmhands had to guide the male horse's mating organ into that of the female horse – quite a dangerous task since the male horse was generally wild and unpredictable. Although we were often chased away by the breeders, we delighted in covertly watching the horses mating through holes in the six-foot-high, solid wood fences that surrounded the farm. Such spy games gave way to fantasies and discussions – childlike and naïve as they were – about the mating process.

On many peaceful and quiet evenings, I would float with a friend or one of my brothers on the River Hornbach using my two-seater *Faltboot*, a collapsible rowboat that was handed down to me by the president of my father's company. This was always a mysterious and somewhat dangerous adventure, because there were rapids between the wild-growing willows. After the rapids, there were larger whirlpools that could cause a little *Faltboot* to capsize, and escaping such a whirlpool was almost impossible.

On the way to town was my elementary school, which is now called *Altes Schulhaus Ixheim* or Old Ixheim Schoolhouse. When I attended the school, there was no indoor toilet, so we had to wait for a recess to go to the back of the schoolyard where the outhouses were. Only in a real emergency were we allowed to go there during class.

For the first day of school, my mother sewed me a small white suit with a jacket and short pants that had a pocket on the right side. Prior to attending school, I had had homemade shorts without any pockets and could not carry any stones. My new pants seemed luxurious at the time. To accompany the new suit, my mother bought me a nice little bow tie. My brothers always wore bow ties when going to work, but I did not fancy mine. As soon as I was five minutes away from home, I removed it. On my way home from school, when I was close to our house, I put it back on. My scheming worked brilliantly, or so I thought. The second week of my first school year, class photographs were taken. Alas, I was not thinking about my little bow tie at the time. When I brought the pictures home, my mother found out what I had been up to, and I was subsequently reprimanded. Luckily, I had other clothes, too, so I didn't have to wear the bow tie all the time. (*Today I almost always wear a bow tie when dining at fine restaurants or attending special events. Mother would be proud.*)

When walking towards downtown, nothing impressed me more than my 1st and 2nd grade teacher's house. At the time, the teacher, the pastor and the mayor were considered the most important people in a village or suburb. The teacher for my first two years was Herr Leonard, a very friendly man and also a close friend of my family. The little boys sat obediently in three straight rows on the left side of the classroom, while the girls mirrored the boys on the right side of the room. We students stayed in the same room for the first two years of school and our teachers came to us.

The boy or girl with the highest grades was always seated in the first seat in the first row. If the teacher had to leave the classroom for some reason, this pupil wrote the names of misbehaving students on the blackboard. The first two years, I occupied the first seat and received my share of threats whenever I put someone's name on the blackboard. Most of the time, I erased the name before the teacher re-entered the classroom. Thus, I had a quiet room and nobody outside in the hall could hear noises. I had a very strong physique, though, and did not fear threats after school. It was still customary to be rewarded for good grades with gifts, but also to be spanked with a thin bamboo rod for bad behavior. This bamboo rod was used across the palm or across the backside. Depending on the severity of the bad behavior, one could earn between one and ten strokes.

In the 3rd and 4th grades, I had a teacher by the name of Herr Kappel, who was a very strict teacher and disciplinarian. Almost every day, a few male students were hit with the bamboo stick on their rear ends and female students on the palms of their hands. I remember well Herr Kappel chasing a scared student over several benches, his bamboo stick in hand. At the end of the room he caught the offender, who promptly got his share. I was never struck by Herr Kappel, of course. I enjoyed the time with him. He liked nature and he had his own cottage three kilometers from the city, where he raised bees for honey and had a large flower garden. He took the whole class to his place on occasion, and some of us even visited with him for a few hours on a Saturday or Sunday.

During my first four years of elementary school, boys quite often measured their strength on the way home from school, and fights erupted nearly every day. I was quite a strong young boy, involved in sports, and I won most of my fights. I never complained to my father. I am certain that my parents knew that I was getting into fights by way of my roughed-up clothes, but they rarely commented on my shenanigans. I knew very well that my father, coming from Bavaria where many fights took place even among adults, was raising me to be tough, to protect and defend myself. Little did I know at the time that my survival skills would serve me well as my country became embroiled in World War II. These 3rd and 4th school years were interrupted by the war, and due to our town's proximity to the front, I was temporarily schooled in Munich, Bavaria and Homburg/Saar, when my family was forced to evacuate. I remained in the first seat until the end of the 4th school year.

Once I entered the Helmholz Gymnasium, however, I became lazier and did only what I had to do to get into the next grade. The Helmholz Gymnasium was a high school known as a *Mathematische Wissenschaftliche Hochschule* (Mathematics and Science High School). The school was good for students who chose to go into engineering, physics or chemistry. Other high schools specialized in old languages, history and education. In Germany, the high schools specialized early. Zweibruecken had four such schools, the standard in most German cities at the time (and probably today). The Helmholtz Gymnasium was founded in 1833, just as the Industrial Revolution began. At first, it was an evening school, but by 1839 it had become a full-time school, catering to students who needed to study new subjects that cropped up as a result of the Industrial Revolution. The school developed methods and equipment for agriculture and exhibited them as early as the famous Industrial

Fair in London in 1851. The school received its name from the distinguished natural scientist and philosopher Hermann von Helmholz.

It was quite exciting to go once or twice a month to Zweibruecken, a beautiful and historic town with 30,000 inhabitants. We either walked from our home to the city, which took about 45 minutes, or we took the train, which I liked best. On our excursions into town or back home from downtown, we had to walk primarily in the road, because there were no sidewalks that were paved or had stones. When it rained or when the dirt in the road was soft after a frost, our shoes and clothes became very dirty.

There was no pavement at the Ixheimer Railway Station, either, just a loose stone floor next to the train cars. It was a high step up to get onto the lowest stair rung of the train, and one had to be careful not to slide down the gravel to the rails. There was only one man selling tickets, loading and unloading freight, and dispatching the train. He had a nice blue uniform, like an Air Force officer's, and a bright red hat. Before dispatching the train, he called at least three times, *"Einsteigen bitte!"* ("All aboard, please!").

I liked the steam engines very much and I wanted, if possible, to be in the first car, close to the engine. We were allowed to open the windows, and it was exciting to travel along the river and close to homes. Sometimes we had to wait in front of a railroad signal near the main railway station in downtown Zweibruecken. At that point, I could have waited forever in the train and smelled the steam of the engine (*as opposed to today, when we rush through almost every moment of our lives*). The captivating *Hauptbahnhof*, the main railway station in Zweibruecken, had five tracks and a tunnel underneath the tracks to access each embarkment platform. Combined with the high ceiling of the station, these architectural marvels were very impressive to me.

Ixheim's bumpy cobblestone road ended at the beginning of the city of Zweibruecken, and a well-paved road took over. It was much easier to walk on. There also were more concrete and paved sidewalks, but not all had such a nice surface. All the sidewalks had to be paid for by the homeowners, and not everyone could afford them. During our visits to the city, I was always impressed by the beautiful castle, once home to the dukes of Zweibruecken, with its large gardens. I also enjoyed the expansive marketplace. On market days, my family visited the many stands where merchants sold beautiful fruits, vegetables, meats and sausages. Most important to me at the time was the stand where my parents bought me ice cream.

When visiting downtown with only my father, we often went into the *Ratskeller*, a restaurant that in most German cities is located next to City Hall. It is generally a gourmet-type restaurant with a beer and wine bar attached. City Council members usually visited the Ratskeller to socialize after their meetings. When we had lunch or dinner there, my father always bought me a smoked pork chop with sauerkraut. Next to City Hall and the Ratskeller was the so-called *Fruchthalle*, a covered market. Originally fish, fresh fruits and vegetables were sold there, but in my time it was remodeled into a theater which was used for plays and to show movies to the Hitler Youth. Very impressive in the inner city were many small canals and some beautiful villas belonging to wealthy people whose names my father told me. Once in a while my father took me to his favorite wine-restaurant, called *Gasthaus Horn*, located on the *Hauptstrasse* (Main Street). He often met friends there over a good glass of wine. My father, a wine connoisseur, could identify the area from which the wine came, as well as the type of grape and quite often the year, without looking at the label.

Also of interest to me were the large churches, military barracks and German military parades in Zweibruecken. Sometimes we visited the *Rosengarten*, or Rose Garden, which I found somewhat boring, except when I could feed the large carp in the garden's ponds. The city had many public wells, similar to drinking fountains in the United States. I liked pumping water out of these wells so much that I often convinced my parents to stop at the wells even if I was not really thirsty. My parents never missed the famous Zweibruecker horse races, and most of the time I was allowed to accompany them. My father always had the same seat, called a *Sattelplatz* (or saddle seat) right next to where the horses entered the race track. That way he could see the horses up close. Taking his seat and station seriously, my father always bet on his favorite horses. I, on the other hand, was mainly interested in the hotdogs and lemonade.

Looking back at my early, innocent days, I can't help but become a bit nostalgic for the drama that I fabricated every day. From fights on the way home from school and illicit fishing expeditions with my friends to eavesdropping on my uncles and feigning thirst in order to pump water at every public well, my life was carefree and pleasant. I felt that I was in control, that my little world was manageable. In fact, I was not unhappy to see my brothers drafted into the military. Their absence would, after all, afford me more freedom to play and the luxury of even more control. Little did I know that not only my world, but the whole world was about to change in ways that neither I nor the most powerful leaders of the day could control. Before long, I missed my brothers very much.

2

Between the Wars: Posturing and Escalation

> It is our intention to organize the moral and cultural blockade of Germany and to divide this nation into four parts. It is our intention finally to start a war without any mercy.
>
> BERNARD LECACHE-LIFSCHITZ
> *Le Droit de Vivre*
> *December 18, 1938*

Germany's relationship with France had a long history of discord. France's urge for expansion (mainly towards the east) led to a war with Prussia and to the eventual defeat of Napoleon III, who capitulated on September 1, 1870, in Sedan with 108,000 soldiers. With the surrender of Paris on January 28, 1871, the Franco-Prussian War finally ended. The peace treaty required France to pay only the cost of the war and to give back Alsace-Lorraine, which it had originally taken from Germany 200 years previously. The French were not dishonored, but the disgrace of defeat had them yearning for revenge.

On every possible occasion, the French expressed this desire publicly. In the following years, they entered into several alliances against Germany and Austria-Hungary. France brought Russia and England to her side, mainly because Germany was growing too strong economically in the world market. Many older Germans believed that France vigorously tried to start a war with Germany and eventually succeeded, in a roundabout way with Germany's partners, Austria and Hungary. It was widely held in Germany that the French financially supported the anarchists that assassinated the Austrian Archduke Ferdinand in Sarajevo, thus triggering the First World War.

After the declaration of war by the Austrians against Serbia on July 28, 1914, an avalanche of war declarations by France, Russia, England, and some of their befriended states were issued against Germany and Austria. France now had her revenge: England moved against her competitor, Germany; Russia attacked East Prussia in the hopes of fulfilling its dream of expanding westward; and Japan confiscated the German colonies in East Asia.

Until 1916, Poland had not existed as a state for 120 years. In 1915, the Germans defeated the Russians, who had occupied this territory, and then helped substantially to create a new Poland on December 6, 1916, making the Poles overwhelmingly happy. But the more the Germans got into difficulties on the western front, the more the Poles started distancing themselves from Germany, even though at this time the Allies treated the Poles with condescension.

To worsen the situation, the United States stepped into the war against Germany on April 6, 1917. There's a Germany saying that "Wall Street discovered war as being good for business." Then, after its defeat in November 1918, Austria-Hungary renounced its ally, Germany, and signed a separate peace treaty.

Germany at this time was still undefeated and had troops far into France, but it was also at the end of its strength. With the commitment by U.S. President Wilson for peace negotiations between equal partners and his promise to stand up for "less expensive reparation costs," Germany laid down its weapons. Although many Germans still think that Germany did not start and had not lost this war, Germany unfortunately became branded as a war criminal and was not even invited to the peace negotiations.

On November 11, 1918, the Germans signed the capitulation documents in the woods of Compiegne, in the belief that everyone wanted peace. But after the demilitarization of the German Army on January 18, 1919, the governments of the United States,

Great Britain, France and Italy, contrary to what they had promised and barring Germany from participation, insisted on draconi-
an conditions. The 14 major points of U.S. President Wilson were
ignored, and uncontrolled revenge and greediness for German
land took place. (President Wilson, therefore, did not vote for the
ratification of the "Dictate of Versailles." On August 25, 1921, the
United States signed off on a special peace treaty with Germany
and Austria.)

During the negotiations in Versailles, the Polish delegation requested land annexations, almost all of which were accepted by
the U.S., England and France. Poland requested a return to the
borders of 1772, in addition to *Oberschlesien* (Upper Silesia), part
of *Mittelschlesien* (Middle Silesia), the city of Danzig, and almost
all of *Ostpreusen* (East Prussia). Only British Prime Minister Lloyd
George prevented such demands. The Poles did not like this, and
using force and terror tried to change the situation, hold down the
German inhabitants, and implement everything regarding Polish
rights and Polish law.

On June 28, 1919, in the Hall of Mirrors in the Palace of
Versailles, Germany had to sign a peace treaty under dishonor-
able conditions. The German representatives even had to sign in
a standing position, although the negotiators (representing all the
other nations) signed while seated.

The victors had dictated that Germany would accept the Treaty
of Versailles and would pay large bills for reparations. Only in the
poorest, most helpless times of emergency, and under great protest, did the Germans sign the treaty. The terms that were imposed
on Germany, without a doubt, planted the seeds for the Second
World War.

After the signing of the treaty, a famine spread through
Germany and then throughout Europe. Inflation and the high
rates of unemployment soon followed. These were the conditions
that led to Hitler starting his party and coming to power.

When the Treaty of Versailles returned Poland to the status
of a sovereign state, Germany was essentially carved into two territories. The larger western section of the country remained intact.
However, West Prussia on the Baltic Sea and East Prussia, also on

the Baltic and sharing an eastern border with Lithuania, were separated by a wide swath of the new Poland, which included the port city of Danzig (now Gdansk). This separation effectively cut off German-controlled East Prussia from the rest of the country.

Many German territories were confiscated, even though 90 percent or more of the people in most states voted to remain with Germany. In 1919, 92.4 percent of the West Prussian population voted to stay with Germany, but the land was given to Poland, to provide it access to the Baltic Sea. This land, which (like Bavaria and my home, the Palatinate) had been a part of Germany for more than 1,000 years, became the main source of conflict between Germany and Poland. Poland now had direct access to the Baltic Sea, and Germany had no more land connection to East Prussia, Germany's corn-producer. Neither the German governing party of the Weimar Republic, nor the Social Democrats (in power at this time) accepted this – what the Germans called – land theft. Germany continuously repeated the request to return the territory, but its influence in world politics was too weak at this time to get it back.

The other territories also voted in 1919, under Allied observation. The results were overwhelmingly for staying with Germany: East Prussia, 97.5 percent; *Niederschlesien* (Lower Silesia), 97.6 percent; and *Oberschlesien* (Upper Silesia), 60 percent. East Upper Silesia went to Poland, and the rest to Germany.

Some Terms of the Versailles Treaty:

- Germany must give up very valuable old Reich territories: Eupen, Malmedy, and Moresnet to Belgium; Northern Silesia to Denmark; parts of Silesia and East Prussia, almost all of West Prussia, and Posen to Poland; the Hultschiner land to Czechoslovakia; the Memelland to the League of Nations (*Völkerbund*) under administration of Lithuania; Alsace-Lorraine to France; Danzig and the Saar area to the League of Nations; and all colonies as mandates of the League of Nations to different countries (since it was claimed that Germany had shown itself to be incapable and unworthy of owning colonies).

- The German military would be limited to only 100,000 soldiers (it was an elite group, and my oldest brother was selected for it);

there would be no more military draft; there would be surrender of all weapons and war materials without reimbursement; all warships must be given up; the Navy would be reduced to 15,000; the whole German Rhineland would be occupied by the Allies for 15 years; and a military-free zone would be installed 50 kilometers east of the Rhine River.

Additional war reparations were: Germany must give up many merchant marine ships, much manufacturing equipment and many factories, large amounts of coal, numerous animals, and the German undersea telephone cable; Germany must bear all costs of occupation forces; Germany must sign to owing 80,000,000 goldmarks and agree to the payment of a still-to-be determined total debt over a 30-year period; Germany must accept the internationalization of Rivers Rhine, Danube, Elbe, Oder and Memel, and of the Kaiser Wilhelm Canal.

As a result of this treaty, 19.4 million Germans came under foreign governance. In the provinces of Prussia and West Prussia alone, 2.9 million Germans came under Polish rule.

In summary, the Treaty of Versailles demanded the following of Germany (the Germans talked of rape).

	Inhabitants	Square km./land
North Schleswig	166,000	3,993
Eupen/Malmedy	60,000	1,036
Saar area	652,000	1,925
Alsace-Lorraine	1,874,000	14,522
Hultschiner Land	48,000	316
Upper Silesia	893,000	3,213
Posen-West Prussia	2,938,000	46,142
Danzig	331,000	1,914
Memel	141,000	2,657
Total	**7,103,000**	**75,718**
German colonies	12,300,000	2,453,000
Total	**19,403,000**	**2,528,718**

With the support of the French Occupation Forces, the Poles confiscated and took control of the whole of West Prussia. Under their National Democratic leader, Korfanty, they increased their tactics of terror against the German population, which was tolerated by the French Occupation Forces. This happened mainly in the remainder of Upper Silesia. Some of the Italian Occupation Forces, which did not accept the Polish actions, were murdered. German partisans emerged and fought against the Poles entering Upper Silesia. Finally, it came to the well-known uprising at Annaberg, where only the French Occupation Forces prevented a defeat of the Polish troops.

Shortly thereafter, the Poles began hate campaigns against Germany. Use of the German language was forbidden in the annexed territory, and mistreatment – including murder – of formerly German citizens commenced. One year prior to the treaty, Poland had started the first concentration camps in Europe. In the first two Polish concentration camps, called Szccypiormo and Stralnowo, 8,000 people, mainly Germans, had been incarcerated.

In 1919, the Poles annexed Lithuania. In 1920, they marched into Russia and took away large territories from the so-called White Russia and the Ukraine. But none of this brought any luck to Poland, for at this time the Polish nation was close to economic ruin and starvation. In 1925, a German-Polish trade war started, in which neither side was innocent.

In 1926, the Poles opened two more concentration camps, Kartuska and Brest-Litowsk, and in 1939 they added Chodzen. Many prisoners died of hardship, hunger and illness. The world, including Hitler, was acutely aware of those concentration camps. Hitler undertook diplomatic – and in hindsight, ironic – efforts to request more humane treatment in the camps.

Even as the Poles gave free rein to their hatred of Germany, in 1930 the German Reichsregierung signed a trade agreement with Poland. In the same year, the German Secret Service uncovered Polish plans for an attack on Germany. The Polish western border was supposed to be expanded to Berlin, and all of Czechoslovakia was to be occupied as well.

From December 1922 until February 1933, an air war treaty was negotiated in The Hague in Holland. It was supposed to make sure that cities, villages and buildings which were not close to the battle zone of a land army could not be bombarded at any time. Due to England's opposition, it was never signed. On the contrary, some English press reports even supported the use of fire bombs, at this time the most effective tool for breaking the resistance of a civil population. (*Probably no one in Zweibruecken, with a population of only 30,000 people, was thinking about an air war, especially one that would destroy a small town without heavy industry.*)

It was reported that, at the 1933 Disarmament Conference, the Poles pressured the French to join them in a war against Germany. "In three days we are in Berlin!" screamed the Polish mobs in the streets. France turned down the Polish request. German records show that Hitler tried many times to find common ground for a German-Polish understanding

After years of unsuccessful negotiations with the League of Nations about demilitarization, Germany resigned in protest in October 1933. An agreement could not be finally negotiated because of England's and France's stubborn posture; they were not even willing to reduce their forces by one soldier. (At this time, the U.S. was not part of the League of Nations.) Many Germans thought that World War II resulted from France and England's incalcitrance, fueled by Hitler's demands to revise the land treaties and by the strict Polish refusal.

German-Polish tension increased dramatically in October 1938, when Hitler repeated his request for a two-mile corridor with a territorial road and railway connection between the larger western section of Germany and East Prussia, through the formerly German West Prussia towards Danzig and East Prussia. In return, Hitler offered to cease attempts to regain control of West Prussia and Posen from Poland. Poland responded with delays, preferring to contact England for advice. At first the talks were positive. But England was always interested in conflict with Germany, and soon the negotiations failed. Consequently, the corridor question led to further tensions. (Hitler's peace-and-compromise attitude was likely only for show, and although it was viewed positively by other nations, it was not welcomed in Warsaw.) France, acted more calmly than England did, but it had also been waiting a long while for revenge upon Germany.

Poland again requested an unreasonable amount of territory. On June 29, 1939, a Polish newspaper criticized the Treaty of Versailles and stated that Poland had been unfairly treated, claiming that the Weser River was supposed to be the western border of Poland. The Belgian newspaper, *"Flaemischer Beobachter,"* wrote on August 3, 1939: "The Poles have lost any sense of proportion and measure. Every foreigner who looks at the maps produced by the Poles, in which a large part of Germany up to Berlin, as well as Bohemia and Maehren, Czechoslovakia, and a very, very large part of Russia are included, thinks that the Poles must be out of their minds."

The Treaty of Versailles was the main reason for Hitler's *révisions politiques*, including the building of the Siegfried Line and, in the opinion of many Germans, the reason for World War II, as evidenced by the following excerpt from a letter written by the German Foreign Minister Stresemann on September 14, 1925: "It is the diabolical nature of the Treaty of Versailles to create continuous unrest between Germany and all its neighbor states. The western allies created the never-before existing states of Poland and Czechoslovakia, only to start unrest."

Henri de Kerilis, a French journalist, wrote in the *Epoque* on July 18, 1939, "If the war should start again, one should not be caught like 20 years ago. Germany is incorrigible and unhealable. One must finally make an end. The German people must be exterminated."

Many Germans I have spoken with remember (and I must add that this may seem one-sided) the countless peace offers and proposals from Hitler to Poland. They saw that Hitler was ready for a mutual agreement with England. With France, he was engaged in forging the best of neighborly relations. He waived the German rights to Alsace-Lorraine, and this was celebrated in the Parliament on September 6, 1939. The relations between Germany and France at this time were not bad. The governor of the state of Palatinate had very close contacts in France, specifically in the border regions.

In a speech in Neustadt, a sister city of my hometown, the governor spoke to his French friends. The following is an excerpt:

> We can be friends forever. Germany is ready for peace, but also prepared for war. The French people have nothing in common with their leaders who encourage war. Let us shake hands at the border. We do not want any conflict with you. But know that here on our west borders is a wall of defense which will repel any aggression and which is undefeatable.

He was speaking about the Siegfried Line.

Border conflict between France and Western Germany had extended over 120 years, and my hometown of Zweibruecken had been occupied three times by the French prior to World War II: under Napoleon I, under Napoleon III, and as a consequence of the Versailles Treaty. (A fourth French occupation followed Germany's defeat in World War II.) These times were marked by arbitrary acts of suppression, humiliation, looting, etc. Throughout these years, the French wanted to see the Rhine River as their eastern border.

This lingering border conflict contributed to France's plan, commenced in 1927, to build a defense system to protect its eastern border from Basel, Switzerland, in the south to the Ardennes Mountains in the north. Construction had begun in 1930 and was completed in 1938. The fortresses, tremendous in size and in number, were grouped together under the name "Maginot Line," in honor of French War Minister André Maginot (1877-1932). The French government was convinced that this defense system could never be defeated. Some of the fortresses along the Maginot Line even bore the French phrase "*On ne passe pas*," or "None shall pass here." But history would soon expose the overconfidence of the French military planners.

Hitler's waiving of the rights to Alsace-Lorraine was played down by France and England to avoid publicity. During meetings at the League of Nations, France protested against the German building of the Siegfried Line, which it felt was a threat. Yet France never mentioned its own Maginot Line, built many years before the Siegfried Line.

One day before the beginning of World War II, Charles Maurras wrote in the *"Action Francaise"* daily paper:

> It is not about Hitler. It is about Germany, the Eternal Germany, the only German question. If it is Bismarck or Wilhelm II, the Weimar Republic or now Hitler, it is always the same. It is about the Big German Unity. The Big German Unity is the enemy. This German Unity must be destroyed.

The Treaty of Versailles made that a reality. German unity was destroyed, and ongoing unrest took its place. Many older Germans are still of the opinion that the Treaty of Versailles, and the later pact between France and England with Poland, caused the beginning of World War II.

3

Escalating Tension Felt at Home

The description of the events leading up to World War II in the preceding chapter is primarily about the big politics. There is another view: the way that the people in the border region where I grew up saw the time from the end of World War I through the escalating tension leading to World War II.

In 1918, they had to live through a period, after the unfortunate capitulation, when German troops marched through the city day and night, coming home from the front lines in France. By November 26, 1918, those soldiers had to reach the territory on the east side of the Rhine River if they did not want to end up in an internment camp. Zweibruecken, on the western side of the Rhine River, was left behind, unprotected. With the arrival of the French Occupation Forces on December 1, 1918, an almost 12-year period of suffering started. This time is marked by rapes, imprisonment, beatings in open streets, deportation of people, humiliation, and other arbitrary acts. Even the mayor was deported by the French.

The total reparation costs for Germany also hit home in my hometown. Zweibruecken had to come up with merchandise (from industry and other businesses) in the amount of 20 million goldmarks, as well as 4.6 million goldmarks in cash. The devaluation of the Reichsmark took away everyone's last penny. Unemployment brought indescribable distress. Due to the occupation by the French, almost any contact with the rest of Germany was cut off, and there were no economic relations with the rest of Germany. When the French Occupation Troops left on June 30, 1930, nobody shed any tears. On July 2, the first 100 police troops from Bavaria arrived in Zweibruecken, and there was a big celebration.

On January 30, 1933, the National Socialists (Hitler's party) won a majority in Zweibruecken and slowly, very slowly, the situation started to improve. The unemployment rate came down until 1938, when a real boom started, as had never before happened in this region. It was the beginning of the building of the Siegfried Line, and many people were making a lot of money.

After all the bad experiences with French Occupation Troops, the reasoning behind the building of the Siegfried Line was easily understood by the people in my hometown, only 10 kilometers away from the French border. People thought that without the Siegfried Line, the French could change their minds and move quickly to "liberate" Zweibruecken again. The Germans did not see the building of the Siegfried Line as a threat; rather, they considered it a crucial means of protection, and they accepted the disruption of their daily lives and the loss of fertile and rich farmland while the line was being constructed.

Only in light of these factors – economic boom and protection by the Siegfried Line – could one understand the high excitement Hitler's visits engendered when he toured our area.

From military fortifications to diplomatic efforts, the people around Zweibruecken followed radio and newspaper coverage of all political developments with great care and attention. They supported Hitler's demands on Poland, but were not happy that Hitler was offering to give away West Prussia. Only Hitler's popularity and Goebbels' brilliant speeches convinced Germans to accept that decision, albeit grudgingly.

No one dared criticize the regime, however: first, because of the new German prosperity; and second, because those who engaged in unruly behavior and dissension would be sent to work camps. One of our neighbors with a known alcohol problem had been taken away by the Nazi secret service, ostensibly to sober him up and teach him that overindulgence was unacceptable. He was gone for six months and returned sober – and not just from alcohol.

Then, on November 9, 1938, Hitler's war on Jews went public all over Germany. On that morning, just after five o'clock, my father and I were driving out of the city for one of the many business trips on which I accompanied him. I heard sirens in the distance, and as I looked back at the city from a hillside, I could see the synagogue in Zweibruecken engulfed in flames. My father's demeanor that morning had turned sober. He seemed at once sad and disgusted with what he saw; on the one hand, because he had several Jewish friends whose house of worship was destroyed, and on the other hand, because he knew the fire had been deliberately set by Nazi party operatives, most likely by members of the secret service. (*I would later learn that synagogues throughout Germany had burned that night, on what is now known as Kristallnacht, or Crystal Night. I also learned that, despite the quick response of the local fire department, storm troopers in Zweibruecken had prevented firefighters from dousing the blaze.*)

Shortly thereafter, even I began to understand the mounting political tension in my country. Grave as it was, it excited my friends and me as we played war games and delighted, childishly, in the intrigue of the potential hostilities. What boy wouldn't find war intriguing? For months, we heard the French military maneuvering and firing long-range artillery from the fortress of Bitche. The newspapers routinely reminded World War I veterans and reservists to be ready, because orders to report for duty could come at any time.

By August 1939, diplomacy had taken a back seat to war posturing, and officials on both sides of the conflict were preparing for battle. The days of August were full of tension for the whole population of Zweibruecken. The Siegfried Line was almost complete, but many construction workers were still present, and the streets of the city were filled with construction vehicles. Some of the workers did not want to be evacuated and leave the families they were living with, and everybody hoped that Poland would accept what people thought was a generous offer from Hitler. From the French people across the border, one could hear that they had no desire to fight for West Prussia, but in the end, the people would not be asked.

After the British and French signed the non-aggression treaty with Poland, the Polish government no longer had to accept any good-will proposals from Hitler. Hitler commented after the treaty was signed: "Germany now has to prepare for war." Food stamps were already printed, but they were held under lock at city halls. Rumors were flying that Zweibruecken was located in the so-called "red zone," the section of land between the fortified and military-occupied Siegfried and Maginot Lines. and would have to be evacuated in case of war. From the other side, in France, one could hear that the population of Alsace-Lorraine was ready to be evacuated to southern France.

As a 7½-year-old boy, I was listening with rapt attention to the frequent news reports that kept us within earshot of our family radio, located – to my mother's dismay – in the formal living room. She spent most of her time in the self-imposed exile of the kitchen, so she relied on me to give accounts of the broadcasts. I always sensed, even though she rarely listened to the reports herself, that she really did want to know the latest news. She knew what war would mean for her family: all of her boys except me would be forced into military service. Having survived World War I, the prospect of a repeat experience must have frightened her terribly.

Special music signified breaking news, giving everyone time to stop what they were doing and gather around the nearest radio to hear the latest report. Reporters used words and phrases like "permanent army concentration" and "evacuation," and referred to Zweibruecken as part of the "red zone." Citing treaties between England and Poland and between France and Poland, reports quoted politicians such as the Polish Marshall Rydz-Smiglj: "Poland wants war with Germany and Germany cannot prevent it, even if it wants to prevent it." I may have been just shy of my 8th birthday, but I knew what that meant – my home, my town, and the people who had worked so hard to build the great western wall of defense would not be protected by it. We lived between the lines.

By mid-1938, every citizen had received a gas mask, and frequent exercises took place on how to use those masks in case of a gas attack. My mother and I participated in those exercises, and for me it felt like I was suffocating. General drills simulated an attack by enemy airplanes. The city became completely dark and looked like a ghost town. Nothing could be seen from the surrounding hills. By spring of 1939, the government began to build bomb shelters, and everyone in the town was assigned to a specific place. Shelters dug into the hillsides were preferred over concrete bunkers. (Later on, when a 500-pound bomb hit a concrete bunker next to the company with which I started my career, 14 prisoners in that bunker were killed, and the bomb went through a concrete wall that was 70 centimeters thick.)

My brother Albert had joined the army during the 1935 reconstruction of the German military. Mother and Father were tremendously proud of their oldest child, because at the time and by treaty, military troops could not exceed 100,000. It was considered a great honor if a member of the family served in the army. Between 1935 and 1939, however, I watched the pride on my mother's face turn to concern and finally to worry. My brothers Edi and Emil, both members of the *Arbeitdienst* (a virtually compulsory quasi-military work unit), were drafted during the summer of 1939, and my father received his return-to-service "request" in mid-August.

Each time she said good-bye to another man in her family, Mother stood in the front yard of our home, hugged and kissed him, and then cried as he walked away. I remember feeling some empathy for her, but I never shed a tear. Rather, I was overflowing with pride that my brothers and my father were serving in the great German Army, and I felt a little slighted that I was not yet old enough to serve my country. The expression "Be careful what you wish for" could not have been more appropriately applied than in my case, for the peril I was about to face would rival that of any romantic childhood notion of the glories of war.

4

The Siegfried Line: The Construction

I have ordered the immediate construction of fortifications on the western border of our country. Since the month of May, the most gigantic fortification construction of all time is underway. I only want to give you a few figures: In this massive project, 278,000 workers are involved. The majority of the fortifications will be finished before the winter of 1938. The total number of bunkers will be 17,000. Behind the defense line, the German population is ready. I have ordered this colossal effort on the western border to protect and preserve freedom.

ADOLF HITLER
September 12, 1938

In 1935, the last of the occupying forces from the Treaty of Versailles left the Rhineland. Following years of poverty and foreign occupation, Germany wanted desperately to stand on its own. So, when the foreign troops departed, planning for a western defense system began.

Younger generations and many foreign observers have raised questions about the nature and the purpose of the Siegfried Line, wondering who conceived of it and decided to build it. Even today a veil of secrecy surrounds these questions. (The elderly people in my hometown knew a great deal about it and its purpose, for the Siegfried Line was an epoch of their lives they experienced first-hand, more than 60 years ago.)

Who thought it necessary to fortify Germany's western border, and was the real reason to protect the borders against French attacks? Did not the French, many years before, build fortresses on their eastern borders to protect themselves against German attacks? This is a paradoxical situation: Each nation, France and Germany, trying to protect itself against the other! By 1936, Hitler had one of the best-equipped armies in the world. Was the Siegfried Line really necessary?

There is a history of building such fortified defenses. Ever since humans have lived in houses, there has been an effort to protect them from enemy attacks. The most obvious approach is to build those facilities as fortresses. Communities have protected themselves by castles, fortresses, walls (like China), and later by whole fortress zones, like the Siegfried Line in Germany and the Maginot Line in France.

At this point it might be useful to review some of the conditions of the Versailles Treaty. Nothing was forbidden to the French, but much was restricted for the Germans:

> It is forbidden for Germany to build on the left side of the Rhine River, and along the right side of the Rhine River up to 50 kilometers east of a line along the Rhine River, to keep fortresses or to build new fortresses.
>
> Article 42

> It is also forbidden in the same zone as described in article 42 to maintain barracks and troop assemblies. The same applies for any maneuvers and for manufacturing military supplies.
>
> Article 43

> All fortress systems, fortresses and defense systems and places in the country on the right side of the Rhine River, up to 50 kilometers east of the river, have to be destroyed. Any new system is forbidden to be built.
>
> Article 180

The Siegfried Line, started in 1937, violated all of these restrictions.

Ultimately, the Siegfried Line would form a perimeter about 600 kilometers long that stretched from the town of Loerrach in the south, along the border of Holland in the north, to the Waal River. Based on the topography of the land, a descent from foothills to flatlands, this part of Germany could easily have been conquered by attackers, and Hitler knew this. Because his political goals for the eastern provinces of Germany, namely reacquisition of the land lost to Poland, he did not have enough troops to protect the west; thus he dealt with the vulnerability of the western border by ordering the construction of a great defense system. At the time, critics questioned this decision to build a defensive line rather than use more tanks and airplanes. Hitler responded that the training of pilots and tank commanders would cost more money and require more time than fortifying Germany's western borders. The final decision to build the Siegfried Line was made in 1936, and by 1937, five hundred bunkers had already been built.

On April 7, 1938, the high command of the German Army initiated the Pioneer Program 1938, which brought the massive defense construction project to a radius of 80 kilometers around and including my hometown. Zweibruecken was assigned to the German Division *Gest.Pi.Stab 17*, staff position 17; and its official headquarters opened immediately in the neighboring city of Homburg.

Construction planners began visiting the area around Zweibruecken in May 1938. At the time, they were not readily recognized by the townspeople. The planners' purpose was to determine the exact position of each bunker and defense system. Surveyors marked the chosen locations with white tissues mounted on sticks. The type of bunker and the firing direction for its guns depended on the topography. Farmers were the first to confront the planners, because their fields were surveyed during the growing season. Nazi party leaders held a number of meetings with them in an attempt to calm them down.

Hitler did not want bureaucracy to play too much of a role in the construction of the Siegfried Line, so all the construction workers were hired and paid by local construction companies. Had construction been overseen by government administrators, it would have been slowed significantly, and as we now know, Hitler was an impatient man. So he required the local construction companies in Zweibruecken, Pirmasens, and Homburg to serve as human resource and fiscal agents. Once contracts were awarded and work was underway, the government reimbursed the local companies for the work completed by their contractors. The average monthly salary was 500 Reichmarks (about $250 today), but with overtime and bonuses for night and weekend work, one could earn double that amount. As a point of comparison, a Volkswagen cost 950 Reichmarks in 1939.

Construction of the Siegfried Line required a tremendous accumulation of building supplies. Huge machines dug sand and gravel from the Rhine River day and night. One-third of Germany's concrete mixers were used in the construction effort, and cement factories were required to commit one-third of their annual production to the project. From one end of the line to the other, as many as 8,000 railroad cars and 15,000 trucks moved freight to and from storage places and out to the construction sites. In Zweibruecken alone, 1,000 trucks were stationed. The constant movement of heavy equipment took a toll on the roads, so crews worked non-stop to repair them and to construct new ones. The frequent accidents that accompanied the increase in commercial vehicle traffic also put tremendous pressure on local police forces. On one hand, they had to maintain order; on the other, they dared not slow down any construction efforts. It was at this time that Germany began to install stop signs at intersections, an idea that came from German citizens who had visited the United States.

Before long, we were informed that our section of the line would be so heavily fortified that the French would never again attack us on our own soil. Hitler declared the stretch of the Siegfried Line from Lautzkirchen to Zweibruecken to Kettrichhof a *Festungsfront*, or special fortress section. (I learned later that only four other parts of the Siegfried Line received similar priority designation.)

There were three defense systems in a *Festungsfront*. Sections of the defense perimeter on either side of it were lined by mine fields. They were filled with light mines to deter foot soldiers and heavy mines to destroy tanks and heavy equipment. In the wider, open fields, barbed-wire obstructions were placed. If enemy troops advanced beyond the mine fields and barbed-wire barricades, they would face the outermost line of the *Festungsfront,* consisting of road blocks, small bunkers with machine-gun batteries, and tank traps.

Germany's enemies knew the Siegfried Line for its distinctive "dragon teeth" tank traps, built of concrete gutters with large humps that prevented tanks from rolling through them. Several other tank trap networks were also in place. All of them were built horizontally in front of the bunkers. In the valleys, different systems were installed. For example, deep holes were dug and filled with water. Tank defense walls, approximately 500 meters long and five meters high, were constructed as dams. Shortly before an attack, the dams could be opened to flood the valleys.

The middle band of defense contained machine-gun stations, artillery, anti-tank weapon installations, artillery observation posts, and heavy bunkers with steel towers. Sprinkled throughout were very small bunkers with small steel observation towers that were only big enough for one man.

The innermost system was by far the most intricate: numerous large bunkers that connected to one another by underground tunnels built deep into the earth, so that only their steel towers were noticeable. In and among these fortifications were smaller, one-man bunkers and observation towers.

At strategically important intersections along the line, a battery of soldiers operated a heavy artillery station protected by four heavy guns. The Germans always positioned special tank defense batteries next to important roads and intersections, as well as in the fields near them. At first, they were 3.5, later 7.5, and eventually 8.8 centimeter PAK units, called "eighty-eight" guns by the Americans. These eighty-eight guns were used to attack tanks and to defend against airplanes.

All the bunkers were located so that they could be covered by at least one neighboring bunker. The same applied to PAK bunkers, because they were located close to the defense lines. Except for the bunker types MM19 and FN, no other bunker type had permanently installed guns. This was done for a simple tactical reason: all weapons used from inside the bunkers could also be used outside. Most of the bunkers were connected by trenches and were bolstered by small machine-gun nests in nearby woods or fields.

Farther inland were the heavy-artillery gun bunkers. These were equipped with 15-centimeter guns. With a range of up to 18 kilometers, they were set in groups of four. With one side open, the heavy artillery bunkers were flanked by smaller bunkers that housed the soldiers in charge. Two shifts of personnel were always assigned to a battery.

In order to make sure that water was always available, some of the main fortresses had their own water wells with electrical pump systems, and the rest had wells with hand pumps. Each bunker had a sewage line, a phone connection, and a manually-operated air circulation system, complete with gas and dust filters. Each had a bunker oven that was used for heating, which could be closed immediately in the event of attack, to prevent gas or water from spilling in through the exhaust pipes or smoke being blown back into the bunker. Each bunker also had an emergency exit filled with gravel at the outlet to protect soldiers against explosives. Some of these exits were eighty feet long and were so small that one could get through only by crawling. Bunkers were stocked with ammunition, food and tools, and they were lit by lanterns. Their primitive furniture looked as if it belonged in a submarine.

Bunkers of the C and D type held between five and ten soldiers, while those of the regular defense B-1 type held up to twenty military men. Six of the B-1 bunkers around Zweibruecken were command centers that could hold up to one hundred men.

In his propaganda statements, Hitler declared the B-1 bunkers invincible, due to their enormous firepower. Sunken two-and-a-half stories into the ground, they had two steel towers, each designed with six outlets for machine guns and heavy guns. Each B-1 bunker was equipped with an M-19 grenade thrower with automated feeder and flamethrowers. Door openings concealed large traps that would make it difficult for the enemy to enter, and other bunkers were situated to protect the entrances. (*After the war, when I explored such bunkers, I almost fell into one of those traps myself.*)

The B systems had their own generators and some had observation towers. These towers were about 80 meters away from the main unit and could only be reached through an underground tunnel. Most of the units had two outside walls with a hollow space between them, to minimize destruction of the inner, main wall by enemy artillery fire.

Although the B-1 bunkers were believed to be invincible, Hitler and some of his generals did not like the location of the command bunkers. They felt that they were too close to the main defense line, and they worried that if they were lost, the whole command would be destroyed.

Construction of the defense line brought much spy activity on the part of France and England. Balloons often floated along the French-German border, and French and English observation planes flew above the construction sites during the daytime. When spies were caught – and many were – their cameras, film, and other materials were confiscated. The Germans knew about the increase in spying, but did not take any drastic action. Instead, camouflage became important to the design and construction of the line. Every construction site was completely covered with wooden boards, and nobody was permitted within fifty meters of a site. Workers removed a minimum number of trees around the construction site, and once a bunker was completed, concrete surfaces were covered with dirt. In some cases, stables, barns or homes were built on top of the bunkers. In view of the massive movement of earth and the construction itself, it is surprising that it was all done by hand and not by machine.

The defense system around Zweibruecken had specific strategic importance. The statistics bear this out. Of 2,999 machine-gun nests in the whole Siegfried Line, 173 were located around Zweibruecken, as were 58 of the 766 defense guns. Of 120 anti-aircraft guns, 46 were stationed around my hometown, including 22 of 66 heavy anti-aircraft guns. Approximately one third of all the defense equipment for the Siegfried Line was placed around Zweibruecken.

By September 1938, 3,800 bunkers were operational, with 2,500 still under construction. Near Zweibruecken, bunkers were positioned not only in the valleys but also on top of the surrounding hills. At other locations, a bunker was positioned only at the end of a valley. One could assume that this layout had the purpose of luring the attackers into the valley, so that once inside, they could be destroyed with every system available.

Communication between single bunkers and the command bunkers was made possible by a field cable network. The cables close to the bunkers were about 2.5 meters underground. A short distance away from the units, the cable was buried only one meter below the ground, because research had determined that damage to the cable system was easier to repair when the cable was closer to the surface.

Some bunkers had central cable stations with a main artery to the phone system of the German Reichpost. (*This German postal system, later called Bundespost, held a telephone monopoly until the year 1999.*) From the central stations, the connections went into a special net called *Georgnetz*, which was a guiding system operated by specially trained postal workers. One of these systems was located in Zweibruecken in the main post office. After a mobilization of troops was initiated, the residents were not able to make private phone calls.

Upon completion of the *Festungsfront* and later, when the Allies had already entered France, Hitler decided to augment the defense system along the French border. A multitude of so-called volunteers (those who did not volunteer were generally blackballed by the Nazi party), including members of the Hitler Youth, was charged with digging tank traps. The corps of volunteers consisted mainly of women and children aged 10 to 14, soldiers who had been wounded and were unable to return to active duty, and elderly members of the Home Defense Units. Incentives for young people to get out and dig included two days of excused absence from school and stamps that could be redeemed for a new pair of shoes. New shoes were a luxury, so you can imagine my enthusiastic participation in the digging project.

Eventually this kind of work, outside in an open field, became very dangerous. The American fighter bombers started to shoot at everything that moved. During such attacks we had to lie down in the holes we had previously dug. First the fighter bombers flew perpendicularly to the tank traps, then they began to fly parallel to the traps, the latter being much more dangerous for us because there was very little cover to hide us. After a number of people were killed during these work assignments, my father forbade me to do this work.

In addition to the ground fortification system, an air defense system was in the works. The first phase called for sixty anti-aircraft batteries of varying degrees of potency. Their positions were said to have been so cleverly concealed that they could also be used to defend Germany against tank attacks.

Hitler ordered his staff to update him regularly on the progress of the Siegfried Line construction. He also visited construction sites himself on at least four occasions, both to witness the progress himself and to deliver his now infamous propaganda – all the while reminding the rest of the world of his popularity. On May 20, 1939, he spoke to the local border residents and declared, "What I have seen of the Siegfried Line has convinced me of its invincible position. With me, the German people give our thanks to everybody who has worked on this defense line, which was built for the safety of all Germans." Even Winston Churchill called the Adolf Hitler of 1938 one of the great statesmen of all times.

Indeed, Hitler's popularity in the west of Germany had increased dramatically in the wake of the Siegfried Line construction. For the first time in many years, people felt safe and protected. During his visits, Hitler cashed in on the citizens' enthusiasm, and he was celebrated as no statesman before when he stopped to talk to people along the road. Since he was a dictator, democratic countries were not likely to understand his popularity, but he had brought Germany out of its great depression in just six years. Germans noticed the differences between poverty and prosperity, and, for a few years at least, were grateful to the *Führer*.

By the summer of 1939, the Siegfried Line was ready for its first test, despite the fact that some parts were still under construction. A practical test actually took place when the French attacked a bunker with a 17-centimeter cannon. It happened near the city of Saarbruecken, and the results were completely contrary to the French goal, because the bunker stayed intact. The French unknowingly provided a great service to the Germans. Hitler used this French attack to foster comprehensive propaganda campaigns boasting about how great his defense system was.

5

The Siegfried Line: In My Backyard

I vividly remember the groundbreaking and construction of the Siegfried Line on the outskirts of my hometown. The excitement and intrigue often made it extremely difficult for my friends and me to make it through the school day. I could hardly wait until the monotony of my academic work ended, so I could play soccer and war games while trying to catch a glimpse of the massive construction project occurring near my home. Suddenly, in many places around town, fifteen-foot-high wooden fences were erected. Everyone wondered what was happening behind those fences, especially since they were heavily guarded and no one was permitted to get close to them. Those who were directly involved in these secret construction operations were not permitted to disclose any information. Eventually, though, we could locate the bunkers of the Siegfried Line with their gun holes nearly concealed by looking for the steel towers of their weapons rising out of the earth.

Chaos reigned in the fields outside of my hometown during the construction. Although the main work was scheduled to occur between late summer and December of 1938, most of the farm harvest was destroyed, despite the farmers' protests, and the hillsides around Zweibruecken were transformed into a construction site of epic proportions, especially to a small boy. To my chagrin, our soccer field became a storage area for the sand and gravel that would ultimately be mixed into concrete to build the fortresses. Despite our disappointment at losing a soccer field, we youngsters were fascinated by the manner in which materials were stored there, sometimes reaching a height of forty feet. Trucks with a capacity of three to five tons drove backwards, on two heavy wooden boards, onto the sand and gravel hills to unload. Occasionally, a truck slipped off those boards and tipped over, leaving the driver injured. The process and its occasional unfortunate outcome appealed to my sense of danger, of course.

The chaos was not limited to the outskirts of town, though. More than 8,000 workers were stationed in Zweibruecken and the surrounding suburbs. For a city of 30,000 inhabitants, this was quite an influx of people. To accommodate them, new housing projects and social centers were quickly built. The locals prepared food for the workers in large central kitchens, and several entertainment venues, including libraries, playhouses and movie theaters, were opened. The local brewery operated around the clock to produce beer for the thirsty laborers. Most of them came from Bavaria, my father's homeland, and they were heavy beer drinkers.

It became apparent that diplomacy had failed, when Hitler officially announced the construction of the Siegfried Line in a speech delivered on September 12, 1938. Less than a month later, he toured my hometown of Zweibruecken and delivered a speech praising the construction of the western front line of defense and thanking the patriots who were so diligently helping to build it at an accelerated pace. He referred to the line as invincible, and for the first time in a long time, the people along Germany's western border felt that we were well protected. Who needed a gas mask?

During his inspection visits, which I remember vividly, Hitler was celebrated like no other statesman in my father's memory. Hitler used the enthusiasm of his countrymen to propagandize and improve the Nazi party's hold on the German population. Instead of holding receptions with mayors and party officials, his motorcade would stop every few kilometers so he could converse with people along the roadside. During one such inspection trip, Hitler's motorcade went right past our home in Ixheim. It was a warm and fairly sunny afternoon, as I recall, and throngs of my countrymen had gathered at the intersection in front of my house, waiting to show their appreciation to the man who had led Germany out of the Depression to unprecedented prosperity.

There were amazing trumpet fanfares. People, including thousands of construction workers, had come from all of the suburbs to catch a glimpse of the *Führer*. Local police, as well as the yellow-uniformed SA (or storm troopers), stood scattered in the street to keep it clear for the motorcade. Considering Hitler's popularity and the graciousness he showed by riding through our town, however, a vast and organized security effort was not required. Onlookers knew how to behave and pushing, shoving or disorderly conduct of any kind was entirely unacceptable.

Wearing their mandatory, party-issued uniforms, the *Hitlerjugend* (Hitler Youth) and *Bund Deutscher Mädel - B.D.M.* (German Maidens Organization), the youth organizations for boys and girls ten years of age and older, formed the first line of defense, so to speak, between the onlookers and the parade route. They stood shoulder-to-shoulder in mustard yellow short-sleeved shirts and black kerchief ties fastened with leather clips at the Adam's apple. Just below the shoulder on the left side of their shirts, the Nazi party's notorious symbol, the Swastika, and an eagle were embroidered. To complete the uniforms, boys wore black shorts and girls wore short black skirts. At the time, I was just seven, not old enough to join the mandatory, Nazi party-sponsored club for youngsters; but I looked forward to becoming a part of the group, sporting my own uniform and playing the organized war games that the older children in my town seemed to enjoy so much.

Since I was small and we were four or five rows deep in the crowd that had gathered on our front lawn and spilled into the street, my father placed me high atop his sturdy shoulders so I could witness the great German hero passing through on his way to the massive construction site just north of my home. As the moment drew near, the crowd began to roar. I looked back over my left shoulder and into my view came a long line of twenty or so official military vehicles driven by uniformed men. Thanks to my lofty perch, before long I spotted *the* car, a shiny, black Maybach two-door convertible, enormous by today's standards, with armed guards clinging confidently and attentively to the front quarter panels on either side. The unremarkable escort cars that went before and after the Maybach contributed to the importance of the event by alerting the crowd that the *Führer* was in their midst. The cheering intensified and my excitement grew as the convertible approached the intersection.

Hitler, standing in the front of the car on the passenger's side, grasped the top of the window. He was clearly moved but not surprised by the gratitude he sensed from the crowd. He raised his right arm from his side into the air in front of him, fingertips outstretched and rigid, while his left hand steadied his stance. It was the now notorious salute. The frenzied crowd erupted in a cacophony of *Heil Hitler*s in turn. Pockets of loud verbal salutes exploded in unison, like firecrackers all around me. A group of people behind me, then a group off to my right, followed by a chorus of 100 up ahead: *"Heil Hitler! Heil...Heil...Hitler...Heil...Hitler...Hitler...Heil Hitler!"* The wave continued, gathering strength as he approached the throng. Directly in front of me, the car carrying Hitler paused briefly, barely stopping, and the smiling leader reached down and shook hands with four or five men in the front row of saluting spectators.

And then he was gone, literally but not figuratively of course. The energy that remained in that intersection was like nothing else I have ever experienced. Partly excited, somewhat scared, but ever mindful of the stature and standing of the man who had traveled past my house that day, I had failed to join my countrymen in the salute. But I watched, clinging tightly to my father's chin, never blinking, saying nothing.

Since he was a dictator, these parades must have been difficult for democratic countries to fathom; but Hitler wanted everyone in the world to know how popular he had become and how loyally his subjects supported him. Hitler's words, when he spoke to construction workers near my hometown on October 10, 1938, demonstrated his appeal for support from the German people:

> Three hundred and fifty thousand of you are actively and currently building the Siegfried Line! You are helping me to bring back 3.5 million people from the Sudetenland into the German Reich. Each of you is therefore bringing back 10 Germans. I hope I can rely further on you in the future.

6

War Erupts

In August 1939, the political situation changed dramatically. Poland chose not to accept Hitler's requests, and the persecution of Germans in Polish territories was stepped up. Invitations to come to Berlin for further negotiations were rejected by the Polish government and answered with threats of war instead.

By August 26, 1.5 million German soldiers were in ready position, and food stamps had been distributed to the red zone population. Hitler, claiming to tire of Polish aggression against former German citizens living in the occupied corridor and the city of Danzig (formerly in the German state of West Prussia), demanded that Poland return the corridor and Danzig to Germany. Poland refused, of course, and – having ratified the British-Polish Non-Aggression Treaty the day before – went about mobilizing the Army and Navy for war with Germany. Using tactics aimed at keeping England out of the war, Hitler made last-minute efforts to negotiate with other European countries, but to no avail. War with Poland was inevitable. Because of Poland's alliance with England and France, Hitler ordered the evacuation of the red zone.

During the escalating tension in the month of August, the mayor of Zweibruecken, Dr. Collafong, knew neither what would happen nor what to expect. Since he had no guidance from the government, he tried something on his own. With two city councilmen, he traveled southeast to the French city of Iffezheim to attend the horse races. He believed that the presence of many French people at the races indicated that war was not imminent. His assessment was incorrect, however, because upon his return on August 28, he was ordered to report directly to City Hall. A crisis team welcomed him with a sealed envelope that he was ordered to open at once. Inside were instructions to prepare the city for evacuation. He was given five days to prepare, process and transport all important files and maps to an office in the city of Kaiserslautern to the east. From there, the documents would be shipped further east to the city of Hof in Bavaria.

From that point on, everyone feared war. No reasonable person likes to think about war, but more and more signs pointed in that direction. Everyone tried to follow their daily routines, but the Red Cross had been ordered to evacuate both of Zweibruecken's hospitals, and the government had confiscated most of the civil service vehicles. Despite these measures, at German and French borders, the farmers remained friends, and border guards still conversed with each other. Even after installment of the border guard battalion (consisting primarily of customs inspectors and World War I veterans) between Zweibruecken and the French border to the south, opposing soldiers retained contact and met daily to exchange merchandise.

The order to draft the reserve units in our area was given, to help in securing the western border from any attack by the French military. On August 28, these reserve units had moved into position about 10 kilometers from my parents' house. Veterans of World War I were also drafted in our area (and in the whole western Palatinate), literally taken from their beds and told to report to the military government in Zweibruecken. This included my father, not only because he had served in the previous war, but because he spoke fluent French and was an experienced reserve officer. After six months, he was released from the Army to return to his company, where he was badly needed.

The official occupation of the Siegfried Line came on August 28, 1939. The 106th Border Artillery Regiment moved into the fortresses near St. Ingbert, a neighboring city of Zweibruecken. The 127th Border Infantry Regiment, headquartered in my town, moved into the fortresses around a place called *Grosser Exerzierplatz* (great parade grounds), today the location of Zweibruecken's airport. (*This airport was built by the Royal Canadian Air Force after World War II ended. For many years, after the Canadians left, it was occupied by the U.S. Air Force.*) After occupying the bunkers, some additional units were moved closer to the French border to secure the fore field. Immediately they had heavy casualties. Those soldiers killed close to the border were returned to Zweibruecken and buried in our cemetery.

On August 31, 1939, all police veterans were drafted, and Hitler issued his command for warfare, No. 1, Chapter 3:

1. After all political efforts to remedy, for Germany, the unacceptable situation on the east borders were exhausted, I decided to solve the border problems with power and force.

2. The attack against Poland is to be executed in accordance with the preparations of Operation *Weis* (White), with a few changes resulting from army organization. The tactical plan and goal will stay in place.
    Day of attack: September 1, 1939
    Time o f day: 4:45 a.m.

3. Commands on the western front will be given after we see the reactions of the French and British to the offensive. Small attacks will be defended, but no major action is to be taken.

4. I order a strict respect of the neutrality of Holland, Belgium, Luxembourg and Switzerland. The German western border will not be crossed under any circumstance, except by my personal command.

On Friday morning, September 1, 1939, Hitler's speech was broadcast over all radio stations:

Seit 5 Uhr 45 wird Zureckgeschossen... Since 5:45 we are shooting back. If now the western statesmen declare that this affects their interests, I can only regret such statements. They cannot for one second prevent me from fulfilling my duties. I have solemnly declared and offered assurances that we are demanding nothing from those western states, and I repeat, we will never demand anything from them. I have given assurances that the border between France and Germany is final. I repeatedly offered to England friendship, as well as cooperation. But love cannot be offered from one side, it must be returned from the other. Germany has no interest westwards. The Siegfried Line is for all time the western border of the German Reich.

And with that, the war began. On that day, Hitler's troops entered Poland.

Those of us who resided in the red zone knew that we were in danger and recognized, almost as soon as Hitler's message was broadcast on the radio, that our lives would change. What we did not understand, and what haunts me still today, is why so many of our border homes and cities had been effectively excluded from Germany by the defense line that was supposedly built to protect us. Why did this line, the construction of which had delivered our town and region from economic depression and restored our national pride, suddenly leave us feeling like outsiders? Despite the frenzy of preparing for the impending evacuation, I struggled with this first in a series of paradoxes that would shape my life.

On September 3, 1939, England declared war against Germany without being directly threatened. It was the second time within 25 years. A few hours later, France also declared war on Germany. That same day, the residents of my hometown were ordered to evacuate.

The construction workers still had to finish the Siegfried Line. When this turn of events took place, it had been 80 percent completed and was already occupied by the military. If this had not been the case, the French Army could have very easily invaded Germany. Everyone in Germany was worried about the war with Poland, because the Polish Army was thought to be the strongest in Europe.

On September 9, 1939, the reserve battalion from Zweibruecken was disbanded and replaced by the 337th Army Battalion, which had its headquarters in Pirmasens, a neighboring city. (*Many American GIs were later stationed in Pirmasens and remembered this city for its nickname, "shoe capital of the world." Before outsourcing shoe manufacturing to China and other countries, Pirmasens had the most shoe factories of any place in the world.*)

The French Army secured a position ahead of the Maginot Line very close to the German border. The French unit involved was the 32nd Infantry Regiment. After fierce fighting on September 10, 11, and 12, the French took the first German territories, only 10 kilometers from my hometown. On October 4, heavy casualties forced the French to retreat from this area to their own country. The French casualties involved 60 dead, 157 wounded, and 11 missing in action. In Zweibruecken and its surrounding areas were the headquarters for the 71st, 36th, 257th, 258th, and 262nd Infantry Divisions, all from the Reich's Army Corps XXIV. Heavy artillery was brought in, mounted on railroad cars.

How did the German Army react on the western front? It followed Hitler's command and waited for instruction. The Germans started a counterattack, and on October 15, all French troops were driven out of German territory and back to Alsace-Lorraine. It was a very hard fight of short duration. On the French side, an elite battalion called Chasseurs Pyrénées fought and was defeated. Many French prisoners were taken.

The fall and winter of 1939 were marked by readiness and constant observation. Workers continued toiling on the Siegfried Line, moving earth and planting trees in order to conceal the bunkers and make them as invisible as possible. French and British weapon systems continued to progress and their attacks became more aggressive. Some of the already finished bunkers were not strong enough to withstand the enemy's artillery rounds, and as a result, the important bunkers were reinforced with thicker concrete walls, increasing from 1.5 to 2 meters in width. Hitler also requested the building of larger fortresses.

That same year, plans were begun on a third construction tier that would further enhance the Siegfried Line. This enhancement was named the Aachen-Saar program, also known as The Construction Program 1939-1940. One important change was to allow more room per person and more space for ammunition and food storage. The new Aachen-Saar bunkers were commonly referred to as the AS. With 90 different bunker types, the Siegfried Line was now one of the most diversified defense systems in the world. In our area we had only seven types of bunkers, even though our defense line was considered by Hitler to be one of the most important in the system.

Many construction workers were still employed in our area, working in two shifts. The French knew exactly when shift changes took place, and used this time to hit us with the heaviest artillery attacks. One day, a grenade hit a bus and almost killed all of the laborers in it. Out of 21,000 projected bunkers, some 17,137 were now operational. Work on the underground connections continued until 1942.

7

Evacuation and Return

Now more than 60 years have passed since the word *"Evakuierung"* (evacuation) was planted in every German's head. Up to that time, it had been barely known to the German population. It was a foreign word. The verb "to evacuate" is defined in German dictionaries as "to empty," or "to pump out," but also in a broader sense, "to free in the form of resettlement and transplantation."

What was the reason and goal of the high ranking Nazis – who normally worked diligently to keep any foreign word out of the German language – in using this word, *"Evakuierung"*? It was to draw attention to the extraordinary circumstances that required resettlement and transplantation of people from German territory.

It had been rumored for months in my town that evacuation could occur on short notice. The threat of war loomed despite resurgent German morale and the perceived protection provided by the Siegfried Line. My father, because he spoke French and we had the advantage of living close to the border, listened once in a while to French radio stations. The French government seemed open to and honest about the eventuality of evacuation for its citizens who resided along the border with Germany. Listening to such broadcasts was stringently forbidden in Germany, but it was just one example of the subversive actions my father would use to defy the Nazi regime throughout the course of World War II.

The focus on preparedness alarmed many of my countrymen, however. Why would evacuation be necessary? The strong German Army and western wall of defense were built to protect us, to be impregnable. At the time, the wave of German nationalism that Hitler had bred usurped all reason, and despite our strength as a nation, it appeared as if the rest of the world was out to get us. In short, we were led to believe that the alliance of bullying countries that surrounded us was jealous of our prosperity. To protect the citizenry of Germany, therefore, we were expected to be ready; and since my town was so close to the border with one of the bullies, we were put on notice.

It is clear today that, despite Hitler's grand plan, my father understood the gravity of the brewing conflict much better than most of his contemporaries, and it bothered him. Perhaps his good nature or his command of the French language contributed to this awareness. Most likely, though, the intense pride he felt in his heritage conflicted with the new national pride that Hitler and his henchmen had artfully imposed upon the country. Regardless, my parents knew they had to follow any evacuation order, and so prepared a middle-sized briefcase with cash, bank savings books, house and insurance documents, a few family pictures, passports, and a small container with washing, cleaning and sewing equipment. A small suitcase was also prepared, with shirts, underwear, and socks for one change of clothes. Mother included a second pair of shorts for me and a second blouse and skirt for her.

Threat became reality when my hometown of Zweibruecken was completely evacuated on September 1, 1939, for the first time in its 600-year history. Not only the city itself, but also all villages south of the city were included. A ten-kilometer strip along the French border was declared the red zone. Below is an excerpt from the official evacuation notice distributed to all people in the red zone.

1. Your house is in the red zone and it has to be evacuated.

2. Precautions have been taken to insure a smooth evacuation.

3. Every person will receive a special passport. Children under 12 are registered with their parents.

4. People who can walk must report to the assigned collection place immediately.

5. People who have been drafted and have no special passport must report directly to their draft place.

6. Only an organized evacuation can be successful. It is forbidden to leave on your own or stay behind.

7. People must have the following: food for three days; blankets; metal dishes; water bottles; underwear; washing, cleaning and sewing equipment; flashlights, passports and family documents; bank savings books; other important documents; and especially your gas masks. All of these items together may not exceed thirty pounds.

8. Owners of vehicles not registered for war purposes will receive special permits and instructions for use of their vehicles.

9. All fires in houses must be extinguished. An official will shut off gas and water lines in your house.

10. All animals must be let free.

Upon receipt of the evacuation notice, dispatched by members of the Nazi party, my mother and I had two hours to gather the required items and report to our collection place, the suburban railway station in Ixheim. During those two hours, my mother seemed confused and anxious, and she cried as she struggled with what else to pack and what to leave behind. She hurried to make sandwiches and even packed spoons, forks and knives for both of us. Our gas masks weighed between eight and ten pounds, and thus consumed one-third of our weight limit. As a result, we could not take blankets or bottles of water. I wanted to take a few things, mainly my miniature toy trucks, but Mother refused to pack them. She thought then, and I understand now, that thirty pounds would be reached in no time. Had we exceeded the limit, something – not likely of our choosing – would have been left behind. Other than my attempt to include toys, I was not involved in packing. Mother checked three or four times to insure that she had turned off the main gas valve and the water lines. She also checked all doors and walked, worriedly but deliberately, through the whole house several times before we left. Citizens like us in the red zone were also required to cover porch lights to prevent enemy aircraft from seeing the area at night.

Like my mother and many of our neighbors, I was devastated at having to leave our animals to roam free. Because of the threat of war, we had purchased two goats, one pig, and five each of geese and ducks. We also had 10 chickens, several rabbits and a cat named Liesl. Just before the two-hour preparation time expired, my father called and told us that he would be staying at a nearby barracks with the company trucks and that we should not let our animals free. He thought he might get a permit to drive into the red zone to feed and water them. My mother and I were, for a moment at least, the happiest people in the world. Not only had we heard Father's voice – a luxury, as many did not have telephones in their homes at the time – but our animals would not be left to fend for themselves.

The harsh reality of the evacuation returned quickly as mother hung up the phone. Being almost eight, I was old enough to sense the emptiness and helplessness around me; but at the same time, I was excited about where the journey would lead us. In retrospect, it must have been horrifying for my mother, a reverse nightmare in which she dreamt of safety, security and normalcy but woke abruptly to confusion, disbelief and uncertainty – all of which magnified exponentially the more alert she became. Three of her four sons and her husband were serving in the war, she had been forced to abandon her home, and her youngest boy carried a gas mask and a suitcase filled with documents rather than his toy truck collection. I was lucky that I did not fully understand the gravity of the situation, but I was grateful that my father would – maybe – be able to look after my animals.

In sweltering heat – it reached 90 degrees that day – a police car equipped with a loudspeaker drove through the city of Zweibruecken and its suburbs, broadcasting the following announcement: "Attention! Attention! The whole population of Zweibruecken must evacuate immediately." The evacuation began in a disciplined fashion, but fear soon gripped the crowds because of possible artillery attacks. For six weeks, the French troops had been holding maneuvers around the fortress of Bitche just across the border. We had heard the enemy artillery exercises, especially at night, so the war declaration heightened our fears when we realized we would be walking – veritable moving targets – as we proceeded to the train station.

My mother and I only had to walk about 10 minutes to the railway station, so we waited until the last moment to leave the house. On the way to the railway station, several neighbors joined us. Everybody talked nervously and quite a few ladies cried. I did not join other children because I had been told by my father and reminded by my mother to stay close to her and to obey all her wishes and commands. It was a sunny day with a few clouds. People were well behaved, but almost everybody cried at some point. At the railway station, twelve special trains waited to transport the evacuees. At the end of each train was a freight car to hold the belongings each family had brought.

Those citizens who were healthy and could walk were asked to assemble in groups and to go to destinations outside the red zone on foot. As the remaining women and children boarded the trains, they appeared sad and insecure, and some were clearly frightened. Some even wondered aloud to themselves, "Did we close the doors? Are the lights turned off? Are the gas and water turned off? What will become of our beloved animals?" I forced myself to overcome some of my own fear to support my mother in my father's absence. It wasn't easy, but I felt a sense of duty to protect my mother.

Saying good-bye to their wives and children drove some men to tears. Nobody knew how long the evacuation would last. But as the train pulled out of the station, most passengers pressed up against the train windows, shoulder to shoulder and two or three deep, all uttering the same, still surprising lament: "Good-bye, my beautiful Zweibruecken. Farewell, my beautiful homeland." I remain impressed today that in a time of such personal and familial stress, most people turned their thoughts to the beauty of their city. Everybody wanted to have a last look out of the windows to see our beloved suburb one more time.

The train departing Ixheim took us twenty kilometers north to Bruchmuehlbach. Located in the green zone inside the Siegfried

Line, residents of the village were not evacuated, but they had been put on alert in case hostilities with France ensued. At the time, though, Bruchmuehlbach was out of range of the French artillery positions on the Maginot Line. A local family took us in and generously gave my mother and me their master bedroom to stay in. I do not recall the name of the family, but they were in their mid-forties and the gentleman worked in the mayor's office. They lived in a very nice, solidly built two-story sandstone building. The bedroom in which we stayed was typical of the time, outfitted mainly with solid wood furniture. Our hosts even cleared a little place in their closet for our clothing. My mother did not unpack much because we had to be ready to leave again on short notice, so our few belongings were left packed and stored in a bedroom corner.

The bedroom, like all German bedrooms, did not have its own lavatory and toilet, but it was much better than our situation at home. The bathroom, including a toilet, was across the hall from the bedroom, and we had to share it with the family who took us in. We did not have bathrobes packed, so we had to check that nobody was out in the hall when going to the bathroom. Living in this house in Bruchmuehlbach was comfortable, since everything was newer and more modern than at home. Almost daily, my mother reminded me to respect the property of our generous hosts – not to look into their drawers in the bedroom or touch anything in the house.

A so-called military station had been established in Bruchmuehlbach to serve breakfast, lunch and dinner for the temporary inhabitants from the red zone. The people who took us in were very generous, though, and invited us to join them for all their meals. The family must have known how difficult the evacuation and abandonment of our possessions had been for us. This was somewhat uncomfortable for my mother, but I enjoyed eating with them. I think a few times we went out to the food station, but my mother did this primarily to see the Ixheim neighbors and friends who had been evacuated with us. I doubt that it was for the government-issued food.

Back in the red zone, only police, soldiers, party officials and those workers still constructing the Siegfried Line had been permitted to remain in Zweibruecken. Immediately after the last evacuation train left, guards with police authority took positions around the city so that thieves would not steal items from the abandoned homes. They also placed signs on every corner warning looters that they would be executed. We later learned that the evacuation of an entire city precipitated some unusual but unavoidable work for those law enforcement officials who remained. At the city's funeral home, for example, there were still cadavers awaiting burial. Many people from Zweibruecken had died in foreign cities and quite a few soldiers – native sons – had been killed during the war with Poland or in border confrontations with France. With the undertakers gone, it became the duty of the police to bury the dead. Unfortunately, it was the rainy season and the police had to dig graves in the pouring rain.

One of the saddest parts of the evacuation for me remains the order that no animal was to be left in confinement; all animals, domestic and commercial, were to be freed. In 1939, Zweibruecken still had its own horse breed, the *Zweibrücker Rasse*. Approximately 100 of these horses were evacuated to central Germany, and the stables became shelters for military equipment. The other, less famous animals in the city did not receive such royal treatment. As you can imagine, many cows, horses, pigs, sheep, dogs, cats, goats and chickens ran around the town aimlessly, while others remained chained – their owners had forgotten to release them in the harried moments of the evacuation. To respond to the mounting confusion, the military suddenly found itself called into action to manage the increasingly chaotic situation. Cows that had not been milked for days were so full of milk that they were screaming in pain, and other animals that had weakened due to lack of food or old age lay dead in the streets. Near my home where the two rivers flowed together, the soldiers lost control of the abandoned animals that broke from the herd and ran into the rivers for relief from the late summer heat. Some drowned and others were rescued with considerable effort. My father, who returned often to feed our family's animals, witnessed the sad situation first hand and offered assistance when he could.

After a few days, the herds were finally contained in the fields and meadows on the outskirts of town. Farm girls and farmers' wives were bused in daily from the green zone to milk the cows, and a relative calm fell over the city. In all, the soldiers helped save tens of thousands of animals from certain death. According to my father, despite this major flaw in planning, the evacuation had been extremely well organized. Not only was the entire population evacuated, so were the hospitals, nursing homes, factories, and the complete administration of the city. After all the hospitals and nursing homes were emptied, the hospitals were taken over by military doctors and personnel, and they were equipped as first aid stations or "field hospitals." The nurses and nuns of the Catholic hospital received the order on September 10 to immediately report to their monastery in Mallersdorf.

One notable exception to the evacuation order was the city's largest company (*coincidentally the one where my career began some years later*), the *Dinglerwerke AG*, which produced equipment for steel mills as well as locks and dams for inland waterways. In direct violation of the government's order that all of the company's employees and management be evacuated together, some of the workers had actually left the city with their wives and children and had begun working in other German cities prior to the evacuation. My father's company, which made barbed wire and small machinery used in the war effort, stopped production for only 14 days. Some of the 300 employees were called back from the green zone shortly after the initial evacuation.

Evacuation of the city government offices, including City Hall, posed a completely different problem. Without the inhabitants, there was little need for such an administration. Those people who had been evacuated, though, needed the former administrators for such official documents as passports and birth certificates. To address this need, satellite offices were established in the cities and towns to which the people of Zweibruecken had been relocated. The Hitler Youth, many of whom were evacuated with their parents, were reorganized in the green zone and kept on Party course.

The Nazi Party was always watching the evacuees and often "suggested" that certain tasks be completed, especially if the Party had offered help to an individual or group.

With the vast majority of the human population safely evacuated to the green zone and soldiers restored to the positions for which they had trained, the German artillery assault began. Grenades launched at France howled over the roofs of my beloved hometown-turned-military installation, and retaliatory French grenades began to explode in and around the vacant homes, churches, schools and offices. My father, having returned to Zweibruecken to restart factory production, allowed several soldiers to live with him in our home. Many of the evacuated residents were unaware that their homes were also being used as soldiers' quarters, and as you can imagine, many personal belongings were stolen.

To maintain communication among the evacuees, a small newspaper called *"Rund um de Exe"* was started. (*Exe – Exerzierplatz* – were the parade grounds in the middle of Zweibruecken where many festivals and fairs were held.) Additionally, the Catholic priest, who had remained in Zweibruecken, would ride his bicycle more than 500 kilometers per week to visit with his parishioners, celebrate Holy Mass, and help them overcome homesickness with news from their hometown.

On the eighth day of our stay in Bruchmuehlbach, the same people who had organized our initial evacuation from Ixheim ordered us to gather our belongings and prepare to leave. Unaware of where the next leg in our journey would lead, we boarded another train. Our belongings were stored above the seats in racks that had nets to hold the bags. The train was crowded but not overloaded, and there was no passport check or anything unusual during the train ride. After we passed Frankfurt, the train stopped at many railway stations to unload people under the direction of Nazi party officials who had accompanied us from Ixheim.

Late that night we arrived in a small city called Babenhausen, southeast of Frankfurt. We must have been unloaded in one of the last stations, because it was already dark and the train was nearly empty. As we disembarked, two small elderly ladies dressed in black, probably 65 or 70 years old, greeted us on the platform and told us that we were assigned to live with them. Since it was dark and we were tired, we could not see much of our new temporary home, but the next morning we realized that our bedroom was located in a special guesthouse at the end of a long courtyard. The two-story guesthouse was very old, but clean and in good shape. It had two bedrooms, a bath and toilet, a living room and a kitchen, all accessible via an exterior stairway. The wooden floors creaked when we walked over them, and I often imagined that I was living in a haunted house. Underneath there must have been old stables or wine cellars. Babenhausen is known, after all, for the famous *Fränkischer Apfelwein* (Franconian Apple Wine). The bedrooms were decorated tastefully, but had not been renovated in many years. Despite their antiquated appearance, the rooms were nicely kept and clean, and the bed covers were thick German down feather comforters, to keep us warm at night. In addition to excellent lodging, under the circumstances, we enjoyed excellent food. Since the food shortage had not yet begun, our kind hosts fed us typical German fare: salads, vegetables, and potatoes for lunch and small cold cuts for dinner, always in plentiful quantity. They probably enjoyed having a young "son" again.

Most days, the landladies took me to the bank of the Main River to watch the freighters, loaded with coal and grain, as they were towed through the town. I also tried my hand at fishing. (*I never caught anything, but the experience of trying sparked an interest in sport fishing that would, later in life, lead to trout fishing in Canada and salmon fishing expeditions in Alaska.*) Babenhausen was a very peaceful place, contrary to the political landscape that surrounded us, and I remained protected – at least for the short term – from the horrors of the war that had begun.

Shortly after our arrival, Mother was able to contact my brother Albert by telephone. After four weeks in Babenhausen, Albert, an officer in the Army, mailed us a special permit and train tickets to join his family in Munich, two hours to the southeast. Without his military standing and influence, we would never have been able to acquire the travel permit to deviate from the evacuation plan.

After a few days, we received a telegram with a notification to report to the *Militär-Kommandatur* (Military administration) in

Babenhousen. They had a report from the *Militär-Kommandatur* in Munich to grant us a permit to take leave from the official evacuation. We were to show this to the local coordinator in order to be officially excused from the evacuation. My mother checked the departure schedule carefully, to be sure that we would arrive in time to board the correct train (as train tickets did not indicate the times of departure). The ladies who hosted us were somewhat sad at our departure, but after we packed our belongings and Mother completely cleaned the place where we stayed, they walked with us to the railway station, onto the platform, and even to the train door.

I was excited to ride in a train again and to see my oldest brother and his family, but my mother was thrilled to be going to see her oldest son and his wife, Friedel, and especially her two granddaughters, Ruth and Isolde. When we arrived in Munich, my brother met us at the *Bahnsteig* (arrival platform), immediately hugged Mother, and refused to let her carry any of our baggage. Outside the railway station, a military vehicle (similar to a Jeep) with a driver waited for us. Albert helped Mother into the back seat, then gave me a boost into the front seat. He nudged me to move toward the driver, then sat down in the passenger seat beside me. How proud and important I felt to ride in a military vehicle between two soldiers.

Mother and I had our own bedroom in my brother's apartment, thanks to my niece, Ruth, who gave up her room and moved in with Isolde. I remember being glad to celebrate my 8th birthday (November 12, 1939) in Munich. It was not a big celebration, but I received some small presents and – what I remember most – a few small chocolate bars. Chocolate was becoming more difficult to come by, so I was especially grateful to have received it

My brother enrolled me in a local elementary school. The school year had already started, so I had some catching up to do. Since we had arrived in Munich during much colder weather, my brother and mother had to buy me some winter clothing. To go to school, I had to get up early in the morning. I walked about 5 minutes from the Lothstrasse to the Dachauerstrasse, where I boarded a cable car. (*Years later, I would learn that just 15 miles from that corner stood the horrible Dachau Concentration Camp, where so many of Hiter's victims insanity perished.*) I had to stay in the tram for about five stations, then get out and walk another three to five minutes. I remember this as clearly as if it were today. I had a monthly tram ticket, and it was fun to ride to and from school. Since I had come from the red zone and had no school supplies, the teacher kindly provided me with books and supplies. There was little difference between the new school and my hometown school, as far as the daily routine and student conduct were concerned. The problem for me was the Bavarian dialect and culture.

After a while, a sense of normalcy returned to my daily routine. While I would have preferred my home and school in Palatinate, at least I lived in a family once again. I knew then how fortunate Mother and I were, and I remain grateful to my brother and his family to this day for their generosity. After school and homework, I was permitted to play in the courtyard of the military housing compound, and eventually found a friend. Evelin lived next door to us and for the first time in my life, I had an eye for a pretty girl. I can still picture her beautiful face, long legs, long and straight blond hair, and pretty blue eyes. She was a year or two older than I, and she attended a private school. I had a crush on her, finding her polite and feminine behavior quite attractive. When we first met, we played catch and kickball in the courtyard and eventually, when the weather turned cold, we moved inside for card games.

Since I was raised in a much smaller town, I found it difficult to make friends with the more cosmopolitan boys of Munich. I struggled to understand their Bavarian dialect and their different behavior. Perhaps because I was a stranger both to Bavaria and to the big city atmosphere, the boys my age seemed taller and more muscular to me. But they were not stronger. As an outsider, I often found myself involved in scuffles, typical in those days, and I was seldom the loser.

In general, I wanted to behave well, especially in view of my brother's family and my mother. While I usually succeeded at winning the scuffles into which I was, more often than not, provoked, I soon learned a harsh lesson: people cannot always be trusted to be honest. One day, the ruffians challenged me to a contest to see who could throw stones the farthest over a garage and barn. Being tough and strong, I excelled at the contest. None of the challeng- ers even came close to my trajectories; in fact, many of them could not even throw their stones as high as the buildings that my stones sailed over with hardly an effort. I was king!

Little did I know that the boys had actually held a contest ear- lier that day. They knew that, on the other side of the garage and barn, construction workers were laying tile for a new building. Not only did some of my stones hit the workers, but also a few of them damaged the new tiles. One of the workers sustained injuries that required medical treatment. Five of the workers came running angrily toward us. As they drew closer, a wave of fear crashed over me, my cheeks reddened, and my stomach began to turn as I real- ized I had been set up by the band of Judas Iscariots. As the men ran after me, I scampered as fast as I could to Evelin's apartment. She must have seen the fear in my eyes, because she quickly let me in and locked the door behind us. The danger had passed, or so I thought.

Later that day, those scoundrels told the construction workers where I lived. Shortly thereafter, they showed up at my brother's apartment, threatening to call the police. As my brother explained that my mother and I had recently come from the red zone and that he was an officer in the military, the workers changed their minds about turning me over to the authorities. They did insist, however, that I visit the man I had injured and apologize. When my mother found out what had happened, she was disappointed in me, but she was not angry. Although I refused at first, she asked me to obey her and apologize to the worker. I visited the worker (and the others working with him) days later, right around the corner at their workplace. I was scared and nervous. One of the workers had a bandage around his head. I approached him and I told him what had happened: that I had been tricked into the stone-throw- ing contest and that I felt very sorry about what had happened.

I was ashamed before my mother and brother that I had caused such trouble. My mother wrote the whole story to my father, but I don't recall ever hearing from him. He knew it was tough to be evacuated and he probably did not want to pour more oil on the fire. At the time, having to apologize was almost as difficult for me as leaving my beloved home along the French border. It was a life lesson that I shall never forget.

In the meantime, my father's employer petitioned the government to release him from military duty so he could return to the nail factory, to restart production of barbed wire and other equipment used in warfare. We were somewhat relieved that he was no longer in an active military unit, so now he could return legally to our home to protect our house and our animals. In fact, we had defied the evacuation command and kept our animals at the house. My father and his pickup truck were stationed in the barracks near the city of Kaiserslautern, just 40 kilometers from our home and 15 kilometers from the red zone. With his special military status, he entered the red zone for work every day and checked on and fed our animals.

After six months in Munich, my father sent us train tickets to Homburg, just ten miles from Zweibruecken but inside the green zone. There we moved in with my uncle, and my father was able to visit us every weekend. We had to sleep on field mattresses on the floor of the dining room. I was enrolled in school and began to make friends again.

We lived very close to the University Clinic, a hospital for wounded and recovering soldiers from all over Germany. Wives, girlfriends and other women – so-called ladies – often visited the soldiers. Since my friends and I played in the nearby woods, we often witnessed their clandestine sexual activities. The couples were so involved with each other that they either never saw us or just ignored us. To spy on them, we approached the area through a closely planted row of evergreens, through which we had to crawl on all fours. Adults probably could not or would not have gone into the thick brush of our hiding place, so we had little fear of being caught. On quite a few occasions we saw couples making love on the forest floor or leaning against the trees. This lasted normally from 10 minutes to half an hour. We sometimes ran away because we thought someone had seen us. The boys with me were all two or three years older, and afterwards we had quite some discussions.

Sometimes we went farther up the street to where those couples had to come out of the woods. We wanted to see how they looked or how their clothing looked. We always stayed at a distance on the other side of the street because we were afraid of being seen, but nothing serious ever happened to us.

After four months in Homburg, my father decided to move us back to our home in Zweibruecken, even though no date had been established for an official homecoming to the red zone. My mother was very excited to return to our house and animals, despite the possibility of war. The threat of hostilities on the western front had diminished and we longed to be a family again. After all, it had been nearly a year since we had left home. Father borrowed a truck from my mother's cousin and we loaded it with all our belongings. The trip was uneventful until we arrived at a checkpoint at the entrance to the red zone. Soldiers and police stood guard there, because only people with special permits were allowed to pass. Father approached the checkpoint slowly, and as the gate opened for an oncoming vehicle, he accelerated through the gate.

The police stopped him, of course, and swarmed to the driver's side of our vehicle. My father never raised his voice. He stated calmly, but in a most determined manner, "I am going forward and taking my family and our belongings with me." The guards replied, "If you continue, we will shoot." My father showed them his permit and said, "I am going ahead and you will not shoot!" With that, he pressed the gas pedal and away we went. Not one shot was fired. My mother and I were shaking and stared straight ahead. We arrived at our home after a silent thirty-minute drive.

Our fear was tempered only by disappointment. While we were happy to return to our home, we discovered that many of the belongings we were forced to leave behind had been stolen. Our expensive stamp collection and some rare books were gone. Saddest of all was the disappearance of a beautiful gold watch with a chain that had been made from a braid of my mother's hair entwined with gold thread. My mother had had it made for my father as a wedding gift.

None of our neighbors had returned to our town, and only a few workers were back. While I had regained the relative security of my home and my parents, I was without friends and school for quite some time. The loneliness I felt then, however, paled in comparison to the danger that would befall me in the months ahead. Hitler was poised to launch a full-scale attack on France, the border of which was located just minutes from my living room.

PART II

8

The French Defeat and German Homecoming

Just prior to my father's courageous display in getting us past the German soldiers at the checkpoint, German troops had entered and taken over Denmark and Norway. We imagined that the British must have been infuriated, since it was widely held that England wanted to build up its empire and influence in Europe. In the matter of these two northern countries, Germany had won the battle – at least for the time being.

Seeing this act of strength on the part of the German military and assuming that tension with France would subsequently decrease, thousands upon thousands of German refugees began to ask, "When can we go home?" Farmers were especially anxious, because planting their crops was overdue. Unbeknownst to them, some of the military units stationed in the red zone had seeded 2,500 hectares of land. While this was far less than should have been planted or would have been planted under normal circumstances, the soldiers' assistance yielded more than 10,000,000 pounds of hay. Imagine how much more would have been produced if land mines and bunkers had not been in the way of a good harvest. Despite the general eagerness to return home to the red zone, the official government-sponsored homecoming had to wait until early fall.

Until May of 1940, the western front was relatively quiet. For months, German troops stationed along the Siegfried Line had been in a holding pattern, operating under the so-called *Fall Gelb*

(Case Yellow) command. The Germans called it *"Sitzkrieg"* or "sit-down war," the French nicknamed it *"drôle de guerre"* or "funny war," and in English-speaking countries, it was known as the phony war. Quite a few soldiers on both sides were residents of the border regions. Everybody in Alsace-Lorraine spoke German. At night, soldiers from the French and German armies frequently met and exchanged cigarettes and food while holding neighborly talks. None of the soldiers liked the war the crazy politicians had created.

On the morning of May 10, 1940, the refugees learned, to their surprise, that Germany had attacked France. Everyone soon realized that Germany would win the war this time. First Denmark and Norway to the north had been invaded. Now the Germans circumvented the Maginot Line to the north via Belgium and Holland.

Hitler had commanded the attack on France through Belgium, Luxembourg and Holland. "Soldiers of the western front," Hitler encouraged his troops, "with this, the hour for you has arrived. Today's beginning fight decides the destiny of the German nation for the next 1,000 years to come. Now, do your duty. The German population is sending their best wishes to you."

All things considered, in Zweibruecken and the western regions close to the French border, things remained relatively calm. Only a few fighter plane scuffles occurred, resulting in several French planes and one German plane being shot down. That first day, though, nineteen soldiers were killed in front of a Siegfried Line bunker during an air attack. They were the first casualties in our area since the war began, and they were buried with full military honors in a military cemetery in Zweibruecken.

The German 457th Infantry Regiment initiated several attacks against France from the border town of Hornbach, just inside the red zone. The regiment would eventually sustain heavy casualties as it pushed into France between the cities of Schweyen and Wollmuenster, and it would see only minor advancement into France.

In the second phase of the attack on France from our area, called the *Fall Rot* (Case Red), another infantry division moved across the border into France slightly to the south, between the cities of Schweyen and Bliesdahlheim. This time, there was very little resistance.

On June 14, eleven German divisions succeeded in penetrating the Maginot Line near the city of Saarbruecken, near my hometown. At the same time, six more divisions entered the French defense line via Belgium, while another division in the Palatinate Forest also made headway. The German military command wisely chose to attack the weakest spot of the Maginot Line, even though from a topographical viewpoint it was the most difficult.

During the next six weeks, breaking news interrupted the radio stations' regular programming with countless reports from the western front, telling of the enormous success of the German Army against French troops. A mood of euphoria gripped the refugees; with each announcement, their confidence in the military and the anticipation of returning home seemed to grow.

Then, on June 21, 1940, all radio stations interrupted their regular broadcasts and listeners in homes throughout Germany heard the deep tone of what sounded like a large bell, and a voice, bellowing, "Attention! Attention! The moment when you heard the sound of the bell, France laid down her weapons on all fronts."

Four days later, another special announcement came from Hitler himself, declaring that France had capitulated:

> German citizens: Your soldiers have, in only six weeks and in heroic fighting, ended the warfare in the Western Hemisphere against a brave opponent. The German soldiers' deeds will go down in the history books as one of the greatest victories of all time. Humbly, we thank God for His blessings. I am ordering to bring out the banners for ten days and to ring the church bells every day for seven days

The leader of our country and the overseer of the rebuilt and efficient German military had spoken. As the national banners of the Reichstag, with their red backgrounds and large black Swastikas, began appearing in windows and on flagpoles on every home and at government buildings, it became evident that things were going well, and the refugees knew it would soon be time to return home.

The French had been convinced that the Maginot Line could not be defeated, and the Germans had let them believe it. Yet, after only three days of offensives, the German armies were successful in breaking through and advancing far into France. The French soldiers were stunned. They felt there was nothing left to do except to surrender to Germany and become prisoners-of-war. France's heavy fortresses, like the one at Bitche, across the border from my hometown, continued to fight. Because it was such a secure citadel, there was no way for the Germans to conquer it. (*In 1993, when my American wife and I visited this famous fortress, we understood why it could never have been taken or destroyed.*)

This stage of the war was over in six weeks. On June 24, 1940, a cease fire was implemented, and shortly thereafter the French commander of the fortress of Bitche surrendered to the commander of the German 257th Infantry Division. The official date in historical documents is listed as July 1, 1940. The 300,000 English support forces stationed in France were allowed to retreat to England at Dunkirk. If the Germans had fought against these troops, there would have been many casualties. Hitler allowed their retreat in the hope that Germany would come to peace with England. With the cease fire, the Siegfried Line and the Maginot Line were both disarmed.

After the war with France ended, tears of happiness flowed freely for those who had been displaced. Everyone was on pins and needles, itching to return home. While my family had done so two months earlier, I had been quite lonely because there were virtually no other children my age to play with and school was, obviously, not in session. I remember being happy at coming home, but the city itself struck me as a very sad place to be. Little did I know at the time that things would eventually become downright mortifying. At the time, though, the damage to structures was limited to some broken locks and blown-out windows. Knowing what I know now, the city had retained its character, and with an organized effort on the part of city leaders and early returnees, it would be back to "normal" before too much time passed.

By June 26, just five days after France's surrender, German newspapers spread the word that homecoming questionnaires were available. In order to return home, one had to secure permission without delay, as it had been determined that returning to the homeland would have to occur in stages. As frustrating as this was for so many who had been displaced by the war, it was necessary in order to prepare the villages and towns for the influx of all the citizens that would ultimately come back. Mine fields had to be cleared and many home repairs needed to be completed, due to damage from heavy artillery fire. Additionally, water, gas and electric service had to be restored.

There were, of course, stories of refugees who attempted to return to their homes without permission. Most of them were turned back and ordered to follow proper procedures. One notable exception was the local Catholic priest. He rode his bicycle to Zweibruecken on back roads and through forests so he could celebrate mass with his parishioners. Nearly 200 people attended his first services.

While the repair of homes and infrastructure were given top priority, food stores were also on the list and they slowly filled up with merchandise. During the people's absence, a heavy March storm had taken down many trees, so it was necessary to clear the side roads of debris. A number of water pipes had also broken. No one in Zweibruecken had wells anymore and all the homes were connected to the public water system. The cold winter had caused many of the pipes to burst, and nearly all of the water meters required replacement. Without safe drinking water and reliable electricity, central kitchens were established that served three meals a day to approximately 3,000 people.

Pioneer military units moved in to start the daunting and dangerous task of locating and destroying mines that had been planted in the surrounding fields. French prisoners were assigned to perform the actual disarmament, supervised by the German Pioneer Units, so that the farmers could use their farmland again.

At first, people were terrified of the frequent explosions. The terror of war remained in their bones. And despite the modern (for the time) mine-sweeping equipment, some French prisoners of war were killed in the operation. The entire process took nearly five months, but when the job was completed, the city of

Zweibruecken celebrated the soldiers who had been responsible for the search-and-destroy mission.

Since most bunkers were permanent, not many guns could be removed from them. Therefore, the main fortresses stayed completely intact. Many curious families took advantage of the disarmament to inspect the bunkers. Men and young boys were especially interested in all the details. My friends and I discovered that we could get into these bunkers after the public visits ended and the doors were locked. All we had to do was squeeze through the narrow gun openings. We often took ammunition and hand grenades from the bunkers and later blew them up. All of the boys my age took part in those dangerous games. Unfortunately, this often resulted in serious injuries. One of my friends lost his left forearm and two fingers from his right hand, and his body was filled with smaller splinters of ammunition. Luckily, nothing happened to me.

There were cosmetic issues, too. The heaviest recorded rain of the century had occurred the preceding fall, resulting in blocked sewer lines and streets covered with layer upon layer of sand and silt. Weeds grew everywhere; in fact, the beauty of the city that had so appealed to the evacuees just one year before was visible only in the lovely architecture and trees. If one looked up, the city appeared, for all intents and purposes, unchanged. Looking down at the ground, however, was quite another matter. In order to bring residents home safely to an inhabitable place, repair work needed to be done.

Zweibruecken was (and still is) known for the largest rose gardens in Europe. More than a third of the rosebuds had died from the freezing winter, and the gardens could not be reopened to the public until after they had received much attention from gardeners. They eventually reopened on May 18, 1941.

More than 50,000 applications to return home were completed by refugees. All were processed as rapidly as possible by city and party administrators assigned to the cities along the border with France; then they were sorted according to city, suburb and village in order to organize return transportation. Refugees were placed in groups according to the location of their homes. On July 18, the first large train transport arrived in Zweibruecken. People who resided in the suburbs were taken in groups by buses from the railway station to a central drop-off location near their homes. The entire process flowed very smoothly and efficiently, and by October 1, the task was finished.

Wreaths made of evergreen boughs and decorated with *"Herzlich Willkommen in der Heimat"* ("Welcome to the Homeland") greeted the refugees as they returned to the Zweibruecken train station. A band, whose members came from the cities of Saar and Frankenholz, cheered the arriving groups and played patriotic songs associated with the Palatinate as each train arrived. Tents with medical supplies and food awaited those with special needs, mothers with small children, and the elderly. Staffed with doctors and nurses, the reception area provided a sense of security to many who had suffered a long year away from home and who were cautiously optimistic about returning to a normal life, now that hostilities with France had apparently come to an end. Doctors in those days made house calls, but with unreliable phone service, it was difficult to notify them when someone was sick. By offering medical assistance as people disembarked at the train station, the authorities did a tremendous service to those in need. The two hospitals in Zweibruecken that had been occupied by the military and the Red Cross were vacated as soon as hostilities with France came to an end. The Catholic nuns resumed day-to-day operation of both hospitals shortly thereafter.

Many residents returned home to find that the contents of their homes had been destroyed either during the evacuation or as a result of looting or artillery explosions on the outskirts of town. It was not unusual for a home to need at least a few new windows and other minor structural repairs. Most of these repairs had been taken care of before people returned, but the insides of homes were often in dire condition. The government established emergency stations where citizens could get furniture, dishes, utensils, and other household items that they could no longer find or that had been destroyed. Support personnel even traveled from other parts of Germany with aid supplies and offered assistance in organizing and distributing wares to those in need.

The reopening of kindergartens and day care centers was essential at this time. With so many men serving in the military, the women had their hands full cleaning houses and clearing gardens and driveways of debris. Regarding cleanup of their homes and homeland as their duty, they felt blessed to have quality childcare facilities provided during the day. Because the task was so overwhelming, however, special work brigades from other parts of the country arrived to provide assistance. In all, they cleaned more than 8,600 residences in 22 villages and suburbs of the city in 87 days. With a core of such dedicated volunteers, it is no wonder that the bakeries, delis and other businesses reopened as quickly as they did. Before long, Zweibruecken was full of life again.

Nobody at this time was thinking about what the future would hold. Everyone was too busy reveling in the present. I, however, had moments of loneliness. Yes, I was very close to my mother and father and was thrilled to be home and with both of them, but virtually no other children my age had returned. With no school to attend and no friends to play with, I spent a lot of time playing by myself, helping my mother with household chores, or waiting for my father to come home from work. One bright spot in my week during the homecoming period was the weekend celebrations that took place in the city center.

9

Air Warfare Development

In the beginning of World War II, the air war was conducted according to international laws. Between September 1, 1939, and May 5, 1940, German, English and French airplanes only attacked military targets.

Then, on May 5, 1940, Winston Churchill ordered the bombardment of the German city of Muenster, long before a single German bomb was dropped on any British city. When Churchill was elected prime minister and war minister on May 10, 1940, he started the second phase of the air war with the bomb attack on the German city of Moenchengladbach. He also ordered the bombardment of the German backcountry. It was the beginning of the air war against civilian populations, which escalated to perverse extremes over my hometown of Zweibruecken. J. M. Spaight, a British supporter of the air attacks, openly attested to the start of the air war on civilians. This is a historical fact.

Berlin was attacked six times by British war planes before the Germans started the first attack on London on September 7, 1940. More than 10 times, German cities had been attacked as the air war escalated, with bombardments on the city of Cologne, Hamburg, and Dresden, and even on Zweibruecken, my little jewel of a hometown. Churchill anticipated the bombardment of London, and by this time had evacuated his London headquarters and located it outside the city.

At the beginning of the war, President Roosevelt appealed to the warring nations not to attack the civilian population. But by the time he sent his own U.S. bombers against German cities in 1943, he had forgotten his own appeal.

The air war intensified into an all-out war. In a later and well-known speech in the Sport Palace of Berlin on February 18, 1943, Joseph Goebbels, the Nazi Minister of Propaganda, asked the German population the famous question, *"Wollt ihr den totalen Krieg?"* which translates into English as "Do you want a total war?" Many Germans still see the beginnings of this in the first bombardment of Moenchengladbach, in which three Germans and, ironically, one English woman died.

The so-called *Luftschutzwache* (guard against air attacks) was meeting frequently, despite the general opinion that the war might soon be over, since Poland and France had given up and the English had retreated to the isolation of their island. In the summer of 1940, 2,000 people in Zweibruecken were trained as guards. Every house had to have special blackout curtains to prevent any light from spilling outside. Over and over, newspapers reported how important it was that no lights should be seen during the night. The British Royal Air Force (RAF), which did not at this time have radar (not until the end of 1941), had very high casualties during daylight attacks and had to switch more and more to night bombardments. Those were not very effective, because quite often they missed their targets. Indeed, the RAF began in July 1941 with its so-called "carpet bombings" of civilian targets, but Zweibruecken was spared until late in the war.

On October 20, 1940, the population of Zweibruecken could hear a large number of heavy bombers flying over the city for the first time. They were heading southeast around 10:40 p.m. and back over Zweibruecken around 1 a.m. By now, people were used to the alarm sirens and were getting somewhat complacent. Fewer people were entering the shelters. Nothing much changed when, on February 8, 1941, four bombs were dropped over Zweibruecken. Almost no one went to the shelters. Only one airplane could be heard, then everything was quiet. In the morning the police found three big holes in a meadow. One bomb had not exploded.

More and more, the alarm sirens were heard. Quite often the bombers were flying over our city to attack other towns. In general, they were the so-called "middle distance bombers," not the heavy kind, but they could carry up to three tons of bombs. At this time they came in small squadrons.

As early as May of 1941, the day attacks increased. Prior to this time only a few sirens had been installed. From this point on, every city had to install sirens in intervals of 500 meters, mainly on top of schools, factories and public buildings. When the sirens were activated, it was a guessing game. Nobody knew if they were going off because Zweibruecken was the goal of the attacks or because the bombers were flying over to reach another city. Precaution was always necessary. Sometimes pre-warnings and main warnings were given three times a day, interrupting the daily activities of schools and work places.

In this phase of the air war, Zweibruecken was not yet a direct target. Even in the attacks on August 16, 1940, and February 2, 1941, Zweibruecken was only a secondary goal. This type of attack happened when there were clouds over the primary target, or some unforeseen event prevented the air attack from taking place as planned. Logically, the RAF selected another city as a second option, in case the first one could not be bombed. Therefore, it was always important to have every home and place darkened at night and to go to shelters during an alarm.

In 1942, the air war intensified. This was the time when the command shifted to British General Arthur Harris, known as "Bomber Harris," and the attacks on Germany increased dramatically. Until this time, the bombers had flown in small squadrons and in waves. With newly-developed radar systems, GEE and OBOE, the new four-engine Sterling, Lancaster and Halifax bombers could fly precisely to their goals. In mid-1942, some of the planes were equipped with the H2S radar systems, allowing the navigator to see the landscape underneath him like a map. This system also made possible the Boy Scout tactic, in which one plane flew ahead and indicated the target with special marker bombs. The rest of the squadrons followed, often more than 1,000 planes, to deliver the rest of the ornance. In the attack on Cologne on May 30, some 1,130 planes bombarded the city, followed the next day by a crushing bombardment from 2,000 planes.

The third attack on Zweibruecken seemed as though it was another secondary hit. On December 6, 1942, it was announced at 7:15 p.m. that enemy planes were about 100 kilometers from Zweibruecken. They were thought to be a lost squadron or some straying two-engine bombers, which at this time could only attack border cities in Germany because of their limited range.

For almost an hour after the main alarm, nothing happened. Around 8:30 p.m., one could hear motor rumbles and then, suddenly, about 50 fire bombs were dropped and detonated. Several fires started and a few houses burned down. Some people were injured, but none were killed.

In case this happened again, the fire departments and special guards conducted exercises two to three times a week. By August 1942, most of the fire fighters had already been drafted by the military. The Hitler Youth and the B.D.M., which included everyone born between 1925 and 1930, were recruited and trained fire fighting duties. The Red Cross units were also reduced as their members were drafted into the military. Hitler Youth units had to take over their work as well. Since I was born in 1931, I did not have to participate yet.

The air war escalated slowly until 1943, when the American Air Force became involved. The 8th Air Unit, formed in England, started to fly air attacks on Germany. The people of Zweibruecken heard more and more sirens as a result of so many squadrons flying over. A new command was given that alarm sirens at night would only be activated when more than 10 planes were in formation. Quite often, the night was filled with observation planes or night fighter planes which came alone. While British operations preferred to use a long, narrow formations for night attacks on industrial and civilian goals, the Americans used *"Bombenteppich"* (carpet bombing) formations.

The Americans were flying in groups of four-engine bombers, like the B17 (Flying Fortress) and B24 (Liberator). Attacks on Germany took place 24 hours a day. The Germans answered with more anti-aircraft batteries, more fighter planes and more shelters. Because the Allied bombers sustained heavy casualties during daylight, they cut back and concentrated more on night attacks. This was easier for them, since the German night defense fell completely apart in 1943 when the Allies started to drop *Düppel* (small aluminum strips). This foiled the radar system on the ground, as well as the German night fighter planes.

As of April 1943, the British Air Force started using liquid fire bombs instead of magnesium fire bombs, which were easier to extinguish. The new bombs caused very large fires. A further escalation took place when the air attacks came from planes now stationed in Italy, although Zweibruecken was still not very much involved in this phase of the air war. No serious attacks were registered in either my hometown or its sister cities.

On August 12, 1943, the police commander of Zweibruecken received a report that British airplanes had dropped small incendiary devices to start fires on the cornfields to destroy the harvest. The population of Zweibruecken was warned to be on the lookout for fires. On August 16, the first attack on Zweibruecken took place by British Whitley and Wellington bombers, each equipped with two engines. The first detonation could be heard on the outskirts of the city in the residential area of Kreuzberg. Several homes started to burn, but no casualties were reported.

Starting in the fall of 1943, the night observation planes, called "Iron Henry" or *"Gustav"* by the Germans, were coming quite often. They shot at every little light they could see. Most of the time, the planes came out of nowhere, shooting continuously, so there was no way to run to a shelter. One just had to lie down anyplace in the house. There were reports that the bullets from those planes went through windows and exterior shutters. Consequently, the blackout demands by the government were intensified.

The cities of Saarbruecken and Saargemuend, about 30 kilometers away, were attacked on October 10 by 46 U.S. bombers. In Zweibruecken, the highest alarm stage rang from 10:49 p.m. to 0:19 a.m. Between midnight and noon, it went on and off eight times.

At the end of 1943 and the beginning of 1944, not one day passed by without alarm, other than Christmas and New Year's, when Bomber Harris gave his crews a few days off. At the beginning of 1944, it was relatively quiet around Zweibruecken, except for the noise from large bomber squadrons flying to and from their targets in the interior of Germany.

Some people in Zweibruecken thought for a while that the air war had forgotten the city. We became used to the Iron Henry and the large bomber formations flying over the city.

But then, on February 25, 1944, around 10:30 a.m., some 246 B17s belonging to 18 different bomber squadrons started in east England and flew in the direction of southern Germany. They belonged to the first U.S. Bomber Division. The mission for 196 of those B17s was to attack the Messerschmidt Aircraft Manufacturer in Augsburg, Bavaria. Fifty others were supposed to attack targets in the city of Stuttgart. In total, the planes carried 168 tons of high explosive demolition bombs. The day produced excellent flying weather without any clouds, and the bomber squadrons received coverage by Thunderbolt B47 fighter planes that were supposed to protect them from attacks by German fighter planes. The Thunderbolts only had enough fuel to fly from England to the German border and back – not enough to fly with those heavy bombers all the way to their goal. They had to waive off battles with German fighter planes and had to leave the bombers to their own destinies.

The heavy bomber squadrons flew in narrow formation very close to one another, and they were not allowed to leave formation even when under heavy anti-aircraft fire. The attacking Germany fighter planes were exposed to a firewall of hundreds of on-board cannons, operated by well-trained gunners. Each of the B17s was equipped with 13 machine guns. In total, there were approximately 300 machine guns firing in one direction against the attacking Germans.

When the heavily loaded formations flew east over Zweibruecken, they were without any Thunderbolt protection. The city of Zweibruecken was at the highest alarm stage, and at first nobody was in the streets. A short time later, the highest alarm was canceled when the planes passed Zweibruecken and flew east toward Augsburg and Stuttgart.

Long before arriving at Augsburg and Stuttgart, the bomber squadrons were already running into trouble. By the time they reached the city of Karlsruhe, the German anti-aircraft batteries and fighter planes were fully engaged. With no Thunderbolts to provide protection, 172 bombers were damaged, some very heavily, and 13 planes were shot down. On the return flight, they continued to protect themselves as well as possible, but waves of German fighter planes continued the assault. Some of the bombers ran out of ammunition.

Around 4 p.m., some of the squadrons flying back reached Zweibruecken. Despite a renewal of the highest alarm stage, not very many people stayed in the bunkers and shelters. People thought that the bombers were on their way home and no longer posed much of a threat. My brother Emil, who was a First Lieutenant in a German infantry division fighting in Russia, was home with us for a 10-day vacation. He was watching the bomber squadrons flying home, and he told us that we could come up from the basement.

People gathered in groups in the street and pointed at the sky; the sun was already on its way westward. One could see the attacks from German fighter planes. They looked like small silver points. A dog-fight started above our city. One of the bombers was emitting a trail of smoke. He was slowing down and losing altitude. We could see parachutes opening, first two, then three, then seven. Two parachutes did not open and the unfortunate airmen fell straight down to earth. The plane was still circling over the city. Every time it came closer to our house, we ran back to the basement. Only my brother stayed outside. Three times we ran back to the basement. Before the bomber squadron flew past Zweibruecken, we noticed a second plane burning. When the plane circling above our town came lower, we could see that one of the four engines was on fire. One German fighter plane followed the U.S. bomber, shot at it again, and then left the scene. For a moment, the bomber was no longer visible, because it flew behind a small hill.

When the bomber came back into view, it was flying only about 600 meters above ground. It looked like the pilot was trying for an emergency landing in a meadow not far from our home. One landing gear could be seen. Burning parts were falling down. Then the pilot directed the plane, probably in a last effort, toward the railway station. Some people said he tried to land the plane on a meadow behind the railway station to save the lives of the people on board who had been wounded. The plane was flying very low when one wing broke off and the plane plunged sideward down onto a house. One of the engines was embedded 27 feet in the ground. The B17 did not have any bombs on board, but it still carried about 1,500 liters of fuel, which ignited immediately. Four airmen in the plane were burned to death. Their remains, along with the remains of the two dead parachuters, were buried a day later in the central cemetery for enemy soldiers in Mainz.

Only one person in the house hit by the bomber died. The soldiers drifting down in parachutes were carried by the wind to the west side of the city. Five airmen came down safely. One was surrounded by a group of civilians and was very shaky. My English teacher in the Helmholz Gymnasium later told me that he landed near her house. She spoke very good English and talked with him, staying with him until the local police took him prisoner.

After the disastrous attack on Augsburg and Stuttgart, the first U.S. Bomber Division had 12 wounded soldiers and 130 missing-in-action, most of whom were probably dead. Included among the missing were the six dead airmen from the B17 shot down over my hometown and the five prisoners.

This dramatic and horrific event sent shivers down the backs of people. Everyone in Zweibruecken was now painfully aware that the air war did not consist only of bombers flying over the city. Something happened in the middle of our city, and a civilian was killed, someone whose family was well-known to us.

When everything was over, I rode my bicycle to the place where the plane had come down. I could not get close, because the whole scene was cordoned off. Since I was with my father and brother during this ordeal, I was excited and not afraid. Although it was quite scary at the time, after a few weeks, I forgot most of the B17 event, because I was involved in other adventures.

As large units of enemy fighter bombers attacked the Siegfried Line and observation planes frequently took pictures of the western wall, looking for weaknesses, it became important for Germany to deploy an air defense. As early as 1942-43, Hitler's plans for a rocket air defense were laid out on paper.

The plan called for a defense system of rocket stations, built 12 kilometers apart. Also scheduled were 600 batteries called *Wasserfall* (Waterfall) and 900 batteries called *Schmetterling* (Butterfly). On the drawing board, the system extended from the Alps in the south up to the North Sea. The concept called for each battery to have eight launch sites, with a capability of 35 rockets that could be fired into heavy bomber squadrons. The weapons could prevent any plane from penetrating German air space.

The defense system was never built. There were no suitable factories or building materials left, and the former defense manufacturing capacity was no longer intact.

It is interesting to note that the 3rd air defense line was to be located north of the cities of Zweibruecken, Homburg and Pirmasens. (*It turned out to be exactly the same spot where the U.S. troops established their rocket air defense system between 1950 and 1970, using Nike rockets. The Nike rocket was supposed to be an enhanced version of the German* Wasserfall *rocket.*)*

---

* *After the war, German rocket scientists were deported in three teams to the United States, France and Russia. The team of scientists earmarked for transport to the United States was headed by the well-known Dr. Werner von Braun. His genius was recognized by Winston Churchill when he wrote that the Allies saved five years of intensive research work just by capturing the German scientists and their rocket technology.*

Ten of these scientists who were working in France were hired later by the German company for which I worked. Eventually the company expanded to the United States, and I became president of a U.S. subsidiary of the firm. With this team, the company built many wind tunnels in Europe and other countries. The most famous was the Hermann Goehring Wind Tunnel, started in the German Oetztal and rebuilt and finished in the French Alps. In this tunnel, half of the Mirage and models of the Concord jets were tested.

The tunnel's fan was driven by turbines of a hydropower station and needed 120,000 HP to operate at full capacity. It had a diameter of 47 feet and contained two counter-rotating rotors. The same team also developed very sophisticated axial flow fans with variable pitch blades to be moved in flight. They are used in wind tunnels, fossil power stations, mines and road tunnels.

In the summer of 1944, we were acquainted with another kind of air war. We called it "Attacks by Jabos." Jabos were Allied fighter planes, mainly P47 Thunderbolts. They were equipped with machine guns and could carry two light splinter bombs. The fighter planes had to accompany the heavy bombers, but until spring of 1944, they only had enough fuel to fly from England to the German border and back.

Right after the Allied troops landed on the Normandy beaches and captured more land, several fighter bomber squadrons were installed on air bases in northern France. Then the Allied Air Force brought in several P47 squadrons to protect the large heavy bombers as they penetrated deep into Germany. At the same time, the P51 went into service. It could protect large bomber squadrons and even have time for separate fighter plane attacks.

In mid-1944, constant fighter bomber runs literally became a plague, attacking day and night. They focused on industrial facilities, but in larger cities they also attacked civilians. They shot everything that moved: women, children and elderly people. They acted like they were attacking on an incentive basis, as if they would receive extra payment for more killings.

On May 1, 1944, one of the Mustang P47s was caught over my hometown, just before turning back to England. In the morning we had sunny weather, but clouds rolled in that afternoon, and once again we had the highest stage of alarm. From a high altitude, we could hear continuous machine-gun fire – fights between German and Allied airplanes. Suddenly, howling motor noises and the firing of machine guns could be heard from close range. Out of the clouds came an American fighter plane, and behind it, a German BF109, also known as ME109. More blasts of machine-gun fire were heard as both planes sped toward the suburb of

---

The company built the first rocket model test stands after World War II in Germany, and I sold them. For this reason, we signed a consulting contract with one of the closest co-workers of Werner von Braun. When failures occurred with the ignition of the third stage of the rockets, we had to simulate those ignitions in high vacuum chambers to produce atmospheric conditions. I was the one to introduce some products in the United States and was assigned to start a fan company in the U.S. The firm was owned by a large German conglomerate.)

Einoed. The American fighter plane went almost straight down after the ME109 gave it a last machine-gun blast. I swung onto my bicycle and quickly rode to the place where the plane crashed. Nothing could be seen but parts scattered over a wide area. The pilot was dead.

At this time, U.S. fighter planes still had many problems with intercepting German fighter planes by themselves. This soon changed. The bomber attacks were coming closer and closer to my town. On May 23, 1944, a large squadron entered the air space in southwest Germany. Equipped with large four-engine planes, it bombarded the neighbor cities of Pirmasens, Homburg, Neunkirchen and Saarbruecken. On May 28, Saarbruecken was again attacked by 331 Liberator bombers. More and more of the Jabos now attacked the cities in our area.

Because the fighter planes flew so fast, there was often very little time to warn the population. It almost did not make sense anymore to issue warnings, because when some squadrons were flying home, others were just entering German territory. By the summer of 1944, the Allies had control of the air over Germany, and their airplanes flew through German skies day and night. For example, on June 26, 1944 – during the day alone – there were 705 heavy four-engine bombers and 678 fighter bombers over Germany. An unbelievable number of planes!

In mid-1944, when the first major fighter bomber attacks started on Zweibruecken, I personally spent most of my time at the bunker across the street from my house. Except for when bombs were being dropped, I stayed outside and watched the attacks. Only when the planes flew toward me did I run inside. The German populace proclaimed many times that the constant attacks were a violation of human rights, yet after the war not one of the Allied commanders, such as Bomber Harris, was taken to court.

Close to my home, about two-thirds of a mile away, an 8.8 (the Americans called it 88) anti-aircraft battery was positioned. It must have been a very experienced unit. They had quite a few rings painted around their guns, each representing a shot-down airplane or a destroyed tank. There were several other anti-aircraft batteries positioned in a radius of about a mile from our house, too.

One day several formations of fighter planes (they always flew in groups of four) appeared – some at higher and some at lower altitudes. All the heavy and medium anti-aircraft batteries started to fire at full capacity. Normally, when such a battle was going on, my father would quickly open the windows, because otherwise the air pressure caused by the 88 batteries would shatter the glass panes. Many times they shattered anyway, but quite often we could save some of the windows.

During this particular attack, one U.S. plane was hit by the 88 guns and plunged into a small valley about one and a half miles from our home. I cannot recall what kind of plane it was, but we called it a Lightning. We feared those Lightnings because they fired their machine guns not only on the way down, but also when they went back up.

Two airmen jumped out of the plane and landed safely on the ground. One airman landed by our church and the other several miles away. With great speed, I rode to the church, even though there were still other fighter planes overhead, not far from us. I was, at my father's request, not to do this, but boys often do what they are not supposed to do. When I arrived at the church, the airman was already surrounded by civilians, and they were close to physically attacking him. At almost the same time, a German officer and three soldiers arrived and chased away the onlookers. They loaded the airman into their vehicle and drove away. I later heard that the soldier was now a prisoner of war, and by the Geneva Convention, no one was allowed to hurt him.

(*After the Americans took over our city, a check-point with guards was established at the intersection right in front of my home, called "Outpost #11." Its soldiers belonged to a unit stationed in Eppenbrunn about 10 miles away. Since I had studied two years of English before the Americans took over, the soldiers used me as an interpreter. One morning two U.S. Air Force officers arrived and asked me if I, or somebody I knew, had seen an airplane shot down in that area. I could confirm it, since I had seen it with my own eyes. They asked about the pilots. I told them that two people had come down with parachutes, and that I had seen one of them personally. The officers were very happy to hear that two airmen of their own unit had landed alive, and that there was a good chance they could survive the war as prisoners. The war was still going on to the east of us. The officers asked me to get into their Jeep and to ride with them to the place where the plane had crashed. Parts of the plane were still lying around, and if I recall correctly, the American officers could confirm from a number stamped on a motor part that it was a plane from their unit.)*

Toward the end of the war, the people of the suburbs of Contwig and Tschifflik had an experience with the fighter planes stationed in France. On August 8, fighter planes flew over the major road going through these suburbs. They were shooting into the streets and into homes. On August 27, they shot at a train carrying civilians, incapacitating the locomotive. The raids went on day after day, weather permitting. The announcer of the air warning system might say that no more enemy planes were in our territory, but that could change 10 minutes later. During all activities, like shopping, garden work, hiking on Sundays, children playing outside homes, etc., one always had to be alert. It was very difficult for farmers and for people who had to transport food because one could not always detect the low-flying planes. Suddenly they would come from behind a hill or small woods, and sometimes, before one could run into a shelter, they were gone.

One morning, farmers were assembled with horses and wagons in front of a school playground. They were fleeing from the villages close to the French border because the fighting front had moved closer. Hitler Youths, now working for the fire department, were present to help feed the horses and to bring them water. Suddenly two fighter bombers came over the hillside and dropped their bombs, which exploded in the middle of the farmers, creating a blood bath of people and horses. Carriages were tangled together. Dead horses were lying on the ground, while other horses were still standing with open wounds. Six people were killed: two young boys (ages 13 and 14), one little girl, and two workers from the railroad who had been standing nearby. Many of the injured were brought to the hospitals. A few days later, a woman also died, from injuries she received in the attack. For the pilots, it was just an attack on the city – they did not have to look into the eyes of the civilians who were killed.

Two days later, more attacks followed. Again a train was shot up outside of Zweibruecken and incapacitated. People nearby left their wagons and fled into the woods. Several civilians were killed.

My brother Edi, who was fighting in the 2nd German Tank Division in Russia, had been severely wounded. An explosive bullet went through his thigh and he nearly lost his leg. When he was transported back in a Red Cross train, marked with the Red Cross sign, the train was attacked by fighter bombers. Lying in a field bed on the train, he was wounded again, with a large splinter in his arm and 18 smaller splinters in his head. Some of the splinters were removed through surgery, but five had to stay in his head and became self-encapsulated. (*He died when he was 79 years old with those splinters still in his head.*)

On September 28, 1944, one of the most memorable attacks occurred. In the morning, a small SS unit with 12 anti-aircraft batteries (with four guns per mount) drove westward through the city. At first no one noticed anything special, since troop movements through the city were going on all the time. Shortly after they positioned their batteries in different locations throughout the city, several Thunderbolts attacked the railway station and the railway system. All hell broke loose. The anti-aircraft batteries fired with all guns, as did the Thunderbolts, circling back around for repeated attacks. The Thunderbolts were part of a squadron whose goal was to attack the railroad system. They fired explosive fire bullets. Several railroad cars parked outside the main railway station were hit. Two of the cars were railroad tankers filled with gasoline. Railway workers saw that gasoline was leaking from one of them. Obviously it had been hit by the Thunderbolts. The railroad workers immediately signaled to the engineer to move the locomotive away from danger, while they tried to uncouple the leaking tanker car.

But then it happened. A fire ball shot into the air about 100 to 120 feet high. The second wagon exploded at the same time. Everything in a diameter of about 500 feet was totally destroyed, leaving a crater in the ground that measured 120 x 100 feet. Only pieces of the two workers were found. Parts of the railroad cars were found half a mile away. People were thrown about like trees in a tornado. There were 13 civilians killed in this attack. Six people died instantly, three died in the hospital the same evening, and the rest died a few days later.

I remember this vividly, because in our house, all of our windows and part of our roof were gone. Carpenters and people fixing windows had to work for 10 weeks to replace all the windows in Zweibruecken. At a distance of one-third of a mile from the explosion, no tiles at all were left on any roofs.

Nobody knew why the 12 anti-aircraft batteries were suddenly moved into my hometown. Later it was said that the two tanker cars did not hold gasoline, but a kerosene type liquid used to fuel V2 rockets launched against England. Some of those V2 rockets were launched in the neighborhood around Zweibruecken, and it was the talk of the city that American spies reported the launch sites back to England, causing the fighter bomber attacks. The V2 launch sites were movable and were changed from time to time.

Late in 1944, smaller cities were also attacked, mainly those that had important intersections and hydroelectric plants. By the end of 1944, the German war-production machine was falling apart.

As the attacks intensified, more people left Zweibruecken every day. My father took my mother to live with relatives on a farm about 20 miles away. At this time Generals Patton and Hodges' troops were already near Saarlautern/St. Avold/Saaralben, about 50 kilometers from Zweibruecken, but still on French soil. A second evacuation of 15,000 people took place from September to November of 1944, but it was not as organized as the one in 1939-40. Most of the evacuees settled about 200 miles to the east, in Baden-Wuerttemberg.

On November 1, 1944, the 8th and 9th USAAF attacked Germany with a total of 324 bombers and 321 fighter planes. The next day they increased the number of attacking aircraft to 1,174 bombers and 968 fighter planes. They added units from the British Bomber Command (B.C.) and the 15th USAAF. In total, there were as many as 2,200 planes in the air over Germany in one

24-hour period, which happened not only on this day, but also quite often on other days. It is almost unbelievable, but it is the truth.

On November 1, 1943, on the German religious holiday of *Allerheiligen* (All Saints' Day), three Thunderbolts fired into a private home in Ingweiler (two miles from Zweibruecken) and totally destroyed it. In another Thunderbolt attack on November 19, 1944, one person was killed in the Spitalstrasse in Zweibruecken.

But on November 4, a new stage of the air war began. On that day, around 12:30 p.m., for the first time a small squadron of two-engine Marauder bombers attacked our area. Their target was an artillery battery stationed in the suburb of Einoed, but some nearby homes were destroyed. The two-engine planes were now stationed in France, and they were used for quick, small attacks. The next attack, which took place on November 30, 1944, involved me personally.

It was a foggy and overcast afternoon. Military vehicles filled about two miles of the main road, from downtown Zweibruecken up to my house in the suburbs. The people in charge felt safe from air attacks on this day because of the weather. Otherwise, their vehicles would have been moved during the night. The whole convoy had been held up, and I was sitting with a soldier in one of the vehicles. I always was interested in trucks, especially in military equipment.

Sudenly we could hear airplanes coming. We wanted to get out of the vehicle, but we could not open the door fast enough. Seconds later, missiles came down in the carpet bomb formation about half a kilometer southwest of our position. The American spies must have found out about the large troop movement, and that was the reason for the bombardment. If the planes had released their bombs a split second earlier, I might not be alive today. The bombs also hit the back yard of my niece's home and a farm about one kilometer away from where we were sitting. Six people on the farm were killed. Next to my niece's home, one can still see today the holes in the ground caused by those bombs. The airguard report about the attack on November 30, 1944, reads as follows:

Starting at 5:45, the 3rd U.S. Bomber Division was flying over our town. Constant flights between 15:44 and 16:00, 20 Marauders over Saarbruecken, Zweibruecken and Landau; 15:46, nine Marauders bombed the area with 80 high explosive bombs (Zweibruecken); 12:45-12:47, heavy bombardment on the neighbor city Homburg.

The Marauder attack happened while I was sitting trapped in the military vehicle. What I did next was not a good idea, and I got reprimanded for it by my father. The minute we were able to open the door of the armored military vehicle, I got out, ran to my home, and grabbed my bicycle. I rode to the place where the bombs had exploded to see what had happened. Other than deep craters, only splinters from the exploded bombs were lying around. I picked up one of the larger splinters while it was still hot and I burned my fingers.

I took the splinter back home, and when I met my father he chastised me severely. At first I did not know why he was so angry, because the Marauders were already gone and there was, in my opinion, no more immediate danger. Then my father told me otherwise. It was not uncommon for some of the bombs to have time-release devices installed for later explosions. Some could have been so-called "blind shells," which exploded when touched the wrong way. Then I understood why my father yelled at me, and it became another lesson for me on the dangers of war, although I kept the bomb splinter as a souvenir for quite awhile. The attack was also sad for the population, because six farm people were killed. More would have been killed had the Marauders not missed their target, including perhaps myself.

After this attack the city officials created additional, and stronger, shelters. Shelters in basements and above-ground were not safe anymore, because of the heavy bombs, which were called *Luftminen* (air mines). Previously, those shelters had been declared safe against machine-gun fire and smaller, lighter bombs. Under the city of Zweibruecken there were some 40 cellars or caves that in former times were used to store ice for breweries. Those cellars and caves were strengthened with heavy support beams and were relatively safe. At the beginning of the air war, those shelters were only used in the highest stage of alarm. Closer to the end of the war, people stayed in them day and night, only coming out to buy food and to breathe some fresh air. The shops in the city at this time were only open a few hours a day, mainly between attacks or alarms.

10

Hitler Youth: Participation Obligatory

When a German boy reached 10 years of age, he was required to join the Hitler Youth organization. It was almost like being drafted into the military. I had to become a member despite the opposition and resistance of my father, but I have to admit that I liked it. At exactly the same time, at 2 o'clock in the afternoon, on Wednesdays and Saturdays, we met in front of the railway station. The first task was attendance and registration in a small book we always had to carry with us. The attendance was signed off by one of the Hitler Youth leaders. Afterwards, we participated in war games, learned songs, marched in large formations through the city, and were active in all sorts of sports, such as soccer, handball, and track and field. To be with other young people in groups like this was just great. Once a month we also met on Sunday mornings to see movies.

We all had a uniform. It consisted of dark blue or black pants (shorts in summer and slacks in winter) and a light brown shirt. We also had to wear a tie that was like a black scarf with a leather knot through which the scarf was pulled and bound. It was mandatory to come to the meetings wearing the uniform and clean shoes. To buy the uniforms, so-called *"Bezugsscheine,"* similar to food stamps for buying clothes, were distributed. The stamps were only a permit to buy the uniforms – one still had to pay the full amount in Reichmarks for them. When joining at the age of 10, we did not get new uniforms. We had to take hand-me-downs from older members who had outgrown them. I hated this and could not wait until I got the first stamps to buy my own uniform.

Although we all liked the war games very much, today I can see that we were taught at the age of 10 to be prepared for real war and fighting. At least once every month we had a war game. For example, *Zugs* (Groups) 1 and 4 from our *Faehnlein* (Troop) had to fight against Groups 2 and 3. The oldest members were in Group 1, and the youngest were in Group 4. A bunker of the Siegfried Line was chosen, for example, and two units had to defend it, while the other two units attacked and tried to take it over. We did not have weapons, so fighting consisted of wrestling, boxing and anything else except killing. Many times we went home with very dirty clothes and injuries. Twice a year we had a big war game. Two groups of about 600 Hitler Youths each started from separate points towards a goal. The group that arrived first had to raise its flag, and the second group had to take down the flag to defeat the first team. If the flag could not be taken down, the first team won.

In those big war games, most of the time real officers from the Army or other military units participated. They were mainly local people who were relaxing and recovering at home from injuries sustained at the front. The officers taught us how to tactically approach fights. For example, our leader one time ordered us to slow down and let the other team get there first. The target was a farm, and it was easier to attack than to defend. The officer assembled a group of about 50 to attack with a tremendous noise from one side, while the main attack took place quietly from the other side. We won the battle. It still amazes me how we young boys were initiated and prepared for war at the age of 10, and how we did not realize it. On the contrary, we liked the games. It is clear to me now that my father recognized what was happening and did not want me to participate, even though he was an officer and generally liked the military, as opposed to the Nazi's aggressive war policies.

Young girls had to go through the same routine, starting at the age of 10 in the B.D.M.. They did not have war games, but they were encouraged to be German homemakers and to bear children for the *Führer*.

None of us young boys or girls recognized at this time that we were being brainwashed to support the Nazi party. We had to memorize the whole biography of Hitler. (*To this day, I still know a great deal of it, including his birthday and birthplace.*) We also were constantly informed about the good deeds of Hitler, such as building the Autobahns and dams with hydropower stations, and developing the Volkswagen, which was sold before the war for 950 Reichmarks. Never were we told anything about the concentration camps and the inhumane treatment of the Jewish people and others who opposed the Hitler regime.

My father hated the Nazi system and the Hitler Youth. Many times during our regular meetings, we marched through the city in large formations. We had to show off how well trained and disciplined we were. Due to my age, I was in the so-called Troop 7 and Group 4, which marched close to the end of the parades. (There were nine troops of 160 in all. Between 1200 and 1500 youths participated.) During these parades, my father often came downtown to run errands, and sometimes, I think, he timed his visits so that he could take some sort of action. He watched where we were marching and often motioned to me, a sign for me to come to him right away. I had to report to the group leader that I had to go to the bathroom. My father would take my hand, lead me to his car, and say, "You're going home with me right now!"

Because I had registered when I reported to the unit, I did not get a demerit when I left early. I did not like it when my father took me out of the marching and singing units, however. I liked being with friends, playing sports and games, listening to the bands, and singing songs. In my age class, I was often ranked first in several sports, and my name appeared frequently in the local newspapers. My father liked to see me active in sports, but he used every occasion possible to keep me away from the Hitler Youth and the Nazi propaganda.

I was blond, blue-eyed, healthy, intelligent, and very active in sports, and I was therefore exactly the type of young boy the Nazi party selected for promotion to become party leaders. The leader of my troop proposed that I be assigned to the NAPOLI, the *National Socialistiche Politische Erziehungsanstalt*, a Nazi boarding school. The pupils who attended those boarding schools were often transferred into schools with university ranking. *(Two of my very close business friends had gone to NAPOLI, and after the war it took a considerable time to get their names cleared. One of them was made a prisoner of war by the American troops, even though he was only 16. Normally, the Allies did not take prisoners from such a young age group.)* I still do not know how my father handled the situation and how he kept me away from the school without our family being put on a blacklist.

Since I was not allowed to attend the NAPOLI school, I had to continue to go to the Helmholz Gymnasium. The Helmholz Gymnasium was renamed *Oberrealschule* (Upper Level School) during the Third Reich, and parents had to pay monthly tuition. Everything had to sound German, and words from the Latin language or any other language were supposed to be used as little as possible. The last school year, 1944, or at least the last days of school were not very pleasant. Depending on the weather, we had daily attacks by fighter planes and heavy bombers. Most of the time around 10:30 and 11:00 a.m. the alarm sirens started. We had to interrupt the lessons and run in an orderly fashion into the basement of the school, which had been turned into a shelter. In the beginning, it was fun and we liked it because we did not have to study and we had no homework. But soon the alarms and attacks turned into a big burden. Sometimes I left school after the pre-alarm, even though this was forbidden. I ran or rode my bicycle, and most of the time I was home before the planes flew over our city and the attacks started. I felt much safer at home around my parents. I always had to avoid main streets because the *Luftschutzwards* (airguard warden) in charge of protecting civilians would have stopped me and ordered me into the closest shelter. Starting in the middle of 1944, the air attacks increased substantially and the school was closed. Until the school reopened, it was a bad time, but it was also exciting.

11

Patton and Hodges Delayed on Germany's Western Border

In the summer of 1944, the trees, hedges and grass had grown up nicely around the bunkers of the Siegfried Line, and one could barely see the concrete units. This was exactly as the architects of the defense line had planned. Some of the bunkers could not even be seen from a very short distance.

On June 6, 1944, the Allies landed their troops in northern France, resulting in heavy casualties. They stayed on French soil. The Atlantic Wall, Europe's most modern system of fortresses, was not able to withstand the massive and brave assault. The Allies were superior in manpower and materials.

Generals Hodges and Patton landed in Europe and led their troops through Italy and France towards the German border. On August 1, 1944, General Bradley transferred command of the 1st Army to General Hodges and became Commander of the 12th Army Group, as well as the newly-formed 3rd Army under General Patton. The latter now advanced from Coutances, exploiting the talent for hard-driving leadership he had displayed in Sicily. By August 4, his spearheads had reached Mayenne, and British Field Marshall Montgomery, still exercising control of ground operations, ordered the first change to the "Overlord" plan. Instead of advancing to occupy Brittany and the Atlantic ports, the Americans only sent minor units in that direction. The 1st Army was to continue its swing eastward, thus encircling German positions in Normandy in a wide loop. Patton was to strike directly across the German rear towards Lemans. The British 2nd and the new Canadian 1st Army (activated on July 23) were to continue attacking southward from Caen.

The Germans were now threatened with close encirclement in Normandy and a wider encirclement on the Seine, but Hitler glimpsed opportunity instead of doom. On August 2, he ordered the German General Field Marshall Kluge to transfer all available tank divisions westward and to strike from Mortain towards the sea, with the aim of cutting off the American breakout. This redeployment was detected by so-called Ultra Intercepts. When Kluge's counterattack began on August 6, it was promptly halted by American forces. The defeat at Mortain, accomplished by attacking and destroying the German tank division from Caen, opened the way for the British and Canadian armies to drive southward towards Falaise. While they struggled to block the German retreat towards the Seine, the American 1st and 3rd Armies were sweeping westward and then northward to Argentan.

By this time, Hitler often gave orders based on stubbornness. However, this was not the case when defending Germany's western border near the Siegfried Line. After the Allies landed in northern France, Hitler released six orders for reinforcement of the western front. On August 12, 1944, he released order No. 61 (reinforcement of the western defense line, also known as the Siegfried Line). This action was part of the plan to retreat toward the German border in order to shore up the defense. In order No. 63, he included some parts of the Maginot Line in the southern upgrade of the defense system.

The importance of the Siegfried Line can be seen in the orders of General and Field Marshall von Rundstedt, the man responsible for the entire western front:

> Starting with the first bunker of the Siegfried Line, we are defending our homeland territory. The Siegfried Line is the strongest defense line of the German Reich. At the places where the Siegfried Line does not yet have enough depth, it is superior to all known defense systems. A breakthrough at any place along the Siegfried Line must

be avoided under any circumstances. If the enemy achieves a break-through based on carelessness or insufficient efforts on our side, this will be treated as a crime against the German people, with direst consequences. The *Führer* will, in such cases, personally hold people responsible. In addition, I make it the duty of every commander and officer to lead by example and to hammer this order into every soldier's head. The troops have to know that they cannot step in good faith in front of the German people if they do not give their best to follow Hitler's orders.

Because of Hitler's orders, the Siegfried Line was now rein-forced at many points. Some bunkers received new additions with the most modern tank defense guns, similar to those used at the Atlantic Wall. One of these bunkers was just 300 yards from my parents' home. It sat in our neighbor's yard with its gun open-ing aimed toward the intersection on which our house stood, and it was used almost daily by civilians seeking shelter from Allied fighter bomber attacks.

In 1939, our area had been given first priority for the defense system, but now it ranked second in importance. The reason was that the main offensive goal of the Allies was not a straight-on at-tack of our area, but rather the lower Rhine region to the north of us. Since our priority had been lowered, there was some neglect of the stronger reinforcement of our segment of the Siegfried Line. U.S. intelligence quickly discovered this oversight and reacted ac-cordingly, noting a weakness that could be exploited.

Even with the pressure at the eastern front of the German Reich, and more action on the western front, Hitler never admit-ted defeat. He saw his last chance to defend the German borders using the Siegfried Line, and without any doubt, this reasoning influenced him to reinforce the western wall.

On August 20, 1945, the neck of the Falaise pocket was finally closed, trapping 50,000 Germans and all the heavy equipment of their 5th and 7th Tank Divisions. The Peiper Unit, involved in the German counterattacks, was also enclosed within the pocket of Falaise. However, the bulk of German personnel escaped and crossed the Seine River in the last week of August. All bridges downstream from Paris had been destroyed by Allied air attacks, forcing the Germans to escape by ferries and pontoons.

After various resistance factions orchestrated an uprising, Paris was finally liberated on August 25 by the French 2nd Armored Division. General DeGaulle, arriving in France under his own auspices, made a triumphant entry into the city on August 20.

The chase from the Seine to the borders of Germany began two weeks after the Normandy landings. Patton departed from his bridgeheads across the river on August 26, and Montgomery three days later. Patton crossed the River Meuse near Verdun on August 30. By September 15, Luxembourg had been liberated by Hodges' 1st Army. Patton's 3rd Army was on the line of the Meuse, and the British were at Antwerp and Maastricht in Holland.

Montgomery's plan to use the Allied Airborne Army to seize key Rhine bridges ahead of the ground advance was code-named "Market Garden." The takeover of the Eindhoven and Nijmegen Bridges by American divisions went according to plan, but eventually Market Garden became a total failure. Within four days, concerted counterattacks restored German control of the Arnheim bridge captured by the British. The advancing British ground forces were unable to reach Arnheim in time to save the beleaguered British force. General von Zangen, the new commander of the 15th Army, energetically gathered remnants and reinforcements to hold the Scheldt banks and islands, while Montgomery was mounting Market Garden in September. The British began a clearing operation from Antwerp on October 2, with the Canadians attacking the south bank. Walcheren, the last German position, was secured in an amphibious operation between November 1-8.

Patton's advance from the Moselle was counterattacked by the German 5th Tank Army on September 18, 1944, but the advance was not delayed for long. Patton's 3rd Army resumed its advance into Lorraine, besieged Metz (which fell on November 22), and then fought its way to the River Saar. By November, Patton had secured bridgeheads at the Saar River only 15 miles away from my hometown. Hodges' and Simpson's Armies later pierced the west wall, the Siegfried Line. The heaviest defense area of the west wall was around my hometown. It is described by several historians as an achievement that came at heavy costs, but compared to storming of the Atlantic wall during the Allied landings in France, the casualties were relatively low. (Penetration through the Siegfried Line around Zweibruecken was between March 18-21, 1945, following the March 16 total destruction of my hometown.)

From mid-November 1944 until the piercing of the west wall by U.S. troops was the most dangerous and difficult period of my life. This was the time of daily artillery fire and attacks and bombardments from fighter-bombers.

The holdup of U.S. troops at a short distance of 20-30 miles was fleeting in terms of tactical warfare. But for us civilians, it seemed endless. It was also a big frustration for General Patton, who wanted to enter Germany as the first U.S. unit, without heavy casualties. However, he and his troops, as well as the troops of Hodges and Simpson, were redirected to the Battle of the Ardennes. If Montgomery would have been a better leader, and Eisenhower had not redirected the U.S. force, the destruction of my hometown and many civilian casualties could have been avoided.

The extensive defeat of the German Army in the Falaise pocket forced the surviving units of Army Group B to retreat at high speed across the Seine River, especially since Hitler had earlier refused permission for a line of defense to be prepared on the River Somme near the next major water obstacle, the Meuse and Scheldt in Eastern France and Central Belgium. The Allies pursued, hampered by shortages of fuel and supplies.

Hitler had ordered the ports along the Channel coast to be held as fortresses. Of these, Le Havre was besieged until September 12, and Boulogne-sur-Mer (the French partner city of Zweibruecken) and Calais fell on September 30. Dunkirk was held by the Germans until the end of the war. This obliged both Montgomery and Patton to draw on supply shipments from across the Normandy beaches. Consequently, the Allied advancement was slowed.

Patton and Montgomery each petitioned Eisenhower, as the supreme Allied Commander, to allot them a major share of the available supplies, thus provoking what came to be called the "broad versus narrow" dispute over strategy. Montgomery insisted that he could break into Germany via Holland if given the lion's share. Patton similarly argued that he might break through the Siegfried Line at Lorraine. Eisenhower diplomatically distributed equal shares. The result – probably inevitable in view of Hitler's mustering of reserves – was that the Allied advance on the German frontier came to a halt in early September.

In an uncharacteristically forceful manner, Montgomery persuaded Eisenhower to allot him the Allied Airborne Army (82nd and 101st U.S., and 1st British Airborne Divisions) to mount an air-ground thrust across the Rhine and protect the Allied advance into the northern German plains. The maneuver, code-named Operation Market Garden, was launched on September 17. As stated previously, this operation was a complete failure. The Airborne Forces swiftly came under counterattack by the 9th and 10th German Tank Divisions. Only the northern span of the bridge across the Rhine at Remargen was taken, and the British were forced, after vicious house-to-house fighting, to relinquish it on September 21. Meanwhile, the British Armored Division, forcing its way through the airborne corridor, was held back by fierce resistance. Despite reinforcement by the Polish Parachute Brigade, the 1st Airborne Division could not hold its position after September 25 and abandoned it at night. The survivors who evaded capture attempted to make their way across the Rhine and back to the Allied lines.

Antwerp had been captured on September 4. Its port facilities, the largest in Europe, could not be used because the estuary remained in German hands. Operations to take the port began on October 2, were not completed until November 8, and were severely hampered by the flooding of certain areas by the Germans. The port was not opened until 20 days later. The 85 days between the capture of Antwerp and its utilization as a port was a period of logistic famine for the Allied Armies on the German frontier. This was also the period in which Hitler developed his plan to isolate the advanced Allied Armies in the west with a bold armored thrust through the Ardennes to the North Sea coast.

The American generals, Hodges commanding the 1st U.S. Army and Patton commanding the 3rd U.S. Army, had been fighting with limited resources while trying to capture ground around Aachen and Lorraine. Hodges, supported by Simpson's 9th Army, advanced to the Siegfried Line. Until the opening of the German Ardennes offensive in mid-December, they devoted their principal efforts to securing river dams. After the 6th Army group of American and French troops landed in Provence in August, they supported Patton and allowed him to make better progress in Lorraine. By mid-December, they had reached the west side of the Rhine vally and the west wall – the Siegfried Line.

Hitler conceived the idea of mounting a winter counteroffensive against the Allies, even while his armies were reeling in defeat in Normandy. He foresaw that, if the Allies could be held on the west wall and along the Dutch rivers, and denied ports of supply along the Channel coast, their long lines of communication would hamper their offensive power and render them vulnerable to a counterstroke. He therefore ordered to hold the ports of LeHavre, Boulogne-sur-Mer, and Dunkirk.

Hitler's concept of Operation Autumn Mist, as it was eventually code-named, was of a thrust by two tank armies from concealed positions in the Eifel Mountains through the Ardennes Forest and across the Meuse to Antwerp, 100 miles away. The operation would not only recapture the port, which the Allies reopened on November 28, but also separate the British and the Canadian Armies in the north from the Americans in the south. Profiting from the confusion this would cause and the time won, Hitler then planned to transfer his reserves eastward to deal a similar blow against the Russians advancing on Berlin.

Rundstedt and Model, respectively Commander-in-Chief West and Army Group B Commander, both thought the plan over-ambitious. During October, they argued for a smaller solution, designed merely to throw the Allies off balance, by a thrust to the Meuse River. Hitler was adamant that as soon as a spell of bad weather promised protection from Allied air attacks, the tanks were to roll. By early December, they were ready. Eight German re-equipped tank divisions and a tank grenadier division were to spearhead the 6th SS and the 5th Tank Armies' attack on a section of the front line held by four somewhat inexperienced and tired American divisions.

Allied intelligence had failed to detect signs of the impending attack and had discounted the likelihood of heavy fighting in the remote and difficult Ardennes. Therefore, when the Germans appeared early in the morning of December 16, they quickly overran the defenders who were able to delay complete defeat only by their brave resistance. Eisenhower's quick reaction helped forestall German intentions. By sending the U.S. 7th Armored and the 101st Airborne Divisions to hold the key junctions of St. Vith and Bastogne on December 17, he insured that the timetable of advance was set back. St. Vith was abandoned on December 23, but Bastogne was held. It became the focus of the American counterattack from the south, begun by Patton on December 22, 1944. On December 20, Eisenhower had appointed Montgomery to coordinate the attack from the north. He was greatly assisted by an improvement in the weather, permitting the resumption of air operations on December 23.

The Germans were also halted that day by a lack of petroleum, having failed to capture the fuel depot on which they had counted for re-supply. On December 26, 1944, the U.S. 2nd Armored Division halted the 2nd German Division at Celles, thus terminating the German effort to reach the Meuse. Rundstedt now proposed that the offensive be abandoned, but Hitler refused. From December 27 to December 30, there was heavy fighting around Bastogne. Hitler ordered the opening of a divisionary offensive in Alsace on January 1, 1945. This was also the day when the Luftwaffe mounted its last large-scale operation; sustaining heavy losses, it destroyed 156 Allied aircraft positioned on Allied airfields in Belgium.

Meanwhile, Montgomery was gathering his forces on the northern flank of the "Bulge." He unleashed a major counterattack on January 3, 1945. On January 7, the U.S. VII Corps cut the Laroche-Vielsam road, leaving only the Houffalize Road as a line of supply to German troops in the Bulge. On January 8, Dietrich, the commanding officer of the 6th SS Panzer Army, was granted permission to withdraw. The Wehrmacht had suffered 100,000 casualties and lost 600 tanks and 1,600 aircraft. The Allies tallied 76,000 casualties. Hitler's strategy set back the Allied drive into

Germany by six weeks, but he lost his last armored reserve in the process. Autumn Mist had proven a daring but costly failure.

In summary, in December 1944, the bulk of the Allied forces were concentrated on the German border and prepared for offensive operations against the Ruhr, Lorraine and Saar areas. Hitler's plan was for the 6th SS Army, under the command of Sepp Dietrich, to drive for Antwerp, while the 5th Army, under the command of von Manteufel, was supposed to support its flanks. Special forces disguised as U.S. troops were to spread confusion in the Army's rear, and parachute troops were to protect Dietrich's initial breakthrough of the American lines. The 6th Tank Army's attack began with a drive to seize ground between St. Vith and the Meuse, but it was halted by the U.S. 2nd and 99th Divisions. Dietrich's armored attack bogged down in the narrow roads of the Ardennes.

A more experienced tank commander, General von Manteufel secured quicker gains, but his axis of advance was a subsidiary one. He was only weakly supported by the 7th Army, commanded by General Brandenburger, and ended up being drawn into a frustrating battle for Bastogne, which had been reinforced by the U.S. 101st Airborne Division on December 17. On December 26, von Manteufel's advance to the Meuse was halted at Celles. Thereafter, the concentration of 33 Allied divisions, strongly supported by superior air power, against 29 German divisions gradually restored the situation. At its deepest, the Bulge had penetrated 70 miles by January 16. All the ground taken by the Germans had been recaptured.

12

Germany's Battle of the Bulge and Peiper's Attack

My research into why the Allies delayed their attack in our area of the Siegfried Line was driven by the desire to know why my hometown was senselessly bombarded and destroyed. In exploring accounts of Patton's troops being moved north to support Montgomery, I discovered the story of Obersturmbannführer (Lieutenant Colonel) Joachim Peiper, a tank commander in the Battle of the Bulge.

Peiper supposedly committed serious atrocities during the German advance, although he strongly disputed these claims. The following description of Peiper's preparations for the attack and his attack methods is presented in a detailed fashion, with the intention of describing how those days of counterattack in the Battle of the Bulge are viewed by many older Germans.

First, something about the preparations for this last major German counterattack. After the German tank units were surrounded in Normandy's Falaise Basin, they lost almost all of their equipment. A few groups of soldiers escaped through a small corridor, but they had to leave behind their vehicles, heavy guns and equipment, in order to avoid creating a second Stalingrad. The Germans had to admit that their 1st SS Tank Division was completely shattered. The division lost at least 5,000 soldiers and all of their tanks and artillery guns. The rest of the troops retreated over the Seine River and gathered in Loan-Marie until August 27, 1944.

Lieutenant Colonel Peiper was still in the hospital suffering from hepatitis. He interrupted his stay to get an overview of what was left of his regiment. He directed his primary attention to the remaining officers. Peiper was one of those soldiers who cared about his officers and soldiers. He was not a father figure, like many of the generals; he was more of a living idol, because of his young age. After Peiper gathered all the information he needed about the survivors, he returned to the hospital near Tegernsee, located in the mountains south of Munich, and stayed there until he was healed.

The defeat of the Middle German Army Group on the eastern front in Russia, combined with the defeat of the German tank divisions on the western front, were signs that the Allies were on their way to ending the war. But the massive Russian offensive came to a standstill in August 1944. A month later, the Allies' attacks on the western front slowed down and their stormy advance slackened. Their units suffered from a classic case of over-work. Another problem was that supplies from England could not be brought to the fighting troops without functioning seaports. Also, the distance grew longer between the landing place for the materials on the northwest French coast and the fighting troops on the German border, creating an additional problem. At the same time, the distance for the German supply lines got shorter.

The weather was very bad and hampered the Allied air support. Large discrepancies existed between U.S. and English strategic war management, specifically on how to advance the war from that point on. The biggest and most important factor for the Germans was their recuperation and reorganization in defending their homeland. They were able to organize a defensive front west of the Rhine River and along the west German border very quickly. This was done by the end of September 1944. Ever since the Allies broke out of the landing zone in Normandy, Hitler searched for an opportunity to regain the initiative on the western front. Here he saw his last opportunity. On the eastern front, Hitler was no longer in control, nor could he improve the condition of military equipment or overcome the lack of fuel; however, the diversified structure on the western front and its smaller size offered him a chance. His opinion was that a successful counterattack would quash the "victory mood" of the Allies and perhaps cause a bigger rift among them. The Allies might consider negotiations for ending the war. Some people around Hitler said that he still thought it was possible to win the war.

Against any military logic, during the planning phase, many things were left to chance. For example, Hitler's only counter against the Allies' air dominance was the traditionally bad December weather. Hitler also counted on the German tank divisions obtaining their fuel from captured Allied reserves. Although the planned offensive was supposed to progress through the Ardennes, in areas only lightly occupied by the Allies, Hitler decided to conduct his main attack via the Maas River, passing by Brussels all the way up to Antwerp. He chose this route after Generals Jodl and Rundstedt presented details for the attack, including several options. The main goal was to cut off the English forces in Holland from the American troops, thus creating a second Dunkirk for the English.

To guarantee that this offensive would be successful, the whole west Army was restructured and all reserves in Germany were mobilized. The center of the attack was to be carried out by the 6th German Tank Army, under SS *Oberstgruppenführer* (Colonel General) Sepp Dietrich, included in the 1st SS Tank Division *Leibstandarte Adolph Hitler* (which will be described later). This unit was reassembled in the region of Muenster on German soil after it had been totally defeated in the Battle of Falaise. The division became the spearhead attack of the total offensive in the Ardennes.

Obersturmbannführer Peiper was chosen to lead the troops and the attack. Thus, the whole destiny of the survival of the German Reich rested on his shoulders. Troops and equipment for the newly assembled division were ready on October 10, 1944, and maneuvers and exercises were held until the second half of November. Brand new tanks were delivered directly from the production facilities to the armies. The 1st through 4th companies were equipped with the modem Panther V tanks, and the 5th to the 8th Companies received Panther IV tanks. (*Experts still say that the Panthers were the world's best tank.*)

Since there were not enough tanks for all units, only Peiper's companies were equipped with them. Peiper's division was ordered to move to the west side of the Rhine River, somewhat southwest of Cologne. The rest of the division stayed on the east side of the Rhine. In this phase of preparation for the Ardennes attack, the Germans created an extraordinary plan. The offensive was called *Wacht am Rhein* (Guard on the Rhine). Nobody on the Allied side recognized the big troop movements and thus did not expect an attack. On December 12, 1944, Hitler called all division commanders to Adlerhorst, his headquarters near Bad Nauheim, where he advised them of the planned attack. On the same day, all units were ordered to be ready.

The Regiment *Leibstandarte Adolph Hitler* (Weapon SS, not the disreputable SS) was grouped into four parts. One part was the tank unit, with Peiper as leader. The Department 501, which normally reported to the staff, was now directly reporting to Peiper. The Department 501 was equipped with 45 Type IV *Königstiger* or King Tiger tanks, which were among the most sophisticated tanks in World War II.

After the groups moved into position on December 14, 1944, the division commander ordered all regiment commanders into his field headquarters near Tondorf and told them that the attack would start on December 16, 1944. Peiper was given the following order: After the 12th Infantry Division broke through the lines near Losheim en route into American occupied areas, he was to move his tanks via Trois-Ponts and Werbomont to the Maas River between Leuttich and Huy. Then he was to hold this position and prepare his units to go forward toward Antwerp. Peiper complained that the roads might work for bicycles, but not for his heavy Tiger tanks. He was rebuffed and told that Hitler himself had selected the route.

Peiper's attack was to be supported by about 800 parachute troopers under the attack name *Stösser*. They were supposed to keep the roads open at the intersection of Monte Rigi towards Eupen-Malmedy. A huge problem was the insufficient supply of gasoline available for the tanks. Peiper had maps marked with the locations of American gasoline depots around the city of Buellingen and was supposed to capture the fuel from them. The length of the attack track was about 25 kilometers, and Peiper allowed all vehicles to move forward only at medium speed. On December 15, 1944, when all commanders reviewed the details of the plan once more, preparations were concluded. Early in the morning of the next day, all tanks, guns and soldiers were brought into starting position.

On December 16, 1944, at 5:30 a.m. in foggy and cloudy weather, the offensive of the Ardennes started with firing from 5000 artillery guns and grenade launchers. The 12th Division with their 48th and 27th Regiments had the order to open the way from the Losheimer Gap to Losheim and Billingen. It took until noon to take Losheim, and at that point the 27th Regiment came to a standstill. Peiper and his tanks were in attack position, but he still had no order to attack. By 4 p.m., he finally received the order.

The tank attack troops left their positions in accordance with the plan, but they ran into problems because the infantry was detained at the bridge (or, more correctly, the lack of a bridge) with their horses and wagons. The bridge had been destroyed by the Germans when they previously left this area. Peiper ordered a Pioneer Company to fill in the ditch so that his tanks could move on. This was accomplished by the time evening fell. After moving to the other side of the ditch, Peiper received an order to change his original route. The Americans had stopped the 3rd Regiment with the 9th Parachute Division, so they could not secure the original route. Peiper then ordered this regiment to counterattack. An immediate setback occurred when it was discovered that the infantry had left this place earlier in the war without clearing the mine fields (as had been ordered), and now no one had maps for the locations of the mines. So as to not lose time, Peiper sacrificed six heavy tanks by having them make a path through the mine fields.

About midnight, Peiper's troops reached Lanzerath. The colonel of the parachute unit was formerly a member of the planning staff and did not have first-hand experience in warfare. He told Peiper that the woods in front of the troops were filled with mines and were heavily defended by the Allies. Peiper therefore changed the spearhead of the attack. He allowed one parachute company to sit on the tanks, and he ordered the three other parachute companies to follow and protect the tanks since they were quite defenseless in the woods. Shortly before dawn, all units were ready to attack. They were met with two surprises: There was no resistance, and there were no mines. The parachute troops did not attack before the tanks, as they were supposed to, but instead stayed in warmer places, such as in the city of Lanzerath, to avoid the cold.

When the Peiper tanks drove with high speed into Honsfeld that dawn, they woke up an American observation battalion. The anti-tank guns at the entrance to the village were unmanned, while the courtyards, backyards and streets were filled with armed U.S. vehicles. Hundreds of U.S. soldiers looked at Peiper's tanks from the windows, probably speechless to see them there. Peiper's unit sent a few rounds of machine-gun fire into the homes and quickly went on towards Bullingen.

The parachute unit was supposed to take Honsfeld. The parachute company riding on Peiper's tanks stayed with the unit until the Ardennes attack was over. The delay at Lanzerath cost Peiper six hours, but the unprepared U.S. observation battalion gave his unit a chance to make up for this delay.

Peiper's tank troops started to attack again on December 17, 1944, around 4 p.m. They reached Bullingen at 7 p.m. Peiper left his Panther V tank and took an armored vehicle with wheels instead of chains. Another commander joined him. (This was strictly forbidden by military procedures, but no accident occurred.) By this time, the Peiper group was somewhat splintered. The *Stösser* attack by the parachute troops under command of v. d. Heyde ended in disaster and did not bring any support for Peiper. The heavy Tiger tanks could not follow the spearhead of the attack, because the roads were not made for such heavy vehicles. Despite a vigorous defense from the Americans, Peiper's group of tanks reached Bullingen at 8 p.m.

When Peiper's forces defeated the Americans in Bullingen, they captured some petroleum reserves and were able to refuel their vehicles. The goal now was to reach the city of Engelsdorf. Peiper reorganized the plan of attack by bringing in the 1st Regiment to support the 10th Regiment. Since German tank commanders always rode at the head of their attack units, Peiper moved from a tank to a captured American jeep. He also ordered his officers to drive as close to him as possible. Peiper reached the intersection of

Baugnez south of Malmedy between midnight and 1 a.m., just as an American truck unit tried to pass by. Immediately a fight started between the Americans and the Germans. This fight became famous and was later called a massacre by the Americans.

With five tanks and five armored vehicles, the head of Peiper's fighting group fired at the American unit. Chaos ensued. The American soldiers left their vehicles, most of which were burning, and some of them came towards the Germans with their hands above their heads. Others ran into the ditches beside the roads and started to fire at the Germans, while yet a third group ran into the nearby woods. As fast as they could, Peiper's tanks attacked the American unit that had now come to a complete standstill. All the Americans within a distance of 60-70 meters gave up. At the time of the initial confrontation, Peiper was somewhat in back of his spearhead. Alarmed by the fighting, he immediately drove to the head of the unit, saw that it was not an important battle, and ordered his tanks to go on towards Engelsdorf. The tanks passed the American vehicles slowly and ordered the U.S. soldiers to head towards the rear as prisoners. Without paying any further attention to them, Peiper ordered his tanks to proceed as quickly as possible.

Peiper and his unit soon changed direction, taking a sharp turn to the south toward route N. 23. During this maneuver, one of the heavy tanks slid into the ditch by the side of the road, a mishap that also was repeated by other vehicles a few minutes later. The rest of the vehicles passed the stranded tanks while several service vehicles tried to pull them out of the ditch.

Meanwhile, German troops coming upon the scene at the intersection 15 minutes later assumed the Americans were an attacking unit, because most of them still had their weapons. Therefore, the second group of Germans immediately opened fire, and several Americans and Germans were killed. The rest of the U.S. soldiers quickly gave up their weapons and were assembled in a nearby meadow.

The captured American soldiers in the meadow took advantage of the time gap between the advance vehicles and the infantry to flee the scene. While attempting to keep those soldiers from escaping, fighting broke out again, and more Americans and Germans were killed. Another group of U.S. soldiers hid in the nearby woods and eventually rejoined their original units.

(After the war, the Americans tried to prove that the Germans purposely fired on the U.S. soldiers gathered on the meadow, and that it was done with premeditation and specific orders. The exact chain of events could not be established after the war. Naturally, if Germans fired on purpose, it was an offense against Geneva Convention laws. The German opinion was that it was not a planned massacre and there was no violation, as this was committed during the war by the Weapon SS. An explanation could only be found in war-related circumstances.)

The troops lead by Peiper came to Engelsdorf around 1 p.m. and met with heavy resistance from American troops. The lead German tank, a Tiger Tank commanded by and officer named Fischer, was hit by a 75 millimeter grenade fired by an American Sherman tank. It immediately started to burn. The driver of the armored vehicle carrying Peiper drove behind a house, while a second armored vehicle was destroyed by the Americans. In the end, the Germans lost one tank and two armored vehicles, while the U.S. lost three Sherman tanks. After the engagement, Peiper waited for the rest of his unit.

Around 4 p.m., he continued his attack via Pont Beaumont and Lodomez to reach the area of Stavolet, which also was heavily defended by the Americans. Without any delay, Peiper ordered an attack. His tanks were at the outskirts of the city just as darkness fell. They tried to take Stavolet at a fast speed, without stopping, because the city was built like a small fortress. Large rocks blocked the natural entry to the city. As soon as one of Peiper's vehicles left a protected spot or entered the city, the Americans destroyed it. Attacking Stavolet with tanks proved to be impossible.

Peiper ordered a unit of 60 soldiers to attack along the street entering the city. This unplanned attack was also stopped by the Americans. Peiper had to suspend any further fighting and wait until more infantry units arrived. The element of surprise was no longer on his side. Around midnight between December 17 and 18, 1944, all of Peiper's attacks came to a halt when a second infantry attack was repelled by the Americans. At this point, Peiper had to wait until the 2nd Tank Grenadier Regiment arrived before he ordered any more attacks. His third attack, on the morning of December 18, was successful.

Two Panther tanks, about 200 meters away from the outskirts of Stavolet, were ordered to drive at full speed and with rapid fire directly towards the American defense line. The first tank was hit right away and started to burn. Because of its speed, it damaged two Sherman tanks in their defense position. The second Panther tank drove towards the bridge, taking advantage of the confused Sherman tank crews. Its goal was to take the bridge and open the way through the street leading to Trois Ponts. The heaviest American defenses surrounded the bridge. The U.S. defense line was supported by tanks closely placed around the bridge and a bit further away on the other side of the slightly hilly terrain. After a heavily fought battle, the crossing of the Ambleve Bridge was accomplished. Without completely clearing the city of American troops, Peiper's units moved on towards the west. At 11 a.m., when they reached the nearby Trois Ponts, all other bridges over the Ambleve and the Salm were blown up. At this point, advancement towards the Maas River was completely halted.

Peiper now made the decision to head north from Trois Ponts to his original goal. This was accomplished via the villages of La Gleize, Cheneux and Rahier. Without any resistance, Peiper passed through La Gleize around 1 p.m., then moved back towards the south and crossed through a side road to one of the few un-destroyed bridges. He was once again on his way toward Cheneux. At this time, the weather changed and for the first time there was a blue sky. Now the Allies could bring back their fighter-bombers. Between 2 p.m. and 4 p.m., the tank groups around Peiper were attacked non-stop from the air. While this took place, Peiper's vehicles were parked on an unprotected street. Three Panther tanks and five armored vehicles were destroyed.

By now the Americans knew the direction of Peiper's attack, and as a defensive move, they blew up every bridge in his way. Just before sundown, Peiper's group reached Rahier, only to find the bridge there destroyed. There was a bridge to the north near Forges, but it was too small for Peiper's heavy tanks. During their search for a bridge that could carry the heavy tanks, the 10th Battalion of the tank regiment came too close to the American lines and sustained heavy casualties. Unable to find a suitable bridge, the whole unit had to retreat.

Once again back near La Gleize, they tried to advance to Stoumont. But Peiper was informed that Stoumont was being defended by large numbers of U.S. forces, with additional U.S. troops on their way from Spa. On December 19, 1944, the spearhead of Peiper's tank group moved westward at 7 a.m. and was confronted by the Americans stationed around Stoumont. These U.S. units were part of the 30th Infantry Division and the 82nd Airborne Division, both of which had a reputation for strong fighting abilities. Peiper decided to defend and hold the bridge southwest of La Gleize, because this position might later prove to be important in the advance toward Stoumont. At dawn on December 19, 1944, Peiper started to attack Stoumont with a tank grenadier battalion. Two parachute companies headed the attack to protect the heavy tanks. Because of the swampy terrain, it was not possible for these tanks to leave the road.

After a heavy tank battle, lasting more than two hours, the infantry could finally enter the city from the south, and it overtook the city. Peiper and his troops then followed the retreating U.S. soldiers and reached the railroad station located three kilometers outside of the city. They had to stop there. The tank units did not have any more fuel or ammunition, and they had to wait until the service units arrived. This was the turning point of Peiper's battle in the Ardennes. It was reported on the same day that the U.S. troops had recovered the city of Stavolet. The German infantry was pushed back into the eastern part of the city.

Peiper ordered another attack of Stoumont, but from the west side, in order to clear it of U.S. troops. He stopped three U.S. counterattacks, but once again he came to realize that he did not have enough fuel to pass over the bridge west of Stoumont. In the early evening, the fighting in the western part of the city started up. Smaller U.S. fighting units, supported by tanks, operated along the route leading to Stoumont. Since the other German infantry units could not secure the street three kilometers from the railroad station, Peiper decided to use his own troops to take it back. All afternoon, Peiper's troops were under heavy U.S. artillery attack.

Peiper established his field headquarters at a farm near the castle of Froid Coeur. This was a holding station for U.S. prisoners as well as a field hospital. After a relatively quiet night, U.S. troops started an attack near the city of Stoumont, but the attempt to simultaneously attack from the west and the north with tanks was a failure. Around noon, however, Peiper's fighting group was cut off by U.S. tank units that had passed La Gleize from the north. This was another blow, since Peiper was still cut off from his German troops at Trois Ponts. Peiper could not respond to such movements, because he had neither fuel nor ammunition for his tanks. In each of the three villages, heavy house-to-house fighting broke out, yet Peiper was able to hold all three.

The German commanders had discussed the plan of attack and decided that if Peiper was cut off, his unit should be freed. Since Peiper was not able to hold Stoumont and Cheneux, it was decided that the last fighting troops would assemble and defend the village of La Gleize, which consisted of only about 30 homes. The order was also given to keep the bridge near Cheneux open. On the evening of December 21, all Germans were ordered to leave La Gleize. All wounded soldiers who were able to walk had to leave with the fighting troops. Some 80 wounded German soldiers and all the Americans were left behind in the field hospital in Stoumont.

The situation for Peiper's group was desperate. There were only six Tiger tanks left. The American artillery concentrated their fire power toward all German defense lines, while American troops were attacking all roads leading to La Gleize. After two hours of fighting, the old defense line was restored, and around 5 p.m. the battle slowed down.

On December 23, 1944, all American attacks stopped. The Germans could not explain why. Peiper had given up all hope of escape. A note was received around 5 p.m. on December 23 hinting that an order was on its way for Peiper to break out of the encirclement, leaving all vehicles and wounded soldiers behind. Peiper was convinced that there would soon be an official order to do so. Unfortunately, the order never came. Peiper made his own decision to leave. His headquarters were in a basement that had vaulted sandstone arches. Everybody was nervous, since there was no official order yet. The faces of the officers and soldiers were marked by fighting and fatigue, but now they were also very solemn. Peiper himself was quiet and calm. He only reacted once, when told that one of his officers had been killed. He gave his commands professionally, with no swearing or screaming. In the last meeting with his commanders, Peiper expressed concern about the wounded soldiers he had to leave behind.

During the night, Peiper met with one of the prisoners, U.S. Major McGown, an officer of the 30th Infantry Division. They reached an agreement. According to Peiper, they did not speak about ideologies, but rather about the sadness and folly of war that made men like themselves fight against each other. (*After the war, during the 1960s, there was quite a bit of talk about the human side of Joachim Peiper. He was mentioned in a book by Toland about the Battle of the Bulge, and his humanity was portrayed in a movie about the tank battle of the Ardennes.*) Major McGown did not talk much about that night, but he admitted that Peiper was a very sympathetic, loving human being. McGown could not understand how such an intelligent and cultivated person could be fighting for Hitler's Nazi Regime. Peiper's final words that night were, "I admit that some unlawful things are happening, but I also think about some good things. Hitler stopped the danger from the Communists and created a better foundation for Europe."

McGown subsequently brought up the subject of the killing of the prisoners. He asked Peiper if he would give him his personal commitment to honor the Geneva Convention about warfare, and Peiper answered, "I give you my word." McGown was part of the prisoner group that went with the Germans. He later escaped.

In the afternoon of December 23, Peiper decided to start his escape. He ordered a German military doctor, whose name was Dittmann, to stay and take care of the wounded soldiers. After all of the vehicles were blown up, the escape started at 2 a.m. on December 24. The escape route had been reconnoitered earlier by a German Navy Second Lieutenant. More than 300 soldiers were

left behind and later taken as prisoners by the Americans, but 800
Germans crossed the River Saim, some swimming and some walking. Six kilometers east of the American front lines in the Salm
valley, they met up with the German army. Effective December 26,
1944, the fighting group Peiper was eliminated.

The original goal for Peiper's unit was to break through the
Allied lines and to advance to the Maas River. Many reasons for
Peiper's failure were discussed after the war. Not only was his
original goal impossible to achieve, but Hitler's main goal for the
Ardennes offensive, which was to sever the English troops from
the American troops, had failed. Hitler's hopes were dashed after
General Patton and General Hodges ordered their troops to the
north to support the British forces. Patton did not like having to
do so. He wanted to be the first one to penetrate into Germany
and cross the Rhine River. He finally accepted Eisenhower's decision to put his troop advancement in Alsace-Lorraine on hold
and move northward, because if the British were cut off from
the Americans, it probably would have further prolonged the war
and caused more casualties on both sides. Eisenhower's decision
proved to be the right decision.

Sources who knew Peiper during and after the war all confirmed that he wanted to be recognized as a soldier and nothing
else. He and all his colleagues did not want to be mixed up with
the political wing of the SS around Himmler and Hitler. All they
wanted to do was to serve as the elite troops of the Weapon SS,
and to be treated as such. Being so young and recognized as a former adjutant to Himmler, Peiper had a black mark hanging over
his head as he entered into the trial that was conducted against
him after the war. The second black mark came from the so-called
"Massacre of Malmedy." Peiper clearly proved that he was in his
spearhead unit, far away from the scene, when the shooting happened. As Commander-in-Chief of the unit, however, he had to
take responsibility for the outcome.

Nobody denies that the political wing of the SS made bad
decisions and performed killings. The responsible people were
prosecuted in Nuremberg and in other trials, and were jailed and
executed. After the war, Peiper was only in his 30s, yet he never

again felt like a free man. People, full of hatred for him, followed him everywhere he went. Long after the war, his house in France was set on fire and he died in the blaze.

How is the Malmedy incident understood in general?

As the bad luck of an American observation unit, which during the battle of Ardennes, suddenly was confronted by the spearhead of a German tank unit on December 17, 1944.

What is the American version?

Survivors of the U.S. observation unit reported that they were shot at, and members of the unit were killed, after they had surrendered.

What is the German explanation?

An American heavy truck unit on its way to St. Vith did not know it was in great danger from an advancing German tank unit and came under heavy fire at a distance of 300-400 meters. While the spearhead of the German unit continued its advance towards Ligneuville, the U.S. soldiers assembled in a meadow near an intersection so they could officially be taken as prisoners by the German infantry following the tank spearhead. Because of bad roads and heavy fighting around Buellingen, the distance between the spearhead and the infantry units was quite large. This gap was used by many of the prisoners as an opportunity to flee. They did not stop at the commands of the few German guards assigned to them and came under fire, resulting in casualties.

The Malmedy Massacre was nothing more than a fight between two units that met each other unexpectedly. It was the kind of military incident that regularly happens in warfare. It was not a deliberate or well-planned massacre, but an incident that occurred in the heat and noise of battle.

German survivors pointed out that two things did not bode well politically for the Malmedy situation. The first was that many German enemies wanted to connect the military SS and the political wing of the SS, even though they were separate entities.

The second is that the British and U.S. Armies already had declared victory, even before the Ardennes offensive was started.

When difficult battles broke out and the Allies suffered a setback, it was embarrassing. The psychological point of the propagandistic warfare should not be left out of the total picture. To offset the embarrassment caused by this military setback, Peiper's unit was accused of unethical warfare. The Army Radio Calais and the *Stars and Stripes* newspaper started a press and propaganda campaign that was totally disproportionate to what had happened. One U.S. First Lieutenant by the name of Pearl said to Peiper, "You have had bad luck. One of the dead soldiers at the intersection was the son of a U.S. Senator. He initiated the whole propaganda and the pursuit."

Other German survivors pointed out that the propaganda was a prelude to the Nuremberg Trials. Starting at the beginning of 1945 and lasting until the summer of 1945, more than 1,000 soldiers of the Peiper Unit were tracked down and questioned about the happenings around Malmedy.

In a trial held at Mauthausen, conducted by a prosecutor named Lieutenant Guth, the following statements were made about Peiper. The research that took place about Peiper painted a very positive picture, in general.

> He was the only one who acknowledged his military rank, and he admitted that at the beginning of his military career he was an adjutant of Himmler.

> It was confirmed that his reputation as Tank Commander and as a fair soldier was never disputed.

> The G-2 report of U.S. Major McGown gave a very positive statement about Peiper's fairness during the Ardennes Offensive.

> The U.S. public was very upset about the events that happened at Malady, and they were looking for a culprit.

> When the U.S. press coincidentally received the name of Peiper, they stamped him as the murderer of Malmedy. He was supposed to be the most hated of men, and enemy number one of the GIs.

> Peiper's destiny was predetermined, because he was an adjutant of Himmler, because the U.S. press had already vilified him, and because Peiper could go undercover and be a threat as a terrorist.

Peiper was asked to demonstrate being a good loser and to admit that he ordered the killing of the prisoners on the crossroads of Malmedy.

Peiper took full responsibility, but only under the provision that none of his subordinates would be prosecuted or sentenced.

The official Malmedy Trial was held in Dachau under case number 6-24, with the United States against Valentin Bersin and others. It began on May 16, 1946. Selected for prosecution were 71 soldiers of the Peiper group – exactly the number of GIs killed. Also being prosecuted were the SS Generals Dietrich, Preiss and Kramer, but since the center point of the trial was the Malmedy Massacre, Peiper was the key figure. Witnesses called were survivors of the U.S. unit.

The main prosecutor, Colonel Ellis, made the following statement: "We will present proof that, for the Ardennes Offensive, guidelines existed to kill prisoners as a revenge for killing of German civilians by the bomber terror on German cities to break German resistance. The 1st Tank Regiment, under its leader Peiper, transmitted this order to his subordinates to fight without mercy and to kill Allied prisoners when the situation required it. This order was read to the officers and forwarded to all soldiers. Based on this order, the soldiers were of the opinion that they could ignore all the laws of the Geneva Convention without being penalized."

Peiper's troops were supposed to have killed Belgian civilians also. The defense claimed, however, that there were some casualties, but that these were partisans and snipers, not helpless civilians.

On July 16, 1946, the courts announced a decision. After a two hour and 20 minute deliberation, which meant two minutes for every defendant, Peiper and the 74 other defendants were declared guilty; 43 received the death penalty, 22 got life in prison, two received 20 years in prison, one received 15 years, and five were given 10 years in prison. Peiper received the death penalty. On July 17, 1946, Peiper was transferred to the U.S. Army War Criminal Prison No. 1 at Landsberg to be executed. There was heavy criticism about the trial procedures, which never had the jurisdictional legitimacy

of the Nuremberg Trials. The German Governmental Research
Institute for Military History went so far as to talk about a derelic-
tion of the law. The verdict at Dachau concerning the Malmedy
affair was of central importance for the Nuremberg Trials. It was
the prerequisite for the later condemnation of the military SS as a
criminal unit similar to the political SS. All during the war, the U.S.
public had seen the SS as an elite fighting unit and not as a political
one. But after the war and during the trial at Dachau, the U.S. public was persuaded to believe that they were the same. In Germany
in general, and specifically with veterans of World War II, this is
still a cause of vexation.

Peiper's death penalty was later reduced to life in prison. After
serving 10 years in the prison at Landsberg, he was paroled and
rejoined civilian life on December 12, 1956. He lived in France for
many years until a fire was set in his house by Communists. He
died in the fire on July 14, 1976.

One might ask why I chose the Peiper group as the fighting
example in Ardennes from the German side. First, I came across
the Peiper story when I searched for reasons why Patton's troops
were delayed from entering Germany in the area of my hometown.
An earlier entry would have saved a great deal of destruction of
historical buildings in the city and avoided many civilian casualties.
After more research, I thought it would interest American read-
ers to learn about the German version of the Malmedy massacre.
Also, the Peiper story demonstrates that, even after equipping the
elite of the elite with the best equipment (like Panther and Tiger
tanks), there was no more chance for Hitler to win the war. It
shows how ridiculous it was to sacrifice more people on both sides,
and it illustrates Hitler's stubbornness in defeat.

A third reason for choosing the Peiper group was the contro-
versy that even today surrounds units of the military SS and the
false comparisons between it and Hitler's criminal political SS. The
military SS was nothing but an elite unit of well-trained soldiers.
One can compare them with the U.S. Marines. I had two brave and
bright cousins who started out as Navy soldiers and then, against

their will, were transferred to the Weapon SS. They were like all of my family, not at all like the Nazis. On the contrary, they were connected to the resistance effort against the Nazis. Germany in general had good soldiers and good military leaders. My father and two brothers were officers. They were no more than well-disciplined soldiers and ordinary citizens without criminal records.

13

My Experience of the Border War

All schools had been closed for quite some time, because of constant air attacks and artillery fire. The roads through Zweibruecken were used to supply the front fighting troops in France with food and ammunition. At first, listening to breaking news three to four times a day on the radio was thrilling. Radio stations would interrupt their regularly scheduled broadcasts to give us updates. As the war dragged on, it became less and less interesting, because newscasters no longer announced that German troops had successfully taken this or that city, and that Germany submarines had sunk many British and American ships. Now, the breaking news reported German troops retreating. This was a prime reason for me to look into other adventures.

About 800 yards away from my parents' home, the little creek Bickenalb (originating in France) merges with a somewhat larger river, the Hornbach. The Bickenalb carries crystal clear water, and my friends and I would fish there once in a while for trout and crayfish, without permission. Suddenly, about another 800 yards upstream, something secret was happening. There were excavations going on behind wooden walls. "What could this be?" we all wondered. After a week, I found out. Covered with green camouflage nets were four anti-aircraft batteries. Each battery had four guns on one gun mount. In German, it is called *Vierlingsflack*. The gunner sat on the gun mount and directed and fired the four guns simultaneously. He could turn the gun mount 360 degrees, like a merry-go-round. The four guns firing simultaneously made the bullets cross each other at a certain height, and it was very effective. Sometimes the soldiers allowed me to take the gunner's seat and to turn it. This happened only when there were no pre-warnings of fighter plane attacks and when the guns were not loaded. Like all war equipment, it was very fascinating to me.

I normally walked early in the morning to this installation, which looked quite harmless. I walked along the little Bickenalb Creek, watching light fog over the meadows, seeing the trout in the water, and appreciating the meadow flowers. Even as a boy, I loved nature and I made many trips with my father and brothers through the hilly, wooded areas and beautiful valleys around my hometown.

Another reason for me to visit the soldiers and their guns was the hope of getting a bite of their breakfast or leftovers, sometimes even a small piece of chocolate. Unlike civilians, soldiers still had enough good food. We had food stamps, but food was not always available, and there was no chocolate at all during this time.

The anti-aircraft batteries were installed on one side of the winding Birkenalb. On the other side was a steep wooded hillside. About 120 feet above the creek was a big old wooden cabin. This cabin had been a restaurant before the war, with a large barn-type building behind it. Both buildings were used for banquets, weddings and other gatherings. Now they housed soldiers. As they were mostly hidden by trees, the fighter planes could not easily see them. When the main alarm sounded in advance of incoming fighter bombers, the soldiers ran quickly down the little hill, and in a matter of minutes they were ready to shoot.

Something else also attracted my attention. At first I was not allowed to come close to the field telephones, called *Sprechfunk* (walkie-talkies). It was, compared to today's modern communication tools, a relatively primitive system, but it was effective. A soldier with headphones was constantly listening to incoming messages. He received encoded and unencoded reports, and he had to write all of them down. A second soldier had to bring the reports to the officer in command. After about two weeks, when most of the soldiers knew me, I was allowed to listen to those messages. I understood very quickly what was going on. All U.S., Canadian, British, Australian and French airplanes entering territory still in German hands were reported, including their most recent flight routes. As long as the fighter planes did not fly directly towards our city, the messages were only of interest if they flew towards cities where our relatives lived.

Our home and my father's factory were located close to a strategically important intersection. Each of the roads led to France, and as I mentioned, those roads were used to transport war materials and food to the fighting troops. The anti-aircraft batteries were therefore located close to the intersection, to keep approaching fighter bombers at as great a distance as possible. The soldiers from the anti-aircraft batteries told me that it was assumed that there would be no attacks from heavy bombers, only from fighter planes. The fighters attacked everything: troop concentrations, regular train and troop transports, the factory of my father, civilians, and farmers with horses. The job of the anti-aircraft soldiers was to protect military targets and civilians as well as they could. At the beginning they were somewhat successful, but later they proved totally ineffective.

When the announcement came that squadrons were now flying east of Metz towards Saarbruecken, we knew that we could be under attack in a few minutes. This was the time when the officer in charge sounded the highest level of alarm and all soldiers scrambled down the hill toward their guns. The guns were always fighting ready, so only a few turns were needed before the grenades were loaded. When the announcement came that squadrons were passing Saarbruecken, Trier or Saargemuend, it was the highest state of alarm for me. I sprinted as fast as I could to my place of safety. A road crossed the Hornbach River, and because the fields left and right of the river sometimes flooded, tunnel-like openings had been built under the road for run-off water. These openings were my hiding place. They were relatively safe. Only if a bomb exploded at one of the openings would I have been killed. I was protected from machine-gun attacks and from bomb and anti-aircraft gun splinters. I felt quite safe in this place and could see what was happening out in the open.

I witnessed the low-flying airplanes and their machine-gun attacks on the anti-aircraft guns. The soldiers operating the batteries had no protection. It is amazing what bravery they showed, day in and day out, risking their lives, and for what? For Hitler's senseless war. During the attacks and counter-attacks, the noise was deafening, louder than the worst thunderstorm. Then something happened that made me curtail my visits with those anti-aircraft soldiers.

On a beautiful, sunny Sunday close to noon, we once again were at the highest alarm stage. It was reported that Thunderbolts were already flying over Saargemuend towards Zweibruecken. I do not know why I did not start right away to my hiding place, but I didn't, and I got caught in the open. All I could do was to lie flat in the middle of a meadow as my father had told me to do, in case I were to come under a surprise attack. I lay there for about a half an hour with my head and nose down in the dirt. This time I did not look at the fighter planes, and I could barely pray a few words. Splinters from the anti-aircraft grenades came down to the left and right of me, and not far from me, bullets from machine guns were pelting the earth. It seemed to go on forever. My blood felt frozen in my veins. I went home, gray in the face, and went right into the bunker across the street to be safe, even though the attack was already over and there was no more danger. I could not tell my father what had happened, or I would have been in deep trouble. For some time, I was cured of my attraction to special phone messages and anti-aircraft weapons, and I did not care for leftover breakfast and chocolate any more.

During the holding pattern of General Hodges' and Patton's troops in Alsace-Lorraine, there was much propaganda spread by Nazi party members in the border cities. One big rumor was that the German troops were preparing themselves to stop the Allies in France with a new counterattack. Then the Allies would be pushed back to the English Channel and destroyed, as had the French and English troops in 1940. My father spoke to us and our neighbors about how it was such nonsense, and he asked everyone to stay calm and quiet. But not everybody was as convinced as he was that the war was lost.

From 1944 to 1945, my father took my mother to a farm owned by my aunt and uncle some distance away from the main danger zone, in the farm village of Grosbundenbach, about 25 kilometers away. On the highest point in western Palatinate, it could be seen from the French side. Situated between the original Siegfried Line and the secondary defense line, it was in the middle of two German defense systems, just as our home lay exactly between the Siegfried Line and the Maginot Line. My mother stayed there about 15 months.

I split my time between my parents. I stayed a few days in town with my father and then a few days at the farm with my mother. Close to the farm was a large military food storage area and a spare parts department in support of the fighting troops who were still on French soil holding back Patton's Army. The supply vehicles for food and spare parts traveled almost daily from the farm village to the troops on the front. In the process, they always passed my parents' home in Zweibruecken. Since we boys were always hanging around the soldiers and their vehicles, most of them knew me pretty well. When I wanted, they would let me ride with them from the farm to my father's house and vice versa. It worked out well for me. Later, when my father's place was under artillery and fighter-bomber attacks almost everyday, I spent more time at the farm.

At first, the days at the farm were quiet and very nice, except for occasional attacks by fighter-bombers. We had enough food to eat, not as much or as varied as I liked, but most of the time I did not go to bed hungry. Although the food was rationed, a little bit was always available. We lived in the farmhouse with six women and three men.

The farm had a sandstone basement with an area for fruit storage. The basement was accessible from outside and always locked. The only one besides my Aunt Maria who had a key to the fruit cellar was me, but nobody knew about this except her. She said to me, "You are the only person here of growing age, and you have to have a little more to eat than the others. Anytime during the day when you are hungry, go to the basement and get an apple, but eat it in some place where nobody can see you." Our meals were based on rations we received from food stamps and what we had from the animals and fields. The portions were somewhat reduced, because Aunt Maria fed two prisoners for whom she did not have food stamps.

The prisoners, a Frenchman and a Russian, lived in separate prison camps and were brought to a central place in the village every morning, where they were picked up by my uncle and taken to the farm. In the evening they had to be brought back to the village, and guards drove them back to the prison camp in large pickup trucks. They were fed at the prison camp in the morning and were given a small packed lunch. In the evening they were fed again at the camp, but every evening Aunt Maria invited them into a small, separate kitchen for dinner before they returned to the camp. If this had been discovered by the local Nazi party members, she would have gone to prison.

The food from the central prison kitchen probably seemed like gourmet food for Stanislas from Witebsk in Russia, but for Marcel from Normandy in France, it was no better than junk food. It was forbidden to have the prisoners sit at the same table and eat with us, but the farm had three kitchens: one for the owners, one for the farm workers, and one where the food for the animals was prepared. Since there were no German farm workers available during the war, the second kitchen was used by my aunt for the prisoners, mainly for lunch and a place to rest.

In the last year and a half of the war, food was not available in large quantities nor in much variety. Most of the farm harvest had to be delivered to a central collection station, but my aunt held back a little for us. My Aunt Maria surely has a place in Heaven, and I can say she was a saint. The entire family was Catholic – so was the Frenchman. In the evening, Aunt Maria locked all the outside doors before she started to serve dinner to the prisoners. The two prisoners got the same kind and amount of food as we all did.

Aunt Maria insisted that the Frenchman say grace before eating. He did it in French, and most of us did not understand what he said. The Russian probably did not have a religion and did not say grace. When it was available, Aunt Maria gave each prisoner a piece of bread and an apple after dinner. They were to eat it at the camp or give it to other prisoners who may not have been treated as well as those at my aunt's farm.

Aunt Maria was very religious and she watched very closely that neither of the prisoners nor any of us cursed. When something went wrong at the farm or with the horses, the Frenchman sometimes said, "*Nom de Dieu*" ("God damn it"). He did not say it often, but when Aunt Maria heard him, she would run to Uncle Otto and say, "Just a moment ago Marcel said 'Nom de Dieu!' Please go quickly and reprimand him!" Uncle Otto would immediately do this, because Aunt Maria was in command of everything at the farm.

After some time with us, both prisoners spoke a bit of German, and my Uncle Otto once in awhile informed them about what was going on in the war. Giving prisoners extra food and talking to them about the war and politics were strictly forbidden and would have resulted in harsh penalties for my uncle and aunt if they had been discovered. (*Both prisoners came back to the farm after the war and thanked my relatives for the humane treatment. They were fully aware of how dangerous it had been under the Nazi regime to feed them and talk to them about war and politics. Also, a number of French prisoners came back after the war to visit our family and thank my parents for their kind and humane treatment.*)

Aunt Marra went to church every Sunday and insisted that my young cousin and I go with her. The adults could choose for themselves. Most of the time, two or three adults came with us, so normally there were four to six of us going to church. There was no Catholic church in the farm village, so we had to walk almost two hours to reach another small community, Wiesbach, where there was a beautiful, very old Catholic church. Every Sunday we had to get up around 4:30 a.m. to prepare ourselves and walk the two hours to Mass. Getting up so early on winter mornings was unpleasant, since it was ice cold in the house in the morning. Heat was never on during the night, only during the day. There were coal and wood-burning stoves in the kitchen and the living room, but none in any of the bedrooms. To warm up our beds, we each had a brick that was wrapped in linen and was heated in the oven before bedtime. Two people had to sleep in each bed, because my relatives took in other relatives, also from the danger zones. I slept in a room with three beds, in a bed with my mother. In the other two beds were two ladies. Since I was getting older, I hated having to sleep in the room with all those women.

It was dark and cold when we started walking to the church, and quite often it was raining or snowing. We did not have good shoes or clothes, because such items were rationed and we had to have government-issued stamps to obtain them. Some years we were not given any such stamps.

We walked first on the road, then across open fields, then through the woods, and only a quarter mile on the road again. Not only did I hate to get up and walk such a distance, but some parts of the journey were much more uncomfortable and dangerous than others. Fighter planes sometimes came by, shooting at everything that moved. On our way to church it was still dark, but going home the sun was shining and we could easily be seen from the air. On three different Sundays we were attacked by fighter planes. We threw ourselves on the ground in a field, and the dirt on either side of us would be flying from all the machine-gun bullets. It was very frightening. Luckily, none of us was ever hit by bullets or splinters. (Maybe because we were so brave to go to church and pray under those circumstances.)

What it felt like at those moments when we were under gun-fire, I can hardly put into words. Our clothes were very dirty after getting up from the ground. Two times we also were under gunfire on the open roads. Most of the time, the roads were lined by fruit trees on both sides (which are still there today). During the attacks, the fruit trees provided good cover for us. Despite the danger, my aunt insisted that we go to church every Sunday. She always said danger in wartime was also at home, and that when our time is up, we could be anywhere. (*How comfortable we are today. We drive to church in air-conditioned and heated cars and do not have to walk for two hours in terrible weather!*)

Daily life on the farm was pleasant most of the time. I was allowed to take part in trips to the fields, especially during planting and harvest time. This involved traveling by horse and wagon. The most exciting part was when we went to cut wood for our wood-burning stoves and to sell to logging companies. Cutting the trees was dangerous and hard work that didn't interest me, but what was really exciting was transporting the logs back to the farm. Because the wooded areas were mostly in low valleys, during the transport uphill to the farm, one of my uncles always had to lead the horses by the head so they would not stop by themselves and let the wagon roll backwards. Another uncle would be at the back of the wagon, operating a spiral brake by hand, and sometimes I was with him. We had to turn the brake very quickly when the horses needed a short break. The spiral brake pressed two wooden blocks against the wheels so that the wagon, loaded with logs, could not roll backwards.

Sometimes life on the farm was boring, mainly on rainy days. I was the kind of boy who always had to be doing something. First I began, without anyone's knowledge, to feed the horses oats two extra times a day, even though they were already fed very well for the hard work they had to do. The horses loved the extra oats and their coats started to shine very nicely, especially after they were brushed. They were cleaned and brushed almost every day by the prisoners working on the farm. They also gained weight, much to the surprise of my aunt and uncle, who also wondered about their shiny coats. The horses grew more restless, and people were surprised by their different behavior. It was much harder to direct them and keep them under control. If the horses were approached by someone they didn't know, they sometimes kicked out their back legs. Sometimes one horse, Flora, jumped up and with both rear legs struck the door of the kitchen where feed was prepared. This made a tremendous noise that could be heard all over the farm. Uncle Otto and Aunt Marie then called out, "Flora!" and the horse stopped.

I soon found out that I could trigger these outbursts myself. One stable door was beside the horse, while the door to the feeding kitchen was behind the horse. From the side door I could reach Flora with a broomstick and poke her on her side rear quarter, which triggered a big kick against the kitchen door. After every attack, Uncle Otto and Aunt Maria screamed "Flora!" and came running to the stable, but when they arrived I had already disappeared around the corner of the barn, and no one could see me. They never found out that I was the culprit who had triggered those noisy outbursts. I knew that my behavior was not fair to the horses, but I justified it by feeding them the extra oats. Whenever I heard my relatives talking about the horses' behavior over dinner, I could not look them straight in the eye.

Then, something very strange happened. Some animals, for example elephants and horses, can remember things they don't like. Apparently, so did Flora! At the beginning of my stay at the farm, when we went to the field or out logging, I was often allowed to ride Flora, but only on the way out. Now, after all the times I had poked her with my broomstick, she reacted differently to me. Whenever my Uncle Albert or Uncle Otto lifted me onto Flora's back, she turned her head and started to nip me. Flora also tried to throw me off her back by kicking up her back legs. After the second or third unsuccessful attempt to lift me onto Flora's back, my uncle said, "We just don't know what's going on with this horse, and you have to stay away from her." My uncle said that Flora had, until this time, allowed almost everyone to ride her. From then on, I had to be very careful not to stand too close to her, especially next to her head where she might bite me or near her backside where she might strike me with her big, heavy back legs. I felt guilty. Nobody but me knew what had happened to Flora, but I stopped my bad behavior. Later on, I told a few friends what I had done to the horse, but I never talked about it to my relatives on the farm or to my parents.

Despite the war, air attacks and artillery fire, we did not lose our humor as boys, and we did some other foolish tricks. As described earlier, the Allied movement in front of the Siegfried Line came to a halt because Patton's and Hodges' troops had to support

Montgomery. The front line at this time was about 40-50 kilometers away from the farm village. One of the supply units for the fighting troops and its storage facilities were located at the village. It also had a service station for repairing heavy equipment. Spare parts and food were stored in the farmers' barns and tightly secured.

Naturally, my friends and I found ways to get into those barns without being detected by the soldier-guards. At this stage of the war, civilians did not have any sweets or chocolate anymore, and we could not at times resist stealing a bar of chocolate and sometimes a bottle of cognac or wine. We entered the barns the same way the chickens did, on the other side from where the guards were positioned. We would eat the chocolate, but we did not drink the wine or cognac. Instead, we took little pieces of bread and soaked them in cognac, and then fed them to the two roosters that took care of the 25 chickens. The roosters got drunk, walked funny, and sometimes keeled over. (*We thought it was funny at the time, but today I would strongly forbid my children and grandchildren from tormenting any animals, even in jest.*)

Sometimes the fun ended differently. When it was dark, boys and girls from the farm village went sledding from the top of the village to the next village down in the valley. We could not do this during the day because of the danger of attacks by fighter planes. One evening I arrived late and thought that the whole gang had already left. I rode down the wooded hills and street about two miles, but when I arrived in the valley, no one was there. I did not know that there had been a pre-warning of an air attack. I had to walk all by myself to the top of the hill, while airplanes were flying above me. Luckily, there was no attack on either village that night. But this was not the only danger. I had to walk for about 35 minutes on an icy road with woods on both sides, and I was afraid that something else would happen and that no one would find me in the snow. I never again went sledding by myself.

One evening, while I was home with my father, a large German Panther tank stopped in front of our house. The SS Sergeant in charge asked my father if he could park the tank in our driveway. On one side of the driveway was our house, and on the other side were trees and tall shrubs, which would shield the tank from fighter planes. The SS tank crew also asked my father if they could stay overnight in our house and cook dinner in our kitchen. My father agreed, probably thinking of my three brothers who were serving in the war and hoping that they would be treated the same way he was treating these soldiers in need.

The young soldiers, who belonged to the SS Unit *Götz von Berlichingen*, came into our house. I'm guessing they were between 18 and 21 years old. The soldiers started to talk about their mission and about their superiority to the American tank units on the other side of the front line. After the war, my father told me how amazed he had been by the determination of those young soldiers. As I recall the conversation, they told us that their unit had only six Panther tanks left, but they were impeding or attacking a much larger American tank force. They said that if they took out one or two American tanks, the remaining 20 or more would turn around and stop fighting. (In reality, the tanks were either from Patton's or Hodges' units and were in a holding pattern because the bulk of troops were supporting Montgomery in the Battle of the Ardennes.) The SS soldiers claimed that the Americans were cowards and were weak. (In reality, they avoided casualties until they were ordered to attack and to fight their way into Germany. The Americans moved a certain number of tanks along the front line to demonstrate how strong they still were, but the same units were used along 150 kilometers of the front line.)

My personal interest was not in the determination or opinions of those visiting SS soldiers, however. I was 12 years old and wanted to see this heavy Panther tank, both inside and out. I asked the soldiers if I could climb on the tank and go inside to observe the driver's seat and the gun turret. As I went to step on the tank, one of the soldiers carrying food into our house stopped me and forbade me to continue. This was very surprising and disappointing to me. My first thought was that I was dealing with arrogant young SS soldiers. They had told my father that they came from the front line to have some repair and service work done on their vehicle. The service station was in Thaleichweiler, about 20 miles east of my parents' home.

The next morning the soldiers left our house in an orderly fashion and said that they would be returning in three days. They asked if they might stay another night with us, and my father said they could. Three days later they came back and parked the tank in the same place. This time the soldiers were much friendlier. They all looked sad, but also somewhat relieved. They now wore clean, good looking uniforms, and the mud had been washed off their tank. I was impressed. This time they invited my father and me to have supper with them, and one of the soldiers cooked a meal. Since we did not have much to eat anymore, I liked the invitation and my father accepted it. We had nice conversations about their families and the cities from which they came, but nothing about the war. We were interrupted every hour or so by U.S. artillery fire, and I ran into the basement shelter, although my father and the soldiers stayed upstairs. At some point the soldiers told me that before they left I could see the tank inside and out, and that I could ask all the questions I wanted.

After dinner, I found the courage to ask them why I was not allowed to see the tank the first time. Again, all the soldiers looked sad and stopped talking. Then one of them told us a story. Their tank commander, whose name was Kremer, had been shot in the head by a sniper or a French Resistance member and had died of his injury. During the fighting in France, Kremer had said that if he died he did not want to be buried in a foreign country. Most of the time, he stood inside the tank with his head outside, to direct the tank's movements and shooting direction. On the evening of the first visit to our house, the soldiers had their commander's body lying in the back of the tank covered with his uniform and his tent. This was the reason they prevented me from going near the tank the first time. They had not wanted to tell us about their dead commander. They also confessed that heavy Panther tanks were very robust and theirs had not been in need of repair, which they could and would have done themselves. They had wanted to fulfill their fellow soldier's last wish by burying him on German soil.

We almost cried. I knew that my father was thinking about my brothers serving as soldiers in the war. Two were officers and one was a staff sergeant. One of my brothers, a first lieutenant in the

German Army, had been declared missing-in-action near Witebsk in Russia, where the Germans lost one of the most decisive battles on the eastern front. (*We never heard anything about his death, despite research still done today by my nephew in Germany. Another brother, who was a second lieutenant, fought in the German Defense Unit in Normandy near Caen, was wounded, and was taken prisoner by the Americans. He was first hospitalized in England and then transferred to a prison camp in Texas. Since he was an officer and spoke English, he was appointed the German commander of the camp. He later said many times that being a prisoner in Texas was the best time of his life. When my parents learned that he was in the United States, my mother said, "Thank God the war is over for him, and I am very happy.")*

By this time, high school students were being drafted and trained on anti-aircraft guns. Others had to build tank traps. I was too young for anti-aircraft defense, but students two classes ahead of me were deeply involved. Most of those young people were not used for fighting on the front, only for home defense. Since they had not been rigorously trained, they were fairly helpless. They had to shoot at well-equipped U.S. fighter bombers and were likely to be killed during an attack.

Three of the young students in classes ahead of me were drafted and stationed at one of the anti-aircraft batteries near our hometown. One was a neighbor of mine, and another was the son of the pastor of the Lutheran church in our suburb. A third was the son of a good friend of my family. My neighbor survived the war without any injury. The pastor's son and the son of my parents' friends were killed by American fighter bomber attacks. Almost all of the students at the Helmholz Gymnasium attended the funeral for these two young men. Some Nazi party members were present and spoke of heroes who died in action for the German Reich. There is no doubt that those students were very brave, but that they died for the Hitler regime is quite doubtful. At this time, nobody believed in a German victory anymore, but no one could speak out openly.

The pastor's son who had been killed by American fighter bombers was an only child, and his parents grieved deeply. The pastor, a friend of my parents, knew that at this time I had a very old bicycle, assembled from parts by my father. We got the frame from somebody, the wheels from someone else, and the rest of the parts from other old bicycles. There were no fenders and when it rained, I got wet and dirty. It needed constant repair and service, but I was very happy to have even such an old vehicle.

About six weeks after his son was killed, the pastor visited my family one evening. With him he brought a brand new bicycle – the bicycle that had belonged to his son. He gave it to me and asked me to keep it clean, maintain it well, and keep it in good shape in honor of his son. I cannot describe how sad we all were, but at the same time how happy I was to get this bicycle. This was a great and generous gesture by the pastor, who said that he did not want any money for the bicycle. What made an even bigger impression on me than this bicycle being new was that it had two gears. It was probably one of the first bicycles of its kind built in Germany. Now I could go uphill better and ride much faster than with my old bicycle. The color was a combination of red and maroon, and there were blue stripes on the frame.

Shortly before the American and French troops took over our area, we hid the bicycle behind straw and hay in the barn because the departing SS troops had told us that the Americans, and more so the French, would confiscate everything they liked. The bicycle of my brother, who was reported missing in action in Russia, also was hidden under straw in the barn. My mother always hoped that my brother would someday come home.

Downtown Zweibruecken before World War II

Beneath a smoke-filled sky, infantrymen of the Third Division advance through the rubble-filled streets of Zweibruecken, March 22, 1945

A side street in downtown Zweibruecken before any debris was cleared away. The ruins of the Luetpold School are visible in the background

During the post-war occupation, the French City Commander walks with the first elected mayor through the remains of Zweibruecken

Zweibruecken at the time of the American occupation. Part of the
castle is visible at right.

The altar of the Catholic church, which sustained the least damage

ABOVE LEFT,
the Alexander-
kirche in ruins

BELOW LEFT,
the Alexander-
kirche restored
after the war.

ABOVE, a view
of both Lutheran
churches, the
Karlkirche and the
Alexanderkirche,
destroyed

RIGHT, the Karl-
kirche restored
to its original
appearance

The first post war newstand, located in the former entrance to a pub, which belonged to the finest hotel in Zweibruecken. The hotel was completely destroyed.

ABOVE LEFT, the destroyed castle, which is located in the center of the city.

BELOW LEFT, the new castle, completely rebuilt and restored.

14

American Intelligence at its Best: Debriefing General Schaefer

The question that was raised around my hometown many times was: Why did Patton's or Hodges' troops not advance into Germany right away? If they had, many civilian casualties and the destruction of many historic buildings could have been averted. The war may have ended several months earlier, and Hitler's senseless Ardennes offensive might not have taken place. Many U.S. and German soldiers' lives could have been spared.

There are probably three main reasons why the 1st Army, commanded by General Hodges, and the 3rd Army, commanded by General Patton, were put on hold in Alsace-Lorraine, only a short distance from the German border and my hometown. The first was the necessity of supporting Montgomery in the Battles of the Ardennes and the Bulge. The presence of the 1st and 3rd armies prevented the defeat of Montgomery and supported his penetration into Germany.

The second reason may have been that the Allies were hampered by shortages of fuel and supplies in the early stage of their advances into Germany. Hitler had ordered the ports along the Channel to be held, which proved to be a good tactical move because it slowed down the Allies. The Germans also did not have enough supplies and fuel, which they wanted to capture from the Allies, but this plan turned out to be a failure.

The third reason might have been to gain time to gather more intelligence about the Siegfried Line, which was a feared defense area. Patton and Hodges, based on their own leadership capabilities and with their well-trained and disciplined staff, could have struck earlier and quickly overrun the German defenses, although this might have resulted in greater casualties. Eisenhower's orders to support Montgomery did not allow Patton and Hodges to follow their own inclinations and recommendations.

For the third reason, the gathering of more information about the Siegfried Line, the U.S. Intelligence units have to be highly commended. The following reminiscences are from Lieutenant General Hans Schaefer, who before the war was Colonel and Commander of the Border Infantry Regiment 127. This regiment was stationed in my hometown, Zweibruecken. After the war, Schaefer wrote about the time he was a prisoner-of-war in France. (*I found this account in the archives of my hometown, on a few yellowed sheets of paper.*)

On August 15, 1944, the Allied landing and invasion began in southern France. A few days later the Army group Blaskowitz was forced to make room and retreat along the Rhone River toward the north. I was ordered to stay put on the coastline. I was supposed to counter the attacks of the invading Allied armies and defend the city of Marseilles with the 204th Infantry Division. We were supported by the Navy, anti-aircraft battalions and artillery units in position along the coastline. After we were captured on August 28th by the French Army, I was detached from the bulk of the soldiers and interned in isolation in Fort Malbouquet in the port of Toulon. On October 19, 1944, I was transferred, together with another German general, to the Americans.

After having spent many hungry days in the French prison, the Americans told us we would have a chance to eat what we wanted. The American staff unit to which we were transported, near Marseilles, was part of the C.I.C. It was supposed to be organized and assembled after a British model. The task was to gather intelligence for further warfare – warfare as seen by military experts and obtained from important German military leaders. They selected military leaders based on rank and previous tasks and experience.

Treatment, food and lodging were exceptionally good, probably in deliberate contrast to the treatment we received as prisoners of the French. We were treated by the Americans as officers and as their equals, and we had many amenities. That all this had a certain purpose was soon understood, based on the conversations and questions.

It was not surprising that we talked about different kinds of warfare and chances for winning the war. Slowly we were led into areas that seemed to be of greater interest to the Americans. The Siegfried Line, where I had served as general and Military Commander of the city of Zweibruecken, was mentioned often. My interrogators knew that I was very knowledgeable of the area. It seemed like the Siegfried Line haunted the American Army leaders. They were very worried about running into heavy casualties, which the American population would never understand and never forgive. All conversations centered around these core questions: What is the Siegfried Line? What is its structure and makeup? How will it be defended? What and where are its secrets that can not be detected from the air?

I had to act diplomatically and not show that I knew the reason for all those questions. It was a little strange to realize that they only had an interest for the area around Zweibruecken, not the whole Siegfried Line. On one hand, they knew that this battlefield was still far away from the front lines, and on the other hand, they would not take any chance to attack fortresses that were strongly built and relatively easy to defend (as they were around Zweibruecken). They showed me pictures and write-ups about fortresses from all kinds of countries, including those from Germany. They hoped I would offer judgments on the structures and their relative defensive values. They seemed to be disappointed when I did not answer right away, and declared myself no expert.

Mid-November of 1944, the American staff was deployed from Marseilles to northern France to be nearer the front line. The new location was the city of Revin by the Maas River, north of Charlesville. From this place, an American officer I knew only as Colonel S. and I drove south in wet-cold winter weather on December 3. We were covered in very thick blankets. We passed the battlefields of Sedan, some of which are the most famous places in the war of 1870-1871. We crossed north of Stenay, the attack area of my regiment in World War I, which fought there in very hard battles and crossed the Maas River. Around noon we reached Verdun. We were driving through the partly-destroyed city, passing the monument of the French soldiers killed in World War I. We arrived on the main street and saw on the horizon the heights of Douaumont. [This was the bloodiest battlefield of World War I, but it had lost all honor when the French surrendered it to the Germans without a fight during World War II.] We stopped in front of a hotel where many other cars were parked. The colonel and his driver entered the hotel. After an endless wait, they came back quite excited. The hotel was filled with French civilians. The American colonel said we had to wait, that we could not go into the hotel with me in my uniform as a German general. I told him, 'Give me your hat and coat, and I will look like an American.' 'Done', said the colonel. The coat was very long and wide because the colonel was maybe 10 inches taller than I was. The coat also covered my boots, which an American officer would ordinarily not wear. The hat with the American emblems fit me very well. As I put my hands deep into the coat pockets, I looked like a real American, much to the colonel's amusement.

With coffee and buttered bread, we waited a good hour in a hotel room. I was curious about what would happen. Finally, someone knocked on the door. A very young and elegant American colonel entered the room. He was introduced to me as Colonel R. He had been ordered to accompany me. We left the hotel the same way we entered, with curious civilians looking at us as we got into the car. We then drove south along the Maas River. My new companion was friendly and told me that he was a staff officer in the 3rd American Army. A year ago, he had been a member of General Eisenhower's staff in England. He married without permission when his girlfriend came to visit him in England. Right after the wedding, he was a personal guest of General Eisenhower, but later he was penalized and transferred to another unit.

We continued our conversation as we drove through St. Mihiel, passing the old fortress of Toul, which had been very heavily damaged during this war. Around 4 p.m. we arrived in Nancy. We stopped on a cul-de-sac in front of a nice-looking villa. I was asked to leave the car and to enter the house, which was protected by three U.S. soldiers carrying rifles. Through a small entryway, I came into the reception area where I met three more soldiers and an American sergeant. He introduced himself in fluent German and said he was a German language teacher from New York. He was now in charge of housekeeping at the villa that was occupied by U.S. officers. One of the soldiers was ordered to serve me. The other soldiers were in charge of cooking and cleaning. After seeing my look of uncertainty, Colonel R. declared that the villa was at my disposal. He escorted me to the second floor into a well-furnished living/bedroom with a large French bed. Next door was a large bathroom, the likes of which I had not seen for quite some time. From the bedroom I could look over a wild garden in front of the villa. In front of the garden, an American soldier with a rifle stood guard. The few belongings I had left I was able to deposit in the armoire.

Just when I wanted to rest on the beautiful French bed, I was told that coffee was being served on the lower floor. I went downstairs to a very beautiful room furnished with cabinets and dishes from Alsace-Lorraine, where I met Colonel S. again, and a lieutenant who said he was Irish. This lieutenant also had been ordered to take care of me. The table was overflowing with beautifully presented foods. I could smell real coffee. I probably had a somewhat astonished look on my face, wondering why I was being given all this beautiful comfort. I was told that Colonel F., with whom I had conversations on the trip from Paris to Revin, had selected this house for me. He said that I had not been quartered in Revin in accordance with my rank, and he wanted me to have peaceful days in an environment appropriate to my rank as a general. I didn't know what to believe, but the Americans' humane and friendly behavior made it worth waiting for whatever was coming. I knew I would find out what their intentions were.

Right after dinner, Colonel F. and Second Lieutenant R. arrived dressed in military attire with helmets that U.S. officers wear in wartime. We went into the living room and I asked who was coming since they were reporting to me so officially. They gave the same story: that a German general deserved better accommodations. They also said that a German general was entitled to such an honor. (Later in my prisoner-of-war days, I was treated quite differently.)

A few quiet and very nice days passed, filled with much good food. The days ended at 10:30 p.m., followed by a late supper. The Americans tried to spoil me. They even served wine a few times. I was driven to a hospital for a check-up of my ears. Several high-ranking American officers visited me. All of them spoke excellent German and most of them had studied many years ago in Germany, mostly in Munich. They were happy to practice their German. Everybody was astonished by my natty German general's uniform with its dark red slacks and playful colors on the jacket. It appeared that military personnel had high respect for a German officer who had served as such even before the war. They were surprised to hear that an officer of my rank met with Hitler very seldom, or not at all, to discuss strategic operations. They were also surprised that I spoke so highly about the good food they had provided, assuming that a general would be more spoiled.

I wanted to walk in the fresh air, but was told by the guard that this was not possible. When I mentioned this to the people serving me, they immediately brought in Colonel R. and we scheduled a walk through the city of Nancy. I was given American military slacks, a coat, military shoes and a military belt. (Later the British took them away from me because they said they were property of the U.S. military.)

The next day, I dressed again as an American and waited for Colonel R. When he arrived he told me that we could not go out anymore. He said that spies had been reported in the area, and that controls in the streets had been increased. Every officer would be checked. Therefore I had to stay inside, but I still had very good food. After a while, Colonel F. visited me and excused himself for not coming more often because he was too busy. Before he left, he asked me if I would give a presentation to several high-ranking American officers about the Siegfried Line, since they knew I had detailed information.

I asked, "Is this the reason for my being here?" and he answered, "No." They were interested in hearing something authentic about the Siegfried Line and its individual bunkers, even though it was not yet decided if the Americans would be attacking it. My first question was, "Where are the American troops with their front line at this time?" They answered, "Today they entered the fortress of Bitche and the Germans are defending the city vigorously." I asked, "How about Saarbruecken?" They answered, "It was already taken by Patton's troops."

The front was moving toward Saargemuend. The next goal must be to take Zweibruecken, I thought. I asked myself if this could be avoided. Could the situation for the city of Zweibruecken improve without my explanations? I did not think so. The road now led, without any doubt, directly from Bitche and from Saargemuend towards Zweibruecken. How could an attack on Zweibruecken be avoided or diverted? I asked the Americans to give me one night to think about the presentation.

I came to the conclusion that I could do more for my home-town of Zweibruecken by agreeing to the presentation than if I turned them down. If I gave a detailed description of the Siegfried Line with its defense systems around Zweibruecken and Pirmasens, perhaps a frontal confrontation or attack could be avoided. Maybe the American attack could be shifted more towards Saarbruecken, where most of the defense systems were already taken by American troops, and from there they could penetrate further into Germany. The next day, on December 9, 1944, I accepted the invitation to make the presentation. I had to prepare myself well, because of my rough English. I asked for maps of the area and for colored pens to make sketches. I received them in ample quantity and dimensions, as well as many aerial photos. From the photos I could see the latest additions to the system, sections that had been completed after I had left the area. I saw the tank traps and their locations.

With the help of Colonel S., I prepared myself and rehearsed several times. I drafted several possible attack directions for the Americans:

1. From Bitche to the north up to the German/French border. From there via Muenschweiler, Wallhalben, in the direction of Landstuhl. [*Landstuhl is one of the largest U.S. military hospitals in Europe, and it was still in operation in the year 2006.*]

2. From around Saargemuend towards Blieskastel and Homburg.

3. From Saarbruecken along the Kaiserstrasse via St. Ingbert, Homburg, and also towards Landstuhl.

I referred to spring flood zones of the Rivers Blies and Schwarzbach between Zweibruecken, Einoed and Blieskastel, and the swamp areas east of Zweibruecken and up to Comwig. [*Author's note: My niece's husband's family owned that area then and still does to this day.*] I marked these areas as dangerous zones because tanks and heavy Army vehicles could become stuck there and come under German attack.

I marked all the fortresses along the Siegfried Line, and I indicated the heaviest armored units, located at the height of the Wallerscheid with Galgenberg near Zweibruecken, and the Gersbacher Heights near Pirmasens as a center of heavy defenses.

After everybody had left, I asked Colonel F. to do me a favor. I asked him to spare my hometown from heavy destruction. I described it to him as a small beautiful town from which no resistance could be expected. I told him that most of my family members lived in this city and that I was worried about them. The colonel said that he was sorry that he could not make promises to save the rest of the city, but he assured me that he would make efforts to spare the part of the city where my people were living. He told me that I should mark on the aerial photos where my family's houses were located and assured me that those pictures would be widely distributed to the Air Force and artillery units. They also would be distributed to the officers of the 3rd Army, which would be attacking the Siegfried Line and Zweibruecken. A major from an Air Force unit of the 3rd Army visited me right after the meeting. I again marked the area, this time in more detail.

This was the end of my stay in Nancy. On December 12, 1944, I was driven with Colonels S. and R. via Toul north in the direction of Verdun. We took a turn through countryside unknown to me and drove until we reached the city of Luxembourg. We stopped in front of a large, elegant house. Here I again met the American diplomat with whom I had spoken briefly before leaving Revin. Earlier, in Revin, we had talked at length about how the German forces as a whole could capitulate, but we could not find a solution. Now, in Luxembourg we met again and I was introduced to another American general who was the head of a Pentagon department responsible for foreign armies. After dinner we had long and interesting conversations, but we could not find a practical solution, any more than before. Germany would be destroyed as long as its armies continued to fight, even without the slightest chance of success. With the provision that only an unconditional surrender could lead to the end of the war, there was no chance that Hitler would give up unless he were killed. We left each other with sad regret at not being able to do anything.

Later I was turned over to the English and I became a prisoner-of-war in England. In April of 1945, I saw a photo in an English newspaper of several layers of rubble and read in shock the caption: "This was the city of Zweibruecken. All German cities will be treated like this when they continue to make senseless defense efforts."

Many months later, I learned from another prisoner-of-war born in Zweibruecken that the area where my people lived was spared from the bombardment by a one kilometer radius. Was it coincidence, good luck, or the American officers living up to their commitment? It is impossible to know for sure.

In the final days of the Siegfried Line, there were several hard-fought battles. In this author's opinion, the most decisive event in defeating the Siegfried Line was the debriefing of General Lieutenant Hans Schaefer, the former commander of the Home Defense Infantry Division located in Zweibruecken. He was extremely familiar with the details of the defense line and the territories around it.

The American military intelligence used Patton's and Hodges' delay very efficiently. The timely information they were able to gather about the Siegfried Line was essential to saving lives. It was based on American military honor, integrity and morale. The members of this U.S. military intelligence unit have to be highly commended. They did not use force, but cleverness and humanity.

15

Passive Resistance and Rommel's Demise

Since living in the United States, and during my travels through many countries, I sometimes hear that Germans did little to remove Hitler from power or to publicly protest against his regime. Sometimes people say this in a polite way, sometimes they say it as an open critique. Many Americans, with the exception of the GIs who lived for a while in Germany, have a negative impression of Germans based on disparaging press reports and movies. I hope I can correct some of this negativity by relating a few of my own stories and experiences.

After the Americans took over my city and country at the end of World War II, most people denied being a Nazi party member or a Hitler supporter. Everybody talked about how they opposed the Hitler regime. Their particular comments may not have been true, but a large number of people and families really did oppose Hitler and his regime. (*Some 10 years after World War II, others started to admit that they had been members of the Nazi party and that they had supported the system. Since the early 1990s, new right wing parties have emerged in Germany and some of their members have expressed admiration for the old system. Luckily, Germany now has strong ties to the United States and the western world. It is without a doubt a solid democracy with a solid Grundgesetz, which is similar to the U.S. Constitution, and the leading parties are in full support of it.*)

My father opposed Hitler from the very beginning, and he was part of the passive resistance. He quite often met in secret with friends to discuss whether anything could be done to oust the

Nazi regime and end the war. This was very dangerous. He and his friends had no doubt that Hitler and his close followers would kill to preserve their power. Here are only a few examples of how my father tried to work against the Nazi regime without being killed or being taken away to a concentration camp.

I will never forget November 9, 1938, the *Kristallnacht* (Crystal Night). About 5:30 the next morning, my father drove out of the city with me, taking me along on a business trip, as he quite often did. On this morning, the synagogue in Zweibruecken was burning (just as all the synagogues were burning throughout Germany). The fire could be seen from far away. Every time we talked about what had happened with family and friends, my father said, "This is the beginning of the end of the Third Reich." At this time, he and most of the people did not yet know about the concentration camps and efforts to exterminate the Jewish people.

Although I was in the Hitler youth, my father was never a member of the Nazi party. One day, my father came home and his face was as white as a ghost's. I heard him talking to my mother and saying, "Under no circumstances. I would rather die than do this." A *"Goldner Phasan"* or "gold pheasant" (the name referred to diehard Hitler and Nazi supporters) had visited the president of the nailworks, and my father had had to participate in the meeting. Neither the president nor the other managers were Nazi party members at this time. The gold pheasant requested that my father and the president of the company join the Nazi party. Both turned him down. He then insisted that one had to join. My father and the president asked for some time to decide. When they met separately afterwards, my father told the president that he would never join the party. The president then agreed to join the party. He knew how stubborn my father could be in personal matters, and he knew that if no one joined, it would have grave consequences for the company, the workers and their families.

After the war, because my father had never been a party member, a fact which was known by the new mayor – he also knew that my father was in the passive resistance – my father and my family were denazified right away by the new U.S. military government. Of the 40,000 inhabitants to be cleared after the war and to be issued a passport, my father and I received passport numbers of 102 and 103. (The president of the company, because of his position and because he was a party member – even though he had joined against his will – was imprisoned in an American camp after the war. It took almost a year for him to be cleared and freed.)

Another example of passive resistance was the treatment of prisoners of war by my father and my other relatives. Special treatment of such prisoners was very dangerous, and heavy penalties, including imprisonment in a concentration camp, were the consequence when people were caught or reported by a neighbor. My parents, as well as my uncles and especially my Aunt Maria, made life much easier for the prisoners working for us on the farm in Grossbundenbach. These actions by my relatives provided me with a model and contributed substantially toward giving me a better understanding of human relations. (*Almost all of the French prisoners visited us after the war and thanked us for their special treatment.*)

My father was in charge of the French and Russian prisoners of war in his factory. He helped whenever he could by smuggling in mail and extra food. After Germany defeated France, prisoners working in the factory could volunteer to work for German families on Saturdays and Sundays, doing gardening, maintenance on homes and cars, and other chores. The prisoners would receive no pay, but they could leave the camp and get extra food, and they received preferred treatment within the camp. One of the French prisoners who came to our house was from the French Navy, and he always wore his blue beret with the red bumble on top. He was very tall and he always drew special attention.

After World War I, my father had lived and worked in southern France for several years, and he spoke French very well. He developed a good relationship with this French sailor, who also was from the south and spoke in the same French dialect as my father. Although the French prisoners were called mainly by their first names at the factory, my father strictly forbade any member of our family to use the first names, and he specifically monitored me. I always had to call the French sailor "Monsieur Schill," even though he was a prisoner. My father told me that I had to respect the prisoners as human beings and speak to them in the manner in which they were accustomed to being addressed in their native countries.

At least once a month my father invited three to five prisoners to work in our garden or house. We could have had all 30 of the French prisoners working at our house once it became known in the camp that they were well-treated behind closed doors in the Beller household. At this time, we still had a reasonable amount of food. It was strictly forbidden to serve alcohol to prisoners of war, but all the Frenchmen, especially those from the south, liked red wine with their meal. We always had some liquor and wine at our house through my father's barter business, and most of the time we had French red wine. While the prisoners worked in the garden or house, my mother would prepare a French meal. Later, she served it to them with some red wine.

Whenever we had the French prisoners working for us, I had to go along the railroad tracks earlier in the day to collect snails. I brought them home in small bags. If I remember right, they had to be cleaned at least 10 times after they were taken out of their little shells in order to be ready for cooking and eating. One can eat only the little part of a snail located outside its shell, but this part can be prepared in many ways. My father knew all about it. The cleaning and cooking process looked anything but gourmet, but the snails, no matter how they were prepared, tasted excellent. At the time, I only got to eat a few of the snails. They were reserved for the French prisoners. (*Today I like to eat snails in fine restaurants as often as I can get them.*)

My father would have received the severest penalties if it had become known that he served wine and good food to the prisoners. And it would have been even worse if it had been discovered that my father passed along information about the war in the prisoners' native tongue so that they could have political discussions. Prisoners of war were completely cut off from war and political information. Because the danger to our family was enormous, I always had to keep my friends as far away from our home as possible during the work sessions with the French prisoners.

What such humane treatment meant to those prisoners, away from their families and homes, can only be understood by people who themselves have been prisoners of war in foreign countries. To spend time with a family, to receive food and wine like guests, and especially to hear news of the war, was for them a tremendously welcome deviation from their camp routine, and it helped to keep depression away and lift morale. A few times I saw them leaving our house on a Saturday evening, saying good-bye to my mother with tears in their eyes. My father always had to escort them back to the prison camp.

Although my father not a guard, he was responsible for the French and Russian prisoners in his factory – mainly for providing them with proper food and making sure it was delivered on time. He also made sure the prisoners kept the prison camp clean. Because the prisoners did not trust each other when it came to food, my father took it upon himself to be present when their food was picked up at a central kitchen downtown. Al the prison food was prepared in large cooking vessels, and the portions were counted exactly. Much of the food came from farms and factories in Frnace.

My father's contact with the chef turned out to be very important. My father quickly found out that the head chef was a Frenchman from Alsace-Lorraine, and that he spoke better German than French. He also had French prisoners as helpers in the kitchen. It was essential that my father spoke French, because nobody was supposed to understand that he and the chef were bartering. It did not take very long for my father to develop a very good relationship with this chef, whose name was Werner.

Werner was a heavy smoker and most of the time he had no cigarettes. The majority of cigarettes produced in Germany were distributed to the soldiers. At home most of the people smoked tobacco planted in their own gardens. (For awhile my father did this, too. When he smoked, we did not need any chemicals to kill flies or other insects in our house. The home-grown tobacco tasted and smelled awful.) Werner asked my father if he could provide him with regular cigarettes, and shortly after, a fine barter business was underway. Werner gave my father real butter, bread, sausage and meat, and in exchange, he received alcohol and cigarettes. Naturally, from every trade my father kept a portion for himself.

Now we had a great source of food and other supplies. With the merchandise from the central kitchen, we could also trade for shoes, clothing, and other items. We had a very good time until the end of 1943. All this bartering was illegal and had to be done in absolute secrecy. My father took those risks mainly for the well-being of his family.

Werner kept increasing his demands, because he had to give some of the cigarettes and alcohol to the people at the central food stations. Because he depended on my father's supplies, he treated not only my father very well, but also my father's prisoners. The portions for them were much bigger than what they were supposed to receive.

There were many prison camps in and around the city. My father always timed his arrival at the central food station for later in the day when most of the people in charge of the food were gone or close to leaving. This made it easier to handle the barter business, but something else was very important to him. Being the last one to pick up food for the prisoners, he always got more food than his prisoners were supposed to get. Werner also reserved the best quality of food for my father.

One time, the Russian prisoners became suspicious. They saw my father taking something out of their food boxes and they assumed it was part of their rations. They felt they were not being treated fairly and asked if they could join my father to pick up their food. Now the barter business was in danger. Werner acted immediately. For the next three days, he gave only the absolute minimum portions of food, which were considerably less than what my father always brought home for the prisoners. Many times my father had an extra large bucket full of potatoes or a couple additional loaves of bread and sausages. These all stopped when the Russians joined my father to pick up the food. After three days and an explanation from my father, they left him alone. Then the barter business blossomed once again.

Another example of my father's activities in the resistance was his meetings with our neighbor's son-in-law. This gentleman was a high-ranking officer in the German Army and the son of an industrialist who, because he owned several companies near the city of

Stuttgart and in England, still had relations with other countries. My father and this army officer talked quite often about possible actions against the regime, but in the end, they were afraid to make a move.

The officer was a neighbor of General Rommel, known all over the world as the Desert Fox, when Rommel lived in Reutlingen in the Meininger Strasse near Stuttgart. Almost no German during the entire war knew that Rommel was not a Nazi, and many still do not know it today. He was a brilliant soldier, but when he saw early on that there was no way for Germany to win the war, he joined the resistance.

Who was Rommel? Many older North Americans and Europeans are probably familiar with his name, but the younger generation may not recognize it at all. Rommel was one of the highest decorated German officers in World War I and the most popular general in World War II. How was his relationship with Hitler and Hitler's Nazi party? As a soldier and general, he undoubtedly obeyed Hitler's commands for a long time. He was known as the Desert Fox from the battle against the British at El Alamein in North Africa where he was far out-manned, as the man in charge of the Atlantic defense wall, and as the defender in charge of the entire German western front. He started to doubt a German victory late in World War II. Because of the weakened German military situation and the faults and mistakes of Hitler as the Supreme Commander, Rommel openly requested a political solution to end the war in late 1943. Because of his forthrightness and knowledge about the failed July 20 coup against Hitler, Rommel was forced into committing suicide.

In September 1944, Rommel was informed that General Speidel had been fired by Hitler as Chief of Staff of Group B, which was fighting at the western front. This front had been falling apart. What Rommel had expected was happening – at almost exactly the time as he had predicted. The Americans broke through a bridgehead in Normandy and progressed first south, then westward to Brittany. They then moved the majority of units eastward in the direction of Paris. On August 25, the English troops fighting to the left of the Americans crossed the Seine River very close to Rommel's former headquarters at La Roche Guyon. By the end of August they reached Amiens. On September 3, they started to enter Brussels. The German troops fled toward the German border to try to form new defense lines along the Rivers Mosel and Rhine. It was the reversal of the war against France in 1940. Everywhere, thousands of German soldiers were captured and marched into Allied prison camps.

Despite this catastrophic defeat, the Germans were able to stabilize their defenses and to fight again, if only for a short time. This took place in mid-September. The loss of German military personnel – in dead and wounded soldiers and soldiers taken prisoner by the Allies – was tremendous. But many escaped eastwards and were quickly reorganized into a new army. Specific and strategic areas (for example, the Schelde River) were newly organized at a fast pace to prevent the advancement of the Allies towards Antwerp. Those strategic areas were quickly built up with a strong defense. At several parts of the front, and at places of advancement toward Germany, the Allies were reluctant to continue their successful operations because their fast advancements also caused some logistical problems that slowed them down. By mid-September, the Allies started to halt their advancement. At the same time, the German Army, which had looked completely destroyed in the Normandy battles, reorganized and picked up a spirited defense.

Rommel had his own intelligence system. He was informed daily about the war situation. He learned early on about the German counter-offensive that took place in the Ardennes. He felt that such an offensive was completely misdirected. He said, "Every shot we are firing from now on against the Anglo-Americans will hit us." *

On September 3, 1944, Rommel was officially fired as Chief of Staff of the Army Group B. Three days later, General Speidel visited Rommel in Herrlingen. Speidel had also been fired without being given a reason. Speidel asked Rommel to talk to Hitler again,

---

* *The account of Rommel's last days is based on "King's Cross: A Life of Field Marshall Erwin Rommel," by David Fraser, HarperCollins Publishers, 1993, pp 529-532.*

to persuade him to take initiative to end the war. Speidel thought that maybe General Gudarian could arrange such a meeting with Hitler. (*One of my brothers fought under General Gudarian.*) But one day later, Speidel was arrested at his house. In the meantime, Rommel was also convinced that he was surrounded by invisible enemies. He had the unmistakable feeling that his house was under surveillance. His wife and his personnel had the same impression. They were of the opinion that the Gestapo was involved, and they feared assassination. Rommel always took a daily walk, usually accompanied by his son, Manfred, and they both carried a pistol. Rommel asked the local military commander to order a military police officer to protect him and his house.

It was a very strange situation for a general field marshall who was not officially named as being under suspicion. Rommel did not have any doubt that Hitler would find a way to execute him, if that were his decision. Hitler's Berlin staff may have been reluctant to openly go against Rommel, but Rommel thought they might do it in a way that they could keep secret from the German people. The only so-called crime that Rommel could have been charged with was his deep-seated and open opinion that the western front had already been lost. He had told this to Hitler and General Keitel several times.

People in Hitler's immediate circle thought that it was dangerous that such a popular and high-ranking commander was so outspoken about the west being lost. The Nazi district governor of Ulm, where Rommel's home was located, warned him and told him that Hitler's Secret Service had already been informed that he no longer believed in a German victory. Since Rommel had told this already to Hitler and the military staff generals, he did not react to the warning, even though it hinted at the most severe consequences.

The same day that General Speidel was arrested, Dr. Stroeling drove to Rommel's home and asked if he could do something to help their mutual friend. Dr. Stroeling himself had his house had thoroughly searched on August 10, 1944. Dark and dangerous storm clouds started to gather over these Nazi opponents. It looked more and more like a catastrophe was in the making. Rommel had known for quite awhile that Dr. Stroeling, a brilliant military leader and the current mayor of Stuttgart, was a staunch enemy of Hitler and his regime. Early in the winter months of 1943-1944, Dr. Stroeling told Rommel that he probably was the only one, because of his popularity as a soldier, who could negotiate with the Allies and lead Germany into a new future. Rommel never answered whether he would be willing to lead Germany after a quick capitulation. He did say that he would talk to Hitler and explain the hopelessness of winning the war. This he did, but he could not convince Hitler.

In early October 1944, Rommel drafted a letter to Hitler in which he expressed his sorrow that Speidel had been arrested, and he declared that Speidel was one of the most brilliant and loyal military leaders. He never sent this letter, since the *Ehregericht* (Honor Court) in Berlin, headed by General Keitel, decided that Speidel was innocent.

On October 7, Rommel received an official request to report immediately to Berlin. The order stated that a special train would pick him up and take him there. When Rommel called Hitler's headquarters to learn the details of the trip, he could not be connected with General Keitel. He talked to General Burgdorf, who was General Schmundts' successor, head of the Army Personnel Department and Hitler's Chief Assistant at this time.

Burgdorf was, as Rommel had been earlier, a professor at the Infantry School in Dresden, and both knew each other very well. Burgdorf said that everything was fine and that they wanted to talk about Rommel's future assignments. Rommel told Burgdorf that he was unable to travel and that he had an appointment with his doctor, Dr. Albrecht in Tuebingen. He also told Burgdorf that Dr. Albrecht had insisted that Rommel make his appointment and had forbidden Rommel to make the trip, for medical reasons.

On October 11, Rommel was visited by an old friend, Major Streicher. They had fought together in World War I. During a long walk, much longer than any time before, Rommel expressed his concern about the way the war was going and the possibility of capitulation. Rommel also told Streicher that he refused to travel to Berlin. He said he did not trust "them" anymore. Rommel said his enemies, whoever they were, were getting closer. Later, Rommel's confidante, Admiral Ruge, visited Rommel for a dinner meeting. The talk lasted until after midnight. The following day, despite severe headaches, Rommel drove with Admiral Ruge to the city of Augsburg. Ruge also told Rommel that he turned down an invitation to go to Berlin because he feared he might not arrive alive.

On October 13, Rommel visited an old friend, Oskar Farny, with whom he had served in the Wuerttemberger Mountain Battalion. Rommel told Farny that he was fully convinced that Hitler wanted to get rid of him.

Some people may have been of the opinion that Rommel was plagued by paranoia. Reality was that his old and reliable intuition, which many times before had helped him anticipate danger, gave him these warning signals. He was right this time, too. In the afternoon after his visit with Farny, a phone call came to Rommel's house. It was the reaction from Berlin to his refusal to travel there. The caller said that the next morning two generals would visit him, his old friend General Burgdorg and his Chief of Staff, General Maisel.

Around noon, the two generals arrived at Rommel's home. Rommel had already told his servant, Loistl, that he was expecting guests, and he asked him to leave the door to the driveway open. Loistl was surprised that the guests' car was parked on the street and not in the driveway. After Loistl announced the arrival of the generals to Rommel, he asked the driver of the car, a *Waffen SS* staffer, to come into the house. The driver turned down the invitation and told Loistl that he had orders and knew what he was doing. At the same time, Loistl noticed a second Mercedes parked in the street, and saw someone in civilian clothes talking to the SS driver of the generals. *

When Rommel first met with the two generals, he sent his son out of the room, and for the next 45 minutes he was alone with them. Burgdorf told Rommel that he had his orders directly from General Field Marshall Keitel and that those orders had come directly from Hitler. Burgdorf told Rommel that it was believed

---

* *ibid., "Kinght's Cross," pp 550-552*

that Rommel was directly involved in the assassination attempt on Hitler and that his guilt was proven by a statement from Lieutenant Colonel von Hofacker. Hitler felt deeply hurt by this betrayal, especially since he highly admired Rommel.

The generals told Rommel that Hitler had decided that the public should never be informed of Rommel's participation in the coup and that his name should not be brought up in connection with the assassination attempt. Rommel was confronted with the statements of von Hofacker and given two options. He could let Burgdorf take him prisoner for high treason and be prosecuted in a court, or he could take the honorable way out, as an officer. If he decided on the latter, he would receive a state funeral with all honors. His family would be completely left out of the situation. Official publications would say that Rommel died a natural death.

General Burgdorf had already brought a quick-reacting, effective poison with him. Burgdorf and Maisel, together with Rommel stepped out of the house and into the garden and walked back and forth awhile. During that time, Rommel went upstairs to the second floor to see his wife, Lucie. On his way up, he called Loistl and asked him to please send his son Manfred to him immediately and, after a half an hour, Aldinger, and old friend and chief-of-staff of Rommel's during Wolrd War I. Then he went to find his wife.

What Mrs. Rommel later reported about her last talk with her husband and their final time together was very dear and detailed, as well as touching. Rommel told her that Hitler left him the choice to stand trial or to take his own life. Rommel had obviously already made his decision before talking to his wife, since he told her, "In about 15 minutes from now, I will be dead." He also told her that Burgdorf and Maisel had brought a quick-acting poison with them.

Rommel informed his wife that he was suspected of being a participant of the attempted coup of July 20. The statements of Generals von Stuelpnagel and Speidel, and by von Hofacker, provided the incriminating evidence. Rommel also told his wife that he did not fear legal proceedings, but he believed that he could never get a fair trial and that he would probably be killed before any proceedings took place. He said good-bye to his wife, Lucie, and then talked with his son, Manfred, informing him about what was happening. After saying good-bye to him, he also said good-bye to Aldinger.

Loistl and Manfred both saw the second car parked near Rommel's house, and several people in civilian clothes sitting in it. It was clear to both that the people in that car were heavily armed. Rommel said good-bye to Loistl in a very soldier-like manner. Aldinger and Manfred walked with Rommel to one of the waiting cars. Rommel was wearing his military coat and hat. In his hand he was holding the *Feldmarschallstab* (his field marshall baton). In the car, Burgdorf and Maisel were waiting. Rommel entered the backseat of the limousine.

Fifteen minutes later the phone rang at Rommel's home. A person from the military hospital in Ulm was on the line. The message was that General Rommel had presumably suffered a heart attack, and two generals had brought him to the hospital. General Rommel was dead.

It looked like Rommel knew about the coup, and my neighbor's son-in-law, who was close to the Rommel family, knew about it, too. On every occasion that he visited his parents-in-law, he spoke with my father, since he knew of my father's opinion and his opposition to the Nazi regime.

Rommel was a soldier and one of the best. He never closed his eyes when moral questions arose that went beyond the strategic and political problems of the German Reich. For example, at Christmas in 1943 he talked to his family about the depressing and oppressing happenings of which Dr. Stroeling had informed him. Rommel told his family about the horrible details and destiny of Jewish people from the area around Stuttgart and Ulm, who were "resettled" in the eastern part of Germany. Stroeling had shown Rommel a report that he had written. It sharply condemned the terrible persecution of Jewish people. Shortly thereafter, when this report became known in Nazi circles, Stroeling was constantly threatened. By then, not many Jewish people still lived in Germany, but Rommel could see the shadows of the concentration camp involvements on the horizon. Rommel's son Manfred wanted to join the *Waffen SS*, but Rommel forbade him to do so. *

Many people today still think that there should have been more resistance to Hitler's regime. There was almost nothing one could do. The SS and SA would arrest and kill anyone, if they found the slightest evidence of resistance against the Nazi regime.

My mother knew about my father's secret meetings and his talks with our neighbor's son-in-law, and quite often during those meetings she was crying and praying. If the slightest suspicion about those talks had surfaced, the Nazi regime would have taken my father, without a doubt, to a concentration camp. Something else could also have happened, as it did in many other cases. The SS would have come in the night to take my father away in a car, and they would have killed him. They took General Rommel away, and he killed himself with cyanide. It was virtually impossible to do anything against the Nazi regime if one did not want to leave family and friends behind and become a martyr. My mother mentioned many times that three of her four sons were in the military. She said that this was more than enough of a contribution by her family to the regime and to the war.

---

* *ibid., "Knight's Cross," p 536*

PART III

16

Attacks on Zweibruecken –
December 1944 - February 1945*

On November 12, 1944, the so-called Home Defense was drafted. This unit was different from General Schaefer's professional soldiers: it consisted of older men and younger Hitler Youth members. When Zweibruecken was evacuated for the second time, all the rules governing the civilian population – curfews, lights out, etc. – were still in place, even until the time when all Germans retreated from France and took up positions in the Siegfried Line. What the German commanders failed to calculate was the rapid movement of the 7th U.S. Army from France toward Alsace-Lorraine and the German border.

On December 12, 1944, the U.S. troops arrived near Rohrbach-Bitche, which is only 10 miles from my hometown. Zweibruecken and the Siegfried Line were now within reach of the heavy U.S. artillery, and severe attacks concentrated on these areas were started on this day. From this point until the takeover of the city by U.S. troops, 20 people were killed by artillery fire in Zweibruecken. This happened even though the majority of people had been evacuated. My family did not have to evacuate, but my mother was living on a farm 25 kilometers away. My parents' house was hit three times

---

This account is based on information found in Zweibruecken's historical archives.

by these artillery attacks, but it was built solidly with walls of sandstone several feet thick, so only the roof and windows were damaged. During these assaults, I most often was in the basement or in
the bunker across the street.

Several small attacks on Zweibruecken came on December 21
and 31. During this time, heavy snow was falling and it was very
cold. The winter of 1944-45 was the coldest since 1941.

The counter-attack that had begun on December 16 failed, even
though it had been initiated with high hopes on the part of the
Hitler and his generals. The Germans called it the *Ardennenschlacht*
(The Battle of the Bulge). This German offensive was probably
no more than a needle prick to the superior Allied Forces. Even
so, perhaps it was a painful one. It brought, for a short while,
some relief for the Zweibruecken area when Patton's troops were
pulled back and moved to support Montgomery. This prompted
Hitler to command an offensive to regain Alsace-Lorraine. It
was called *Unternehmen Nordwind* (Operation North Wind). Close
to Zweibruecken, near Lauterbach and Blieskastel, the 36th and
559th Volks Grenadier Division, the 17th SS Tank Division, the
25th Tank Grenadier Division, and the 21st Tank Division started
a massive counteroffensive against Patton's thinned-out troops,
and right away there were some successes.

For a short while, Zweibruecken was no longer in reach of the
U.S. Artillery. The attack was supported by the German Air Force
and had a two-fold goal. The first was the support of the Air Force
for the ground troops, and the second was referred to as *Bodenplatte*
(Ground Plate). With over 1,000 planes, the German Air Force
attacked airports in France and destroyed 479 Allied planes on
the ground. The Germans lost 277 planes. But after *Bodenplatte*,
all German reserves were gone and not much of the Air Force
remained.

After the Allies woke up from the surprise of the attack, the
German planes quickly experienced the superiority of the Allied
Thunderbolts and Mustangs. Some BF109 fighter planes came to
support the light German bombers, but they were almost power-
less against the Mustangs, each equipped with six machine guns.
One of the BF109s was shot down in the Zweibruecken suburb

of Moersbach, its pilot ejecting and parachuting safely to earth. A light German bombers was caught by Mustang fire, burned, and fell down west of Zweibruecken. The three young airmen died. The plane went down next to a large farm, and the farmer allowed the airmen to be buried in his private cemetery. (*One of the pilots' fathers paid for the tombstones of the three airmen after the war, and the graves could still be seen when I visited in 1999.*)

On January 2, 1945, a Russian prisoner was killed in Zweibruecken by fighter plane attacks. That day, between 8:28 and 11:20 a.m., attacks came from as many as 175 fighter bombers in the small area of Zweibruecken/Pirmasens/Saarbruecken, a radius of not more than 35 miles. Between 12:20 and 3:20 the same afternoon, 11 fighter bomber formations were flying over Zweibruecken and a few neighboring cities.

Early in January, the U.S. Air Force was planning another big attack on Zweibruecken and its sister cities. January 3 was chosen because very good weather was predicted. The attack became number 778. The orders given were similar to those from the attack on December 28, 1944:

> Goal 03-01-45
> Target No. 6: Zweibruecken
> Target: Railroad junction/marshaling yard
> Target point: about 75 meters behind the track change station
>   in direction of the suburb Ernstweiler.

Because of the identical target, this attack was a copycat of attack 776 that had taken place on December 28, 1944. For Zweibruecken, two bomber brigades (Brigade 466 with 28 B24s and Brigade 467 with 28 B24s) were chosen. One plane each from the brigades 453 and 458 had gotten lost from their original units and therefore were included with brigades 466 and 467 to bombard Zweibruecken. In the morning, when a Mosquito observation plane came back from its flight over Germany, the weather report was no longer good. Nonetheless, the formation got underway at 8:00 a.m., with 11 squadrons and 311 B24 bombers. Their load was 833.5 tons of bombs, about 10 percent of which were firebombs. The schedule started with the lighter, high-explosive bombs, about 250 lbs. each. Their purpose was to take off the roofs of houses. When the wooden structure on roofs was uncovered, the firebombs were to be released. This easily set homes on fire. The attack was executed as planned.

At approximately 9 a.m., the whole squadron of planes left Norwich on their way towards the South. Before they passed the Channel, approximately 50 Mustangs from the 56th Brigade joined the bomber formation. Just three minutes earlier, at 8:57 a.m., the planes from Brigades 466 and 467 left the Norwich airspace. They were flying in widespread formations because there was little defense from remaining German fighter planes. The first and second brigades were staggered by one hour, which was about a distance of 350 kilometers.

Most of the planes carried 20 times 250 pounds of high-explosive bombs and about two times 500 pounds of firebombs. The contingent for my hometown was 974 high-explosive 250-lb. bombs, and 91 500-lb. firebombs. In addition, two planes had five so-called M47 fireboxes on board. The high number of firebombs is astonishing, because in the city of Zweibruecken, almost all of the houses were built of sandstone and bricks, and those houses were not easily set on fire.

Over the white cliffs of the English coastline, the planes had the first change of course, towards Boulogne-sur-Mer in France. (*Boulogne-sur-Mer today, like Yorktown, Virginia, is a sister city of Zweibruecken.*) From there, the deadly formation flew to its target of Zweibruecken. At 10:35 a.m., formations 466 and 467 were flying over Reims in France and at 11:10 a.m. they changed course again above Zabern, in the direction of Karlsruhe. In Zweibruecken, the highest alarm stage sounded, beginning at 10:45 a.m. There was hope that the squadrons would continue to fly towards Karlsruhe, but such hopes were soon dashed.

Over Hagenau, a beautiful little city in Alsace-Lorraine, 56 four-engine bombers turned again. They flew over Rimschweiler (a suburb of Zweibruecken where my mother and my deceased German wife were born) and then directly toward their goal of Zweibruecken. Since visibility was bad, they were flying by radar H2X towards their goal, the railway station, which could not be seen from the air. Starting at 11:29 a.m., more than 1000 bombs fell through the clouds. Only a few hit the railway system; the rest fell exactly into the middle of the city, including the downtown area. The heart of my beautiful hometown sank into rubble. Even though the attack lasted only three minutes, it was devastating. Immediately, fires started all over. The firefighters were housed in the basement of the castle. The right wing of the castle was hit by a heavy bomb, which fell all the way through several floors into the basement. A wood-fired oven fell over and started a large conflagration, which almost completely burned the castle down. During the following days and nights, the firefighters had their hands full fighting all the fires across the city. They worked until they were completely exhausted.

Besides the castle, the City Hall, the Alexander Church and the Catholic Hospital, many more public buildings burned. The beautiful tower of the Alexander Church, which was built in the Tuscan style and was the landmark of Zweibruecken, completely burned to the ground. Slowly, more firefighter brigades from other cities arrived. Before they could come, they had to take care of problems in their own cities, which fortunately were not as bad off as Zweibruecken. In total, 17 units from other cities were present.

To extinguish the fires, a great deal of water was needed, but in those winter days of January, it was -7o Celsius (approximately 20° Fahrenheit), and water froze immediately when exposed to the air. Luckily, the firefighters had planned ahead (as early as March, 1944) and parked their vehicles outside the city in a little wooded valley, so they were available immediately after the attacks. Despite so many firefighter units, the city burned for many days and was still burning when the next devastating attack came on January 7, 1945. Not only were the firemen interrupted during this later attack, but also it was difficult for the Red Cross and other helpers to come to their aid. Nine people died in the attack of January 3, 1945, countless civilians were injured, and 11 firefighters sustained injuries.

It is of interest to report that all three attacks had the railroad system designated as their targets, but because of the weather, the inner city was hit twice, taking the brunt of the bombardment. As a result, oce again another large number of people fled the city to go east.

The bombers of the 467th U.S. Brigade landed at 1:58 p.m. at their home air base in England without casualties, and those from the 96th Brigade followed at 2 p.m., also without casualties. In the debriefing reports, one can read that no more anti-aircraft attacks or fighter plane attacks occurred, despite several batteries of anti-aircraft units positioned around Zweibruecken. (*I still wonder, why did those senseless attacks not stop, then?*)

Zweibruecken was luckier on January 5, 1945, when the 20th Division, with three bomber groups, attacked Pirmasens with Brigade 466, St. Ingbert with Brigade 93, and St. Ingbert and Pirmasens with Brigade 448. Each brigade consisted of 31 four-engine B24 bombers, accompanied and protected by 70 P51 Mustangs. Although the squadrons flew overhead, that day no bombs were dropped on my hometown.

But there was no rest for Zweibruecken, even though at this time there weren't any artillery attacks, because of the ongoing counter-offensive in the Ardennes and Operation North Wind. On January 7, 1945, Zweibruecken was again under attack, this time by three bomber groups. Once again the goal was the railway system. They did not hit the railroad station, but the inner city, and this time with more devastation than on January 3. The attack was under the command of the 2nd Bomber Division. The bomber groups started in England, in a reverse formation. At 10:23 a.m., Brigade 453 left the air over Greenwich; at 10:26 a.m., Brigade 389 left, and two minutes later, Brigade 445 took to the air.

After about half an hour, all 11 squadrons, totaling 253 planes, were en route. From the first to the last plane, the distance was 100 kilometers. The distance from brigade to brigade was 10 kilometers, or about 10 minutes. Each plane had its special place and it was not allowed to leave formation. Even though there were no more German fighter planes in the air, the 361 Fighter Plane Group was asked to accompany the bombers with 94 P51 Mustangs that were stationed in St. Dizier in northern France. The 64 bombers, with the target of Zweibruecken, were carrying 1080 x 250 lb. high explosive bombs, 82 x 500 lb. firebombs, and three so-called "fire buckets" or M47s.

The fly routes of those bombers were the same. Only shortly before the target did they part. The 453rd Group was flying towards the city of Zweibruecken, via Mittelbach, and over my home at 12:12 p.m.; later the 445th Unit came from southwest, flying via Wattweiler. They bombarded the city. The 389th unit attacked the railroad and the suburb of Einoed, flying in via the village of Webenheim at 12:25 p.m. All the groups were flying at an altitude of 7400 meters, where the temperature was -36° Celsius. The day before, on January 6, it had been -11° Celsius. Since there was a thick layer of clouds between 1000 and 3000 meters altitude, the planes had to release their bombs again by the H2X radar system. This system projected a picture on a round disk almost the same as a map. Not all bombs fell into the city. In two planes, several bombs got stuck in the bomb shaft and had to be released by emergency procedures. Shortly after 3 p.m., all planes landed back in England.

Once again, the main part bombed was the remains of the inner city. Two industrial facilities were also hard hit, one now owned by the American John Deere Company, and the second owned by the Mannesman company, which is well-known in the U.S. For all other attacks, the fire engines had been moved to safe places outside the city, but this time there was no time to get them out. Most of them were destroyed. There was no more fire fighting possible in the city. Quite a few fire fighter units from neighboring cities came to help. One unit was dispatched under the command of the Catholic priest to help him save his burning church and his burning home next to the church. Many other houses just burned to the ground because there were not enough fire engines or fire fighters available. During the attack on January 7, 39 people were killed: seven Germans and nine Russian, one Dutch and 14 French prisoners. The local report about attack 785 reads as follows: "Thirty-nine people dead, 24 people wounded, 30 more homes totally destroyed, damage to many industrial facilities, and many homes still burning."

Aerial photos were taken later by British observation planes and other aircraft. A plane from the 540th Squadron, 106th Photographic Group, flew several times from east to west over the city. Unlike the day of the attack, the sky was very clear. The plane took 25 photos from an altitude of 4,000 meters while flying three times over the city.

Zweibruecken looked like a dead city. Once in a while, a military vehicle or an ambulance carrying wounded soldiers from the front to the field hospital in Zweibruecken could be seen. The few people left in the city, like my father and me, were either at their workplaces or at home or in shelters. One did not go into the streets very often.

On the day of attack 785, January 7, I could have been easily killed. The highest stage of alarm was sounded. I was standing in front of the shelter at my father's factory, waiting for the soldiers to return from the front and give me a ride back to the farm village to be with my mother. From the moment the soldiers arrived, I could already hear the engines of the airplanes. Since airplanes were in our area almost every day, the soldiers did not pay much attention to the airplane noises that day. They normally only went undercover when they were directly attacked by the fighter planes or when bombs came down.

The soldiers said to me, "Quick, hop in the car and let's get through the city to the other side, where it is safer." This was one of the few times I was really scared. I remember it as vividly as if it happened yesterday. I asked the soldiers to wait just a little longer, to see if the planes were flying towards another target or if they were going to attack Zweibruecken. At the same moment, we could hear the bombs howling through the air. The soldiers left their car and jumped into the shelter with me. Loud bomb detonations followed. Then we could hear the planes flying away. The soldiers and I waited for about half an hour, in case there were time-release bombs.

After I said good-bye to my father, who had been in the basement shelter of our house, we drove towards the city, which we needed to go through to get to the farm. We could only drive about three-quarters of a kilometer and that was all. We tried several other roads, but there was no way to get through. We had to go all the way back and take a roundabout detour through villages around the city. Had I not persuaded the soldiers to wait a few minutes, all three of us could have been killed, because we would have been in the middle of the city by the time the bombs fell. Soldiers who had fought in many battles were more hardened, and I knew that they drove through artillery fire and other dangerous situations many times. I and other civilians were more careful, even though I spent most of the time just outside the shelter watching airplane attacks. Only when I saw fighter planes flying directly towards me and coming close, or when they released bombs, would I jump into the shelter or bunker.

I was much more careful when it was overcast, because one could not see the airplanes before they came out of the clouds. One time, I was standing on top of the bunker and I could not get inside quickly enough. The air pressure recoil of a bomb blew me off the bunker, and I broke my right ankle. I was screaming because I thought I was hurt more seriously, and my father came running to me. Even though the fighter bombers were still flying around and attacking, my father carried me to his car and drove me to the hospital, using narrow side streets where we could not be seen so easily by the fighter pilots. In the hospital, quite a few people were lying on stretchers, but I didn't care, because I was in real pain. I had a few bruises, but nothing more serious than a broken ankle.

All the doctors' offices and operating rooms were located in the basement of the hospital building. Being in the basement and in a building with a large red cross on top of the roof made me feel safe. After waiting about two hours, the doctor straightened my ankle and put a cast on it. I went home with my father, who was not happy with me. He knew that I always waited and came into the shelter or bunker late. Sometimes it was very scary to me and sometimes I saw those attacks as games. I started to walk on the cast too early, because I was again running into the shelter late. The cast must have moved somewhat and my ankle never healed correctly. (*Today it still looks as if I have two ankles on my right foot. I never had any pain or other problems with it; it just doesn't look perfect. The injury did not bother me when, after the war, I played semi-professional soccer for six years in a league comparable to a U.S minor baseball league. I stopped playing soccer when I began my professional career. I may have had a chance to play in the top league, but my professional career was more important to me. The span that I played soccer after the war was the best and most problem-free time in my life.)*

Fighter bomber attacks were going on daily. On January 13, 1945, a freight train was stopped about one kilometer before entering the railway station. One of the fighter bombers saw the train and attacked it. Suddenly there was a tremendous explosion. In a radius of about 100 meters, everything was flattened. Whatever windows remained intact in the city after all the previous attacks were now blown out. It turned out that two of the rail cars carried ammunition, and this caused the tremendous explosion. Luckily no one was killed that time.

On January 14, 1945, the fighter bombers exacted a deadly harvest of prisoners. The prisoners were used to build tank traps, which I sometimes also worked on, earning stamps to obtain shoes. All of the Hitler Youth were involved. We all came under fighter bomber attacks many times. On January 14, the fighter bombers were shooting the prisoners in the open fields like rabbits. The prisoners could find no cover at the places where they worked. Fifteen Mustangs attacked again and again. Nerve-wracking noises from the planes' machine-gun attacks intermingled with the screams of wounded and dying prisoners. Twelve of the prisoners were killed on the spot, and 30 were lying around wounded for quite a while. Only when the "All Clear" sounded could they be transported to hospitals. The prisoners could not understand why their own friends were killing them.

During a Marauder attack on January 16 at 12:40 p.m., another prison camp was hit and three Russian prisoners died. In the evening of the same day, around 8 p.m., two female Russian prisoners were killed by bombs. On January 21 at 8 a.m., another prisoner was killed. On January 24, around 8 p.m., a Russian prisoner was killed by fire from a machine gun aboard an American plane, a so-called Iron Henry. On February 2, an Italian worker was killed near the railway station.

After the German counter-attack, American troops had re-treated further into France. Very soon, however, they fought their way back to the German-French border and again established their artillery base near Bitche/Rohrbach. They could reach our city by artillery, and the grenades of the 44th U.S. Infantry Division were causing many casualties. Artillery attacks resumed around December 1944, but reports on casualties were not available until February 5 and 7 of 1945. The Catholic Hospital, at the time be-ing used as a military field hospital, was hit despite the red cross on the roof. As a result, the remaining 15 patients were placed in the basement.

In addition, on February 1, 4, 10, 11, and 26, prisoners died from Allied attacks. The reports read: "8:23 a.m., 11:19 a.m. to 12:58 p.m., 12:40 p.m. to 14:41, incoming of several squadrons of fighter bombers at altitudes between 2000 and 2700 meters. Bombardments in the suburbs of Langental and Etzelweg (half a kilometer away from my house). Departure of the planes after the attacks in westward direction."

On February 28, beginning at 8:58 a.m., Marauder planes flew eastward over Zweibruecken. One of the planes released several bombs, and they caused big holes in the Hofenfels Strasse. Three city workers were ordered to go there and close the holes in the street. At 4:35 p.m., suddenly four fighter bombers came across the hill. Two of the city workers were killed instantly by the bombs ex-ploding around them, and one died half an hour later. Already that same morning, two Russian prisoners had been killed by Marauder attacks.

The few people who were still living in their homes listened incessantly to reports about incoming planes. The majority of the remaining people were constantly in shelters. If everyone had gone to the shelters, the city would not have had so many casualties on the last attack on March 14, 1945. Most of the people were care-ful, and they were now living like moles underground. Today, no one can imagine that you needed about three hours to go from one side of the city to the other, which is not more than one and a half miles wide. One could not go more than 50 to 70 meters without having to jump under cover from artillery and plane attacks.

17

Final and Devastating Air Attacks on Zweibruecken

On March 1, 1945, Marauder attacks killed 11 Russian prisoners in Zweibruecken. On March 2, two Germans were killed. Why were so many prisoners killed? First, there were not enough shelters. But mainly, Russian prisoners thought that they were on the side of the attackers and that they would not be targeted; thus they stayed in unprotected areas. The pilots could not see the difference, however, between German civilians and Russian prisoners from the air.

On March 10, five people were killed about one block from my home. One was the mayor of our suburb. The plane came across a small wooded hill (the place where I spent many hours playing) and flew across our house. Having released its payload a few seconds earlier, the bombs could have easily hit on our house. We were lucky again. From the small wooded area to the place where the bombs exploded is about 1,000 meters as the crow flies. The planes flew with a speed of about 400 km/hr, which means that the people killed could have heard the noise of the plane's motor only a few seconds before they died. The pilot probably released his bombs without a specific goal. He certainly could not have known that he would kill the mayor and destroy his home. The mayor was the father of one of my best friends.

The following days, until the so-called "Black Wednesday of Zweibruecken," were not much different from the previous ones. Several French prisoners were killed by another Marauder attack.

It was tragic to live through the whole war and last so many years as a prisoner of war, and then to be killed at the last minute.

The final and total destruction of Zweibruecken began on March 14, 1945. It happened under the direction of the Royal Canadian Air Force, which ironically chose Zweibruecken for one of its European air bases after the war.

To understand the attack, one has to look at the goals and reasons of the Allied nations. It is helpful to know some of the instructions of the "Combined Chiefs of Staff" that were formulated on January 1, 1943, in Casablanca. The most important tasks were to destroy the German military machine and to demolish the industry and economy of Germany. It was important to confuse, as well as to demoralize the German people, to the point where the resistance would be totally broken. This "Casablanca Directive" was the foundation for the strategic air war during World War II.

In the case of Zweibruecken, this directive was not applicable, because 90 percent of the population had already left the city. What did apply to the attacks were the words of the English Air Marshall A. Harris: "We shall bring Germany to its knees with terror bombardments." This statement came close to the truth, because on March 14, 1945, General Patton's troops were already at the border of Germany, only about 15 kilometers away from Zweibruecken. There was virtually no more resistance left in the city and its environs, and little more in all of Germany.

The only reason for the late bombardment on March 14 could have been the Siegfried Line and its reputation as a defense system. German General Schaefer, who had been debriefed by U.S. Intelligence forces, may have drawn too strong a picture of the Siegfried Line, specifically the area around Zweibruecken. General Schaefer's statements also could have been the reason for a somewhat slower and more careful attack on the Siegfried Line by Patton's troops after they returned from their support of Montgomery in the Battle of the Bulge. But Schaefer's statements should not have provided any reason for the total destruction of Zweibruecken and Homburg. At the time of this bombardment, both cities had absolutely no strategic importance. Most of the people were already gone. No German troops were in the city, and even the field hospitals had been evacuated to the east of the Rhine River. All factories had been shut down, and all important equipment and machines were installed in cities east of the Rhine, far from Zweibruecken.

Compared to other German cities, Zweibruecken had a relatively low number of casualties, as a result of good planning and preparations by the people in charge. The main reason was the evacuation of most of the civilians in time; another was the use of the caves or old ice cellars, located deep in the hills of the inner city. The caves were discovered in February 1944 and were completely restored. In total, the city had 13 of those caves available for use. At the beginning of the air war, people only went there during the highest stage of alarm, but at the end these refuges became their homes. During the final attacks, specifically the one on March 14, only about 4,000 people were in town, plus 1,000 prisoners and a few German soldiers.

The goal of the air strike must have been the inner city, because nothing else was left. The excellent American intelligence units must have known what was going on in and around Zweibruecken in the final phase of the war. More is written about this senseless destruction in later chapters focusing on the conclusion of the air war

On the evening of March 14, the Royal Canadian Air Force flew toward Zweibruecken with 196 four-engine bombers, guided by 34 Pathfinders. A second formation flew with 161 planes towards its sister city of Homburg. Between 8:14 and 8:24 p.m., the Canadian squadron released 3154 (*imagine 3154!*) high-explosive bombs and firebombs, including some "mine bombs" with a weight of one metric ton each. In total, there were 801.9 metric tons of high explosive bombs and 12.2 metric tons of firebombs. The city became a burning and smoking pile of rubble, and this in a time span of only 10 minutes! Because most of the inhabitants were hiding in shelters deep in the hills, and many had already left the city, "only" 89 people died. My father survived, even though he remained outside during the whole attack! He ran to the shelter too late, and since it was completely filled, he could not get in. Luckily, our suburb was not hit near our shelter. At the time,

General Patton's troops were already on the French/German border, with some already in Germany.

The day began with crews, as well as support personnel, conducting routine trial runs from their airports in England. Around noon, five Mosquitos flew from the 8th Brigade to collect weather data for the night attack of the heavy bombers. On Bomber Harris' program for that night were Zweibruecken and Homburg, a double attack on two cities that were only 10 kilometers apart. The timing was the same for both cities.

During air attacks the weather was very important. On Zweibruecken's night of destiny there were no clouds in the sky, not even at the starting place in England. Sunset was at 6:24 p.m. and the full moon was late at 2:15 a.m. The temperature near the ground was around 0° Celsius (32° Fahrenheit), with light winds of about 20 miles from the north/northeast. All in all, the bombers could not have wished for better weather.

The Command Operational Order for the 14th of March was given in the usual way, by teleprinter, from the headquarters to the Bomber Command in High Wycombe and also to all bomber groups. Bomber Group 6 was directed towards Zweibruecken and Bomber Group 4 was directed towards Homburg. One hundred ninety-five heavy bomber crews prepared themselves for Zweibruecken and 127 for Homburg. Added to their number were 34 Pathfinder airplanes.

At 1:30 p.m., the crews were given their targets, and navigation meetings took place. Together with the Mosquito crews, local geography was discussed from pictures taken on September 29, 1944, and January 15, 1945. Prominent targets were marked. In Zweibruecken, they represented the horse racetrack and the railroad station, among other things. On the airfield, the ground crews filled the airplanes. Each four-engine plane took on 6,300 liters of gasoline. The amount was calculated in such a way that a maximum number of bombs could be carried.

The relation of heavy-duty explosive bombs and firebombs was based on the objective. It was known at the Bomber Command that in Zweibruecken, as well as in Homburg, there were buildings and houses not made of wood. The group attacking Homburg was loading 458.7 tons of high-explosive bombs and 11.3 tons of ignition and marking bombs. The group attacking Zweibruecken was loading 801.9 tons of high-explosive bombs and 12.2 tons of ignition and marking bombs. Special firebombs were not loaded. The main group each carried one 4,000-lb. HC bomb and approximately 14 x 500-lb. bombs, and therefore fewer 500-lb. bombs. The Halifax had only 500-lb. bombs on board

The 4,000-lb. high capacity bombs were the most feared, as they were capable of destroying whole blocks of homes. The British called them "cookies." Those bombs also took off roofs within a large radius, opening access for firebombs to ignite the homes and for the explosive bombs to go all the way through to basements.

Between 4:16 and 5:03 p.m., the 195 bombers of the main force took off from 14 airports in Eastern England for the approximately seven-hour flight to Zweibruecken and Homburg. Squadrons 415 and 425 started with one plane per minute, in total 14 planes in 14 minutes. (The starting times of the planes attacking other cities in Germany were different. Nevertheless, there was such air traffic over England that it was called a very dangerous adventure by the experts. The people in charge were happy when there were no casualties.)

Around 5:22 p.m., the starting signal was given for the faster flying Mosquitoes and around 6:25 p.m. for the PFF. They were located 100 kilometers south of the bomber airports, and they all were instructed to arrive at Zweibruecken and Homburg at the same time.

Near the city of Reading, west of London, the squadrons gathered in formation, which was called a bomber stream. Even though the Allies had complete control over the air in Germany, the Command chose to fly a detour that had proven successful before, across the Channel in the direction of the Somme River. Shortly afterward, they changed their course for the first time. The bombers sped over Laon in France at an altitude of only about 1,000 meters to avoid German radar.

Over the city of Verdun, the bombers made their second course change. Up to this point the bomber group flying toward

Homburg had taken exactly the same course as the squadrons flying toward Zweibruecken, which were flying over the French city of Diedenhofen at 7:50 p.m. The Pathfinder group was at this time at the end of its approach. It was divided into primary blind markers (PBM), blind illuminators (BI), visual illuminators (VI), and supporters (S). The success of a bombardment depended on finding the targets, and the development of radar made it easy. Even when the sky was covered with clouds, the pilots found their goal, guided by the Master Bomber.

The squadrons going to Homburg was about 15 minutes behind the one going to Zweibruecken. They would arrive at their goal when the attack on Zweibruecken was already almost complete. In the cities below, one had the impression that the same planes first attacked Zweibruecken, and then Homburg. This was not the case; even the Pathfinder planes were different. Except for the 5th Squadron of the 8th Bomber Group (PFF), the group attacking Zweibruecken were all Canadians, but the group attacking Homburg included the British, French and Australian air force. The Canadian group attacking Zweibruecken was the 6th B.G. and the 405th Squadron 8th B.G.

The remaining four squadrons were from the 8th B.G. and were all British. In this squadron was the so-called Master Bomber. In total, the 8th B.G. had 11 Mosquitos and 23 Lancaster bombers, and the 6th B.G. had 97 Lancaster bombers and 98 Halifax bombers in its group. The Bomber Command of the RAF with its headquarters in High Wycombe, west of London, consisted of nine bomber groups in total. The staff of the 6th Bomber Group, with a total of 14 squadrons, was in Allerton, 190 miles north of London. This was the bomber group located the farthest north.

The flight of the Zweibruecken bomber groups was camouflaged in different ways – there were sham fights and cover attacks. Some were sent towards Kaiserslautern and Bad Kreuznach to irritate German night fighter planes. Others (40 to 50) feigned an attack on Wiesbaden, then attacked Zweibruecken between 8:27 and 8:40 p.m. from an altitude of 5,800 to 6,500 meters.

Because of the feigned attacks on other cities, the German defense failed completely. When the approximate direction of the bombers was known, three groups of German night fighter planes started in southwest Germany, but they were flying towards Wiesbaden, which was the wrong direction. Therefore there was no defense at all around Zweibruecken and Homburg. The German planes flew too far north towards Bad Kreuznach and only one Halifax #230 of the 429th Squadron registered an attack. At 8:05 p.m., the gunner at the end of the plane registered an unknown plane behind him at an altitude of 1,200 feet. At a distance of about 250 yards, he could identify the plane as a German ME 109. The Halifax immediately made a course change to escape, and the ME 109 turned back. The presence of the 109 was also registered by other planes, but none of the bombers shot at the ME 109.

The warning system for the civilian population failed completely. The 8:05 p.m. report stated that no enemy planes were over German soil. At the same moment, the first plane, or Master Bomber, was over Zweibruecken. Because the German defense was fooled, there were almost no casualties among the attacking aircraft units. The Master Bomber, as well as all the bomber groups, were already in the air over Zweibruecken at 8:05 p.m., but the attack was delayed by one minute because a few markers were still missing. They were immediately called in by the Master Bomber. The Master Bomber was from the 608th Squadron, as was his backup. They carried the responsibility for success.

In the attack on Zweibruecken, three different kinds of radar systems were at work. The attack began with the far radar "Oboe," then continued with "GEE," and then finally "H2S." The latter two identified the goal in more detail. The British Oboe system was similar to the German "X-Verfahren." They determined the position of a plane by contacting two radio stations. The Master Bomber and his back-up, the Controller, both had receivers on board. Both stations might be located in northern France. The plane would be flying on a beam "A" from the north with the PFF directly towards Zweibruecken. Station 13 would have its beam directly over Zweibruecken. On the cross point, the Master Bomber would hear a pipe tone in his receiver, which would confirm the finding of the goal. Now the H2S system of the Master Bomber would go into action. The unit had an antenna directly underneath the plane and could give a map to the plane's navigator. Bodies of water could be seen better than anything else. The same radar system was also on board several other planes.

The city of Zweibruecken, which was chosen for carpet bombardment, was divided into two sectors. Marking the target very precisely was the most important task. The city was completely in the dark after the arrival of the first planes. As the aiming point, a place directly in front of the castle was chosen. It looked like a "V" made by two trees, and it was prominently visible from the air. The Master was directing the Mosquito XVI, RV 301 of the 109th Squadron to the aiming point (AP). Exactly at 8:08 p.m. the Mosquito was flying at an altitude of only 800 meters over the AP and was setting red markings on the ground. The Master, circling at an altitude of 5,000 meters, was controlling the exact marking of the AP. It was perfect.

When the attack started, the time over the target was "H" minus 7 minutes. By radio, the Master advised the Marker and the Illuminator. By 8:08, the Mosquito KB 411 with red T.I. supported the marking on the ground. By 8:09:30, the first blind illuminator, a Lancaster of the 635th Squadron, set his first red/green markings. At 8:09:48, the first target was illuminated with flares. "H" minus 6 was the time. Now more markings followed. By 8:11, the first side markers were setting their red/green target indicators. The first Markers were already beginning their second round and were releasing their 1,000 pound and 500 pound bombs.

The Markers and Illuminators of the 635th and 405th Squadrons constantly improved the red/green markers and constantly renewed them. The units of the 635th Squadron were flying at altitudes between 1,200 and 4,600 meters, and those of the 405th were flying at altitudes between 4,300 and 4,500 meters.

From all directions, 23 four-engine Lancaster bombers sped over the city at about 160 miles per hour. Of the faster flying Mosquitoes, only five were in action together with the Master, and five were flying in holding positions outside the city. They were backups, but they were not needed that evening because the marking was perfect. Plane number MM123 of the 109th Squadron was not participating in the attack, due to technical difficulties, and neither was the Lancaster PB915 of the 639th Squadron, because of difficulties with the GEE and H2S radar systems, although it dropped its firebombs in the middle of the red/green markings. Shortly after the "flares" appeared, the targets set in England could be seen very clearly. Because weather conditions were so good, the marking target was very precise. During the attack, the 635th Squadron dropped 69 white lighting bombs, as well as three red and 20 green markings. The attackers still had 55 light, high-explosive bombs left. The 405th Squadron dropped 70 white, four red, 20 green, and 70 light, high-explosive bombs of 500 and 1,000 pounds. An unknown number of T.I.s were dropped by two Mosquitoes of the 608th Squadron, as well as twelve 500-lb. bombs that caused numerous small fires. The fires, combined with the markings, lit the way for the main bomber group. If somebody in the city had the right radio and frequency, they could have listened in on the conversations between the Master and the other planes, probably even at the exact time of 8 p.m.

The target locating of the main attack force took place by a radio navigation system "GEE." It was comparable to an invisible trellis net across all of Europe. The senders on the ground gave impulses to this net in such a way that they could identify the position of the bombers from 10 kilometers away. From Saarbruecken, about 30 kilometers away from Zweibruecken, the bombers could already see the markings and easily find their targets.

The attack on Zweibruecken was a so-called "sector attack," meaning that the bombardments were done with time-delays and in sectors. The width and the length of the destruction was predetermined. By command of the Master, the first bombers took course for the final attack. The delay applied only to a few planes and was determined by the altitude of the flight and of the sector. The delay was only from one to five seconds. At 8:14 p.m., the Lancaster NG 280 of the 424th Squadron dropped from an altitude of 4,160 meters and at a speed of 170 miles per hour. This was the first bomb of the main formation, and it was a 4,000-pounder called "residential house killer." Following this first bomb, four 250 pound and eleven 500 pound high-explosive bombs were dropped.

The main attack began with 12 planes of the 424th Squadron. Shortly thereafter, the 419th Squadron, with 15 planes, and 430th Squadron, with 14 planes, followed. At 8:15 p.m., the Master Bomber stopped the dropping of markers and illuminating bombs to reorganize the targets, because several bombs did not hit their marks. The Master also ordered complete radio silence between planes, to better direct the attack.

The severity of the bombardments then escalated. Now the 427th and 434th Squadrons joined the main force of the attacking planes. Each plane's flying time across the city was only 8 seconds. By 8:16 p.m., 16 bombers and several marker and illuminator planes were, during a time-span of 10 seconds, over the city at the same time. A number of small explosions were again seen by the crews, most of them with flames in the red to orange spectrum, followed by smoke. The Master ordered dropping bombs on those targets, which still had well-placed markings. At 8:16 and 8:18 p.m., the Mosquitos of the 608th Squadron (PFF), which had already set markings at the beginning of the attack, dropped four 500-pound bombs from each plane, from an altitude of 6,700 meters, into the middle of the red/green markings.

The 433rd, 432nd, 408th, 425th and 429th Squadrons also joined the attack, but a little further apart from one another. Therefore the 408th Squadron was done by 8:18:05 p.m., while the 433rd Squadron with the Lancaster ME 457 dropped their bombs by 8:28:08 p.m., already one minute after the master had terminated the attack.

When the first difficulties within the attacking units occurred, there was radio interference and some of the planes only understood part of the Master's orders, and sometimes they could not hear them at all. Dark smoke was covering the city and the markers and illuminations, making it hard to see targets. The Master ordered his men to drop the bombs towards the black smoke. At 8:18 p.m., the 415th Squadron attacked, followed by the 428th and 431st Squadrons at 8:19, and the 426th at 8:20.

During the whole attack, no German night fighter planes were in sight. Anti-aircraft batteries were firing, but not very heavily or effectively. Only one Halifax RG448 was hit by a grenade splinter

– at 8:17 at an altitude of 4500 meters. The splinter entered the wing of the plane. It probably was by sheer luck.

By 8:18, crews were already observing big explosions in the target area. At 8:19 the Master once again ordered that all communication cease, so as not to endanger the attack. From 8:19:04 until 8:20:05, the air over Zweibruecken was so crowded that serious difficulties occurred. Several of the planes' crews complained about this later during the debriefings. The Halifax NR127 of the 415th Squadron was hindered by another plane while dropping bombs and had to quickly change course to avoid a collision. At 8:16:05, the MZ435 of the 420th Squadron had to change its approach to avoid collision, as did plane #180 of the 425th Squadron. Since those planes were equipped with special cameras on board to document the attack, there was quite a mix-up after their pictures were developed.

The same close call happened to NR228 of the squadron. This plane's special camera was installed so that it could take photos while in a straight horizontal position and at a specific altitude and time when the first 4,000-lb. bomb exploded. To prepare the target for photos, some of the planes dropped flashlight bombs, including the Halifax NA183. On the evening of March 14, 122 photos of Zweibruecken were taken, and only three of them were unusable. Those night photos were compared to the photos taken the day after the attack and provided a record of the destruction.

In summary, in a very short time span, from 8:19:04 to 8:20:05, there were heavy, four-engine bombers flying over and bombarding a city whose downtown was already almost completely destroyed and was already burning in all corners! What a senseless undertaking!

Smoke rose into the sky up to 8,300 feet. It covered the markings, so the Master again ordered more bombs to be dropped into the smoke. The Master had difficulties with his orders because the crews were undisciplined and constantly talking with one another. It took his strong command to restore discipline.

Each plane needed about four seconds to drop its bombs and about eight seconds to fly over the target. Immediately afterwards, a course change was ordered. In general the bombers flew at an altitude between 3,800 and 4,700 meters over the target, some lower. The ME 498 of the 428th Squadron flew the lowest altitude at 2,700 meters.

At 8:21, three explosions were seen. The attack stopped immediately at 8:21:05. On the east side of the target, two explosions were also seen at 8:21 and 8:23. At other places, two smaller explosions followed at 8:22 and a very large one at 8:23. The NR 256 of the 429th Squadron observed an explosion that threw debris up to 700 meters in the air. Grey and black-brown smoke rose after two blood red explosions. The heaviest explosions were observed in the inner city. The bombers departing towards the south observed many smaller explosions, probably from time-delayed bombs or from fires.

The Master officially stopped the attack at 8:25 p.m. He left behind a dead city. The target area of downtown Zweibruecken was no longer anything but burning rubble and ashes. There were 89 dead civilians lying underneath the mass of debris. Fortunately, most people had already left the city.

The debriefing of the Number 6 Bombing Brigade the day after the attack went as follows:

> The weather was clear with a slight haze over the target. Visibility was good. The target was well marked with red and green T.I. points and illuminating flares. Crews bombed on the T.I. s and target area according to the Master Bomber's instructions. Parts of the built-up area could be identified under the light of the flares. Fires appeared to be taking a good hold. Smoke covered the target, at times obscuring the T.I.s and rising to 5,000 feet. Numerous explosions were reported, some especially large occurring at 8:20:25 and giving off clouds of black smoke.
>
> Light H/F was experienced by some crews, bursting from 8,000 to 1,5000 feet, some in barrage form and some predicted. Slight L/F was reported. There was slight damage to aircraft by flack.
>
> An attack was reported on the outward route and a ME 109 was seen in the target area. Fighter flares were seen after leaving the target and there was some evidence of S/Ls cooperating. 754.7 tons of high explosives were dropped."

After the attack, the bombers left the target area very quickly. They flew towards Bitche/Luneville, and from there, course WNW 300° – their first turning point. They headed for Reading, England, and from there, the individual units flew to their respective home bases. The first Lancaster arrived at Downham Market at 10:40 p.m., and the last one landed at its home base at 11:06 p.m. The Mosquitos flew much faster and had returned earlier to their home bases.

The first plane from the main strike force landed at home base at 11:10 p.m. It was the Halifax PN 238 from the 426th Squadron. The last plane landed at 0:47 a.m. on March 15, the Lancaster ME 501 from the 427th Squadron.

The home-flying crews saw the destruction, especially those flying over the sister city of Homburg. The sky was red for 80 miles, according to a report by one of the crews.

The crews did their duty and just thought about their techniques of attack and of the readiness of their planes. That they had just killed numerous people and destroyed a beautiful city was not on their minds. The crews had fulfilled a calculated assault that encouraged the killing of helpless and defenseless people. Proudly they announced, "And again another German city has ceased to exist."

Over Nancy, on the flight back, the 426th Squadron had a bad surprise. Suddenly there were big searchlights and a heavy-duty flack attack of friendly fire. The planes started wild course changes, and one plane dropped the valid marking sign for the day. When American ground forces realized their mistake, they stopped the attack right away. What the German anti-aircraft could no longer do, the American flack almost accomplished. Other than this mishap, the return flights were normal.

The navigator of the KB 794 of the 428th Squadron complained during the debriefing that they had to fly too low because there were no navigation lights over England. It was normal that some planes had bombs left, so-called "hang-ups." Those bombs could not be released the normal way and had to be dropped into the ocean across the Channel at a specially determined place. Most of the bomber crews had to do this manually, and the person in charge had to crawl into the bomb shaft secured by a rope. The 429th Squadron had, on this night, the most hang-ups. Four planes each had one, and the KB 786 had two 550-pound bombs left. It was important to dump them into the ocean, because they could have come loose during landing and created a catastrophe. Other planes from the Squadron 432, 425, and 427 also had 500-pound bombs left. In total, eight planes had bombs left.

Neither the 8th Bomber Group nor the 6th Bomber Group had incurred any losses. Only three planes had to turn early before they reached their goal; four planes altogether had to carry all their bombs back. The Halifax 134 of the 425th Squadron had heavy oil leakage from the starboard side motor and had to turn back over France at 6:20 p.m.

The Halifax NP708 (432nd Squadron) had motor damage and turned back by 7:16 p.m. The outer starboard motor stopped running, but it continued to fly toward Germany. Close to the French border the motor started again, but by this time, the plane had lost too much time and was behind the rest, so it turned. Navigation problems also caused the Halifax MZ (415th Squadron) to turn back. Each of the three planes dropped their bombs over the Channel into the water.

A strange thing happened to the Halifax NP742 of the 408th Squadron, which was in formation until Zweibruecken. At 8:09 p.m., the crew saw from a distance the red markings, but when they were ready to drop their bombs at 8:20 p.m., no more markings could be seen. The plane circled a second time and saw some markings but could not determine their correctness. Further, the Master did not give clear commands. The crew turned around and took the whole load of bombs back to the base in England. A total of 11.12 tons of bombs did not go down on Zweibruecken.

An unusual situation faced the Lancaster NN777 of the 424th Squadron, which started at 4:33 p.m. from Skipton-on-Swale. Bombardment and return flight were progressing without problems. After an almost seven-hour flight, the plane was descending to the home base. Suddenly all control instruments failed, and it quickly lost altitude. The pilot had to land the plane ahead of his own airfield in Dishforth. It was a crash landing with heavy damage.

The navigator and the bomber were slightly injured. The rest of the crew (five persons) had no injuries. Investigations followed, but what technical problems happened to the plane remained a mystery.

Further problems that night: the Halifax MZ435 (420th Squadron) was hindered by another plane while dropping its bombs at 8:16:05 p.m.; the other plane came too close. The starboard engine outside of the Lancaster ME393 (Squadron 427) failed. The plane had to fly back to home base with only three engines. The plane landed safely at 11:52 p.m. The Lancaster NG232 (433rd Squadron) faced lesser problems; it lost the rear machine-gun stand as well as the GEE chain. About five other planes had problems with their navigation systems. The whole system was lost in the NG344. The pilot had to fly behind the next plane, with only the flames coming from the engines of the plane flying ahead of him for orientation.

Two Lancasters, NG 459 and RA 509 (433rd Squadron), had problems during camera flights because of strong turbulence from fire and explosions. Also, the radio contact was very bad from time to time. Some planes came into difficulties because of interference. The KB733 (419th Squadron) was in quite some danger and had to quickly change its course to avoid being hit by bombs released from higher-flying planes.

Despite good weather, no anti-aircraft defense, and excellent Air Force personnel, not everything went according to plan. If one compares this attack on Zweibruecken with attacks on other German cities, however, one could still call this a "smooth ride." That is why many pilots reported very good results. The Halifax NA203 (425th Squadron) reported: "Looked like one of the best efforts." One can understand the debriefing of the 415th Squadron leader: "Crews excited and optimistic. We will continue to handle the enemy non-stop." The new German generation would say this sounds like encouragement to bomb civilians, which they might have expected to hear from German Propaganda Minister Goebbels, but not from the English forces.

On March 15, Marauders and fighter bombers constantly bombarded the Siegfried Line, concentrating on the most heavily fortified area (where Zweibruecken's Airport is located today), and more people fled the city. The attack on the previous day was so devastating that nearly 500 of the remaining population panicked the next day. They ran out of the city, but nobody knows why they all ran in the same direction and up the same street. An observation plane had noticed this exodus, and less than 10 minutes later, eight fighter bombers attacked the fleeing civilians, consisting mainly of women and children. They flew above the crowd at very low altitude, firing left and right, and releasing high-explosive bombs. People were lying down in ditches, but because the fighter planes flew in the same direction as the street, there was virtually no cover for the people. The bomb explosions and machine-gun fire severed branches from trees and sent dirt and stones flying through the air.

Mothers and children were screaming hysterically. Over and over the planes attacked the helpless people. When the planes finally left, the street from the Kreuzberg to the suburb of Moersbach was in chaos. Mothers were running around confused, looking for their children. Others were running into nearby woods. Some vehicles had been hit and were on fire. Dead and injured people were lying everywhere, as were many dead horses. Many people just left their horses with their wagons and fled into the woods. Of the animals that were left without food, some died, some survived until the American troops arrived. This story has been documented by at least 50 of the 500 people who were fleeing the city that day.

I personally witnessed the air attack from the highest point in western Palatinate. On this day, the 15th of March, I was with my mother in a farm village less than four miles away from the massacre. I was running back and forth between the shelter and outside to watch, as the planes circled close to where I was, and then out to attack the people fleeing from the village. At the time, we thought there must have been a movement of a very large military unit to draw such a prolonged and violent attack.

On March 16, 1945, two days after the devastating attack
on Zweibruecken, the cities of Wurzburg and Nuremberg were
bombarded. To put the destruction visited upon Zweibruecken
in perspective, it is instructive to compare the attacks. During the
main asssault on Wurzburg, a city much larger than Zweibruecken,
Allied aircraft deployed 389.3 tons of bombs (its inner city was
also destroyed). Yet Zweibruecken had to endure more than *twice*
that amount, 789.8 tons of bombs.

18

Reports and Opinions on the Zweibruecken Bombing

Why did Zweibruecken come under such heavy bombardment. The debriefing reports of the main force (found in British archives) offer no explanation. They read:

> Halifax, Lancaster, and Mosquitos attacked the city of Zweibruecken in clear weather with only light haze. The target was marked with green and red T.I.s and was illuminated. Parts of housing areas were identified in the light of the dropped T.I.s and illumination bombs. Many fires and explosions were observed. The goal was to block roads and railroads and to destroy enemy troops and anti-aircraft systems. No attacks were reported, only light fire from heavy and lighter anti-aircraft batteries.

In the night report #865 of the Bomber Command 14/ 15 of March 1945, one can read:

> 221/230 heavy bombers and Mosquitos are attacking the city of Zweibruecken and 151/161 are attacking the city of Homburg. Both bomber squadrons carried marking bombs, and the whole attack on both cities was done by request of the Army.

Somewhat contrary to this report was a protest of General Patton, which reads as follows:

> The bombardment of German cities, very shortly before our troops are entering Germany, is a poor choice. In many cases it is almost impossible to advance through those cities, because most of the

streets are full of debris and cannot be passed. As a consequence, our advancement will be delayed. It should be given a lot of thought if such a kind of war is damaging us more than our enemies.

The results of the evaluation of the air photos taken after March 14, 1945, confirmed General Patton's observation.

The downtown area of Zweibruecken pictures burning rubble and total destruction. Two bridges are heavily damaged, roads are blocked, many factories and public buildings are damaged or destroyed. Concentrated damages are in the downtown area northeast from the railway station, but heavy damages are also observed up to the barracks west of the hospital and east of the barracks near the railroad tracks. The railroad locomotive depot is destroyed. Most of the rails are disrupted by bomb craters. Part of the remaining railway station is destroyed. Roofs of the railroad platform have fallen in. More detailed data to this report are to follow.

This was the immediate interpretation of report #K4014 from March 18. 1945. The report was based on 20 air photos taken on March 15 between 1:15 and 1:45 p.m. by a Mosquito of the 542nd Squadron, flying at an altitude of 5,000 meters above the city. The overflight also indicates total domination of the Allied Air Forces. There were some anti-aircraft batteries left, but they did not fire any shots. In total, the Mosquito flew four times across the city.

Photos were also taken of the Siegfried Line. This was done for a specific reason. The Army or the 3rd U.S. Division of the 7th U.S. Army had asked specifically for those photos, to prepare themselves better for the penetration into Germany across the Siegfried Line.

Looking at those photographs that were made public after 30 years, one can observe that the order by the Bomber Command almost completely failed and was purposely changed. The order only was to attack and destroy the public transportation network with railroads and roads, as well as military targets, so why was the target area set as the castle, in the center of downtown Zweibruecken? The total destruction of the city was not crucial in the long-range goal of supplying the front-line German units, nor was it a factor in blocking their retreat. Only four of 18 bridges could not be used;

14 were completely intact. The east/west axis where the German troops remained before and after the bombardments was intact, as well as the main north/south crossroads. The post office and railroad continued to operate. The trains could not go through the railroad station, but could closely approach it from both directions. Only at night did traffic continue, because during the day the fighter bombers ruled the skies. For a long time after the war, the local Germans called the official, published order of the British Bomber Command a lie. The British and U.S. populations were always told about bombardments of strategically important targets. In reality, the target of the flight crews was the triangle perimeter in front of the castle, which was the center of downtown Zweibruecken. After the war, the inhabitants talked (and some older people are still talking today) about the revenge on German civilians ordered by Churchill himself and by Bomber Harris, although no one can prove what their actual motives were. Most of the younger generations are caring less and less, but people like myself and my family still care, because this horrible time occasionally still haunts us, sometimes in the form of bad dreams. Many actions were necessary to remove Hitler from power and to stop the slaughter of innocent Jewish people and people from other European nations, but all too often, the attacks on civilians seemed to go overboard.

Zweibruecken was not the last city to be wiped out by the efforts to destroy "civilian enemy morale." The last bomber command attack was on the city of Kiel in northern Germany on April 26, 1945.

When the end of the war was in sight, Churchill sent a memorable personal telegram to the commanders of the Royal Air Force on March 28, 1945:

> To me it seems the moment has come where one should rethink the bombardment of German cities based on the objective of increasing terror, even if we use other motives. Otherwise, we will take over the power and control of a country that is totally ruined. We might not be able to find housing or barracks for our own occupying forces, not to mention houses for the German population that is left... I'm of the opinion that more military targets should be the goal, primarily for our own interest as opposed to the interest of the

enemy. The Foreign Minister spoke to me on this subject, and I feel we have to concentrate more on militarily relevant targets like refineries, traffic intersections and areas right behind the front lines. This approach has to have preference over attacks of terror with arbitrary destruction, even if they have been very impressive.

The commanders of the RAF protested. They said the telegram gave the impression that Churchill had never ordered the bombing policy called "enemy morale." On April 1, 1945, Churchill released a cleverly formulated memorandum. He avoided a direct reference to the notorious fire bombing of the city of Dresden, and replaced the word "terror" with the phrase "area bombarding." Unfortunately, this change of the "bombing policy" came too late for my beautiful town of Zweibruecken. On March 20, 1945, the front reached the city, which had been completely destroyed, and it was taken by Patton's troops. For Zweibruecken, World War II was over.

Now, let's discuss somepossible reasons for the bombardments of civilians and German cities, as seen from a military and political viewpoint. How could it happen that a city like Zweibruecken was hit so hard, especially at a time when no more German soldiers were in it? The German troops (an Army and S.S. unit which first fought in front of the Siegfried Line) left the outskirts of the city and the city itself without any significant fighting. No great resistance could be expected from the civilians, because only about 3,000 to 4,000 women with children and older men were still in the city. The rest had been evacuated. American Intelligence knew this. To understand the situation a little better, one has to go back into the history and politics of the air war.

Right at the beginning of World War II, the air forces of every country involved were brought into action to meet strategic goals. This began with the war against Poland and its capital of Warsaw as a military target. The city was furiously defended by Polish troops despite three calls for capitulation. The Germans then declared it a fortress and bombarded it. Following the British commitment to support Poland, the RAF first bombarded German ships in

Wilhelmshafen on September 4, 1939. On September 5, another British attack followed on military targets in the German cities of Cuxhafen and Wilhelmshafen.

Only two months later, on November 13, 1939, the German Air Force attacked military targets in England for the first time. Despite the attacks, nothing negative was reported because they were carried out in the frame of the "Hague Air War Regulations" against military objects. Therefore the danger of an all-out air war was considered highly unlikely at the beginning of World War II. Hitler had declared on September 1, 1939: "I do not want a war against women and children. I ordered the Air Force to only attack military goals." The RAF was also ordered that "attacks against targets which can endanger life and property of civilians are forbidden."

But as soon as Churchill was elected Prime Minister and War Minister, the politics drastically changed. Over the objections of French General Gamelin, he ordered the bombardment of the enemy's interior lands. On the 11th of May 1940, the periphery of Moenchen-Gladbach was bombarded. Four people were killed. This was seen in Germany as the sign for the start of an all-out air war. Following this, the Propaganda Minister Joseph Goebbels, in his famous February 18 speech to the German population, asked, "Do you want a total war?" adding, "Churchill has started it already a long time ago." This was politics as seen by the German people. Moenchen-Gladbach was only the beginning of attacks on civilians, even though the "Hague Air War Regulations" declared those attacks as criminal war actions.

On May 16, 1940, another British air attack followed on Muenster. On June 7, 1940, the French sent a bomber to attack Berlin. The German capital was the goal of British air attacks six times. The German Luftwaffe answered the first time with a retaliatory attack on London. Even my hometown was attacked by British bombers on August 15, 1940, just when everything had settled down after the return of the inhabitants who had left during the first evacuation. The damage on Zweibruecken at this time was minimal.

From the German viewpoint, it is mentioned many times that the Germans showed great reluctance to retaliate against civilian targets, and stated over and over that they lived up to the Hague Regulations. The history written by the victorious powers lays all the blame for the bombing terror on the Germans, so much so that it is completely believed by many in today's younger generations. In my hometown, one can often hear remarks that the Germans started the bombardment on England.

Many people think mostly of the fair treatment they received from the American troops entering Germany, and also of the CARE packages that the American people sent after the war.

Because of those good deeds, people quickly forgot the bad. But many do not know what they are talking about. One of the supporters of the British attacks on the German civilian population admits his support with the following statement:

> We began the bombardment of targets in Germany before the Germans started to do so in England. This is an historically proven fact. We gave up the privilege to keep our cities intact and sacrificed London while we completely destroyed the German cities.

This statement was made by J.M. Spaight, the Principal Secretary to the British Air Ministry. His admission and many others of a similar nature make it understandable that many Germans still harbor some resentment against Great Britain and especially against Churchill, who they believe was lying and covering up his orders.

A woman by the name of Fraulein Feulner wrote in her diary about a discussion with an American officer. She talked to him in the barracks of Niederauerbach, a suburb of Zweibruecken, where about 10,000 Russian, German, and other prisoners were gathered after the war. Six German girls from the newly established German city government of Zweibruecken were employed to register their names and give them new passports to transport them to their home countries. This all was done under the supervision of American troops. Fraulein Feulner reported that during one of those working sessions, she talked with an American officer about why the city was destroyed and asked about the claim that the Americans were responsible. The answer of this officer, whose name was Neidling and who spoke fluent German, was that this was the fault of the last S.S. City Commander, whose name was Sarnow. The Americans, via radio, had ordered the city three times to capitulate without any fighting, but the answer was always the same: "The city will be defended until the last soldier." Therefore, they had assumed that the city and the bunkers of the Siegfried Line surrounding the city were fully occupied and well defended. As a consequence, the bombardment was requested from the Air Command in England. The answer hit us hard. The total destruction was based on the answer of a single German!

Fraulein Feulner wrote her observations in a letter to the mayor of the city of Zweibruecken on December 1, 1986. (*The mayor, Werner von Blohn, is a personal friend of mine, and I served under him and another mayor for seven years as a city councilman in Zweibrücken.*) The mayor had asked the *Historischer Verein Zweibruecken*, a non-profit historical society, to investigate deeper into this situation. The research work was done by the president of the society, Karl Hudlet, and he wrote the following in a letter to the mayor:

The research regarding the statements of Fraulein Feulner with the gentleman who wrote the history of the S.S. Division *Götz von Berlichingen*, have the following results:

The last German troops which defended the city and its outskirts in March 1945 were units of the S.S. Division *Götz von Berlichingen*. In the division was an *Obersturmbannfuehrer* (lieutenant colonel) by the name of Sarnow. He was the leader of all supply units. In March 1945, he was Commander-in-Chief in Zweibruecken, and his headquarters were in the *Wehrbezirkskommando* (central military station) in the southern section. In connection with the removal of the troops reporting to him, the last one left the city by his command. During the bombardment of the city, Obersturrnbannfuehrer Sarnow was in the basement of the military command station, which was spared by bombs. Sarnow himself wrote the statement for the military history of his division as follows:

'As the German division by Zweibruecken took new positions on the hills around Zweibruecken and stabilized those, I was with some other leaders and sous-leaders, promoted to fighting commander, to also support some Pioneer Units in charge of blowing up important bridges and other important targets. I also was responsible for the supply of those fighting units. We fulfilled the orders given to us until we were freed of this task via radio contact by the Division Headquarters. This was the time when the fighting troops had moved into position in the second defense line east of Zweibruecken about 20 to 30 kilometers away.'

Even if the statements of U.S. officer Neidling are correct, the facts are different. The question still remains: Why was there bombing on Homburg on the same day, on the sister cities of Pirmasens and Neunkirchen the following day, on Bad Duerkheim on March 16? The argument of Officer Neidling was probably an excuse because he was part of an administration unit. The fighting units under Patton's command had already been at the outskirts of Zweibruecken on March 13 and 14. They moved through the Palatinate towards the Rhine River by Ludwigshafen-Mannheim and further towards Nuremberg, Munich and Salzburg. As an aministrator following behind, Officer Neidling probably felt bad when he was confronted by this young German girl, and he might have tried to fabricate an excuse.

19

Allied Troops Storm the Siegfried Line and My Hometown

The main attack by U.S. divisions began on March 15, 1945. That morning, the U.S. artillery began preparations for the take-over of Zweibruecken and Pirmasens with heavy gunfire by 16 batteries. This was to pave the way for the 3rd Infantry Division of the 15th U.S. Infantry Regiment. By then, the German troops were reduced to one-quarter of their original strength. In the sub-urb of Wattweiler, the German troops were already defeated. That evening, the 19th German Volksgrenandier Division retreated into the bunkers of the Siegfried Line.

On March 16, the 7th Allied Infantry Regiment marched with-out resistance into the village of Altheim on German soil. The 15th Infantry Regiment was already in Hornbach. On March 17, the complete 3rd U.S. Infantry Division was ready to take over the west wall (Siegfried Line) in the area of Zweibruecken.

At 5:45 a.m. on March 18, the American Infantry started to attack. Airplanes were providing support. Their flight routes were well planned, helped no doubt by the debriefing of German General Schaefer by the American Intelligence.

That morning, very heavy fighting erupted in front of the 17th SS Tank Grenadier Division in Mittelbach. The whole staff and command units of the division, located in the center of the suburb, were thrown into the middle of the fighting. The 17th SS Tank Grenadiers defended the troops in front of the Siegfried

Line against two U.S. divisions until, with heavy casualties, they retreated into the bunkers on the evening of March 18.

The 16th *Volksgrenadierdivision* (People's Grenadier Division) defended the section in front of the Siegfried Line until March 19, when they also had to retreat. The three German divisions were supported by what was called a "fortress and people battalion."

The German situation was now catastrophic. The core of Germany's defense was in the Siegfried Line, but it was already broken by American troops in several places around the Saar area. The German troops in the way of the 17th SS Division had fought for every bunker, even though there were not enough soldiers to occupy them all. The greatest value of the Siegfried Line had been the unique defensive arrangement for each bunker, but with the reduced number of troops, it now had to be abandoned. Only 30 to 60 percent of the bunkers and fortresses could be occupied, because manpower was so reduced

For the same reason, the artillery had to move into different positions and relinquish their defense against the tanks. Four 8.8 tank defense guns could not be moved quickly enough into their new positions at the site of the Pheasant Woods and were blown up before the U.S. troops could move closer. (*The remains of those guns could be seen for almost 20 years after the war was over. The Woods were originally part of a pleasure and hunting castle built by French King Louis XV to house his exiled father-in-law, the Polish King Stanislas. The castle is now a hotel, and my wife and I often stay there when we visit my hometown.*)

Many other heavy artillery and tank defense guns could not be moved back towards the Siegfried Line because there was no longer enough fuel. One battery was stationed at the farm village called Grossbundenbach, where my parents and I survived the last day of fighting in our region. This battery was deserted by the German troops and turned into scrap metal several years later.

Just a few miles northeast of Zweibruecken, along a line of the suburbs Lambsbor-Oberauerbach-Fehrbach, a new defense line was established, with Grossbundenbach in the middle. Tank blockades were built, including one constructed of heavy railroad beams, not more than 80 yards from my parents' house. The vanguard of American tanks fired into the traps, and big bulldozers cleaned the roads.

On March 17, 1945, 11 German soldiers were killed in heavy fighting in front of Mittelbach, just a few miles from our house. They were quickly buried on March 19 in a mass grave, still wearing their uniforms. Hundreds of soldiers died in these battles around my hometown.

Suddenly, on March 19, several German airplanes arrived and entered the fight, but in no time they had to flee because of the large number of Mustangs in the air. One German plane that was shot down that day fell to earth about half a mile from my home.

That evening, U.S. troops were already a half mile from my home and the city. Early the next morning, the 30th U.S. Infantry Regiment started to invade the city through the suburb of Ixheim, where I grew up. While the U.S. troops took the city without heavy fighting, the airplanes were still attacking fleeing German soldiers and civilians. March 20 was the last attack on Zweibruecken from two fighter bombers.

On March 20, 1945, the only sirens that were still intact, in the suburbs, could be heard in the city. In the inner city, everything was destroyed. The sirens started because several squadrons of planes were flying over the city to bombard other German cities not yet occupied by the Allies.

The following description is based on the original American military reports of the events from March 18 to March 21, 1945, the final days before Zweibruecken and the Siegfried Line fell completely to the Allies.

March 18, 1945

The hour "H" is 4:45 a.m. The 7th and 15th Infantry Regiments are selected to attack, and the 30th Infantry Regiment is on hold in back-up position. For 20 full minutes, uninterrupted artillery fire is shot into the buffer zone fields and the bunker areas.

The 1st and 2nd Battalions of the 15th Infantry Regiment start at 5:45 a.m. behind a constant artillery fire. Pioneers with explosive devices and with earth-moving equipment are involved. Immediately, heavy defense fire begins by the Germans. Forward movement is very slow.

At 9:30 a.m., Company A reaches the first defense line consisting of concrete fortifications. Heavy fighting takes place throughout the morning. At 11:30 a.m., Company A breaks through the defense line. Company C needs four hours to reach the defense line, but once there can't immediately break through. At this point the Germans fight with everything they have left to protect the Siegfried Line. Company B passes the tiring soldiers of Company C and immediately initiates heavy fighting that lasts all day and most of the night.

Shortly before midnight, the Germans counterattack to the Wallerscheid (*site of the U.S. Air Force base established after the war*), which is located on the periphery of Zweibruecken. The first U.S. Battalion of the 7th Infantry Regiment runs out of ammunition and is forced to retreat. Tanks are held up by tank traps, with one tank stuck in the concrete fortifications. At 4:55 p.m., the battalion breaks through the first two defense lines and passes many Germany troops still in their bunkers. The Americans decide to take the bunkers at a later time. At 6:30 p.m., the battalion reaches the farm *Muehltaler Hof* (*only a half mile away from my parents' house*). At this point the battalion comes under heavy German gunfire. One Sherman tank is lost. The Pioneers are not able to create a path through the concrete fortifications for the tanks of the 756th and 706th tank units.

At 7:30 p.m., the 3rd Battalion with its Assault Company 1 starts to attack and meets the German troops that were overrun in the first attack. The same thing happens to the south. The Germans start an infantry counterattack against the 1st Battalion, but are pushed back to their starting position. Near the end of the day, the 7th Infantry Regiment has conquered 1,500 meters, broken through the first and second defense lines, and is at the hills of Zweibruecken with a view towards the city. Fighting continues throughout the night.

March 19, 1945

To lighten some burden of the 7th and the 15th Infantry Regiments, the general in command decides to attack Zweibruecken with the 30th Infantry Regiment. The attack comes in two lines, one directly from a wooded area (*within view of my parents' house*). After four hours of artillery fire, the 1st and 2nd Battalions break through the defense lines of Zweibruecken. The 1st Battalion of the 15th Infantry Regiment takes over protection of the flank. Company G of the 2nd Battalion captures four bunkers in the morning. Close to noon, the 2nd Battalion is 2,000 meters southwest of the suburb of Contwig and comes under heavy German artillery fire. It also encounters hundreds of T&S mines, which slow down its advancements. It is the biggest concentration of mines the division has faced.

The combat is fierce and bloody. Corporal M fires a machine gun into a bunker. The Germans stop fighting back. Several U.S. soldiers blow up the hood of a bunker with TNT and take eight prisoners. In another case, an American sharpshooter kills five German soldiers in just a few minutes. The 1st and 3rd Battalions of the 7th Infantry Regiment are pushing the attack northwards, passing bunkers still occupied by Hitler's troops. German defense units try to stop the advance, but without success. U.S. troops are now very close to the River Schwarzbach, which flows from east to west and passes through Zweibruecken.

March 20, 1945

The 2nd Battalion of the 30th Infantry Regiment captures a bridgehead across the River Hornbach in Zweibruecken. The soldiers use a bridge that the Germans blew up. Although badly tilted to one side, it can still be used. (*For decades after the war, we referred to this bridge as "the crooked Hornbach bridge." It was located where we used to bathe and swim in the summer, since there were no public swimming pools anywhere. This bridge was replaced some 20 years after the war.*)

The 3rd Battalion cleans the fields around the bridgehead of smaller German defense holds. (*It was in one of these holds that my friend and I searched several weeks later for food and instead found partially buried German soldiers.*) During the night, small groups of observation units from this bridgehead are sent into Zweibruecken. The 1st U.S. Battalion of the 30th Infantry Regiment is ordered to take Zweibruecken. (*It is amazing what they accomplished in such a short time!*)

The 1st and 3rd Battalions become involved in heavy fighting with German infantry soldiers dug into trenches. Heavy 8.8 artillery fire from the Germans supports the soldiers. This artillery fire comes from batteries now located around the farm villages of Grossbundenbach and Moersbach, suburbs of Zweibruecken on the northeast side. (*Those battery stations were the reason my family had to leave the village and wait in the nearby wooded valley.*) As a result of the fighting, two German batteries are destroyed and 60 prisoners are taken. The way is now clear for the 6th U.S. Tank Division.

Company E of the 3rd Battalion in the 7th Infantry Regiment occupies a German bunker at 2:30 a.m. In total, the battalion takes six bunkers occupied by the Germans. These are the bunkers that the American troops passed up on the first day of the offensive. The 1st and 3rd Battalions move forward to the north. By 8:25 a.m., they take 35 German soldiers as prisoners. At 11 a.m., a part of Company E of the 7th Infantry Regiment meets part of the 30th Infantry Regiment behind the two churches of Ixheim. (*I was baptized in one of the churches and attended Mass there for many years.*) The 7th Infantry Regiment leaves around noon and takes over another suburb called Niederauerbach. At the same time, the 15th Infantry Regiment successfully breaks through the German line. The Germans are now retreating with high speed. Around 4 a.m., Germans attack Companies F and G. Later that morning the attack slows down. The 2nd Battalion now advances into the suburb of Contwig without any German resistance.

March 21

Around 4 p.m., the 15th Infantry Regiment attacks the Siegfried Line from the back, advancing from the villages of Stambach and Walshausen, six kilometers east of the Siegfried Line. No longer is there full resistance. Only a few single bunkers respond. The 1st Battalion of the 15th Infantry Regiment moves eastward towards Dusenbruecken and Winzeln-Windsberg, both suburbs of Pirmasens. (*This town and its suburbs became well-known to many GIs after the war, as quite a few lived there with their families.*)

In only three days, the 7th U.S. Army broke through the legendary Siegfried Line. It was able to do so with an overwhelming force of soldiers and equipment. The German defenders had been decimated and were exhausted. But it was not easy for the U.S. troops; they had casualties, too. Urgency dictated that the dead German soldiers' bodies be rolled into their tents and buried quickly. Later, they were laid to their final rest in the military honor cemeteries in Zweibruecken and Pirmasens.

Already on March 21, the newly established U.S. Military Government declared a curfew in Zweibruecken and its surroundings. That meant that, until March 26, it was not possible to search for survivors. Therefore, only corpses were later found in the rubble. Eventually, people were allowed to leave the shelters from 12 noon until 1:00 p.m. to get a little fresh air. People whose homes were still halfway intact were allowed to go to them, but the curfew was still in effect.

20

My Family Survives the Allied Bombardment and Invasion

How can I convey what it was like: The countless hours of weary sitting and waiting in wet, cold cellars and bunkers while listening to heavy explosions of bombs and grenades from artillery? The experience of those fearful days that all of us endured was beyond words. The screaming of mothers and children in the shelters during the attacks was almost unbearable.

The daily news reports no longer had German troops taking towns or territories. Instead, it was reported that they were defending against Russian troops and holding their lines. It was reported that fighting in the Battle of the Bulge was see-sawing without the Allies gaining any territory, despite substantially increasing their forces.

In the war reports, one could read about heavy fights on the Mosel River. One also could read about attacks from German submarines close to the English coast. The radio stations from Saarbruecken and Kaiserslautern broadcast very little. Nothing exciting was going on in the vicinity of Zweibruecken. The whole situation was marked by waiting, waiting, waiting. We felt prepared for anything, even the possibility of seeing American troops at our door, but we were not prepared for what actually happened on the evening of this March 14, 1945.

While the U.S. troops got ready to penetrate into Germany, life on the farm was getting unpleasant and dangerous. During daytime attacks of fighter planes and artillery fire, I started to feel quite uneasy. There was a woman living at the farm across from us who had been evacuated from a farm closer to the French border. The two of us seemed more frightened than anyone else in the neighborhood. We both felt safer in the special reinforced basement shelter, or at least very close to its outside door, so we could jump inside when attacks happened nearby. This shelter was across from our farmhouse in the basement of the neighboring farm. It had two entrances: one end was accessible directly from the street and protected by heavy railroad beams, to prevent splinters from bombs and grenades from penetrating into the shelter; the other end could be reached from the first floor level by way of extremely steep stairs. In the early stages of bombardment, all my relatives, including my mother, stayed in the farmhouse, but during night attacks, they got out of bed, dressed, and came to the shelter, too.

But by the end of 1944, when I was with my father, we still only went to the basement when a large squadron of heavy bombers was announced. We stayed in the house for attack planes that came late at night. Usually they just shot a few machine-gun rounds above the roofs and quickly disappeared. They were night mostly observation planes whose motors sounded like an old sewing machine. These raids were called Iron Henry attacks, and it was recommended to stay away from windows and doors when they began.

There were three phases of air attack warnings. The pre-warning signal was a long single tone of all sirens in the area, interrupted only three times. The main warning was a siren very much like the sound of ambulances in the United States, but it came from the same place as the pre-warning. The end of the attacks was announced with a long, single uninterrupted tone. This signaled the time when everyone could emerge from the bunkers and shelters. The radios in family homes, offices and factories became a mainstay. During the last two years of the war they were on constantly, because they sometimes broadcast warnings of air attacks.

When the pre-warning and main warning signals were activated during night attacks, mothers had to dress themselves and their children very quickly. During day attacks they had to take food from the stoves, collect important papers and a few other valuables that were already packed up, and run into the shelters. Sometimes this happened twice during days or nights, and in rare cases, three times. Can you imagine how children reacted to being abruptly awakened and taken from their beds? I vividly remember shivering while running in the rain to the shelter with my mother. Not only were children shaken awake from a deep sleep, but we often had to wait two to four hours in the cold, wet basements and bunkers without any heat.

After an air attack, no one but the official helpers were allowed to come out of the shelters. Only when the airplanes were long gone, and it was confirmed that they would not return, were people allowed to leave the shelters.*

It was generally dead silent in the streets during alarms. All one could hear was the noise of the bomber squadrons attacking in the distance. When they came close to our city, we usually sat in the shelters in total silence. Sometimes people prayed. My father, however, would often sit on a bench in our yard during an alarm or an attack. Sometimes he even slept outside through alarms. He had been in World War I for four years and had experienced many dangerous situations. Only when our city was bombarded would he come into the shelter.

It is impossible to describe the bombardment of March 14, 1945. It simply goes beyond human imagination. One could compare it somewhat, but only somewhat, to an assault of tornadoes without the availability of police, doctors and ambulances.

---

* Nothing official can be found in German archives about what happened during the air attacks in World War II, except the following statement: "Any documentation and publication of air attacks is strictly forbidden." Even in newspaper death notices, it was not allowed to refer to them. The Nazi government's reasoning was that a lack of documentation prevented the enemy from learning about the consequences and successes of any air attacks. (*I learned from one of the historians that the only material available is from photos of British observations planes, which are stored in British archives. Bombardments of my hometown on September 29, 1944, on February 15, 1945, and during the evening of the heaviest attack on March 14, 1945, were included.*)

The day began like many other days. The weather was beautiful. Most people had stayed overnight in the shelters. They were rushing before dawn in the dark streets. Some went home to pick up belongings, others were buying food. The most important tasks were done at night, including the mail. Even during the darkness, it was dangerous to come out of the shelters because of the artillery fire.

Even though Zweibruecken had been under frequent air attacks for some time, the main attack on the evening of March 14 came as a surprise. Most surprising was that it happened with such force and vehemence. Nobody expected such an attack anymore, because almost no military forces were left in town. The American troops were literally on our front doorsteps.

During the main attack on March 14, my father was still at the factory. He normally did not go into shelters, but this time he tried to. He was running to the shelter but could not get in, because it was filled to capacity. People in my suburb did not stay in their own basement shelters, but rather went into the bunker of the Siegfried Line located across the street from my home; this location was less than half a mile away from where the first bombs exploded. Therefore, he saw the whole attack from outside the bunker, and he reported that it was as bright as during full sun.

I will never forget that night, as long as I live. I was with my mother on the farm, located approximately 10 air miles away from the cities of Homburg and Zweibruecken. Since the farm was at one of the highest elevations in western Palatinate, I saw the lights over Homburg and Zweibruecken. Even from where I was, it was so bright that one could read a newspaper. Everybody from the village was outside, watching the inferno and thinking that this was perhaps the end of the world. Our greatest fear was that my father would be killed, since we knew he very seldom went into shelters. Luckily, he survived.

About a week before the U.S. troops took over our village, the woman from across the road and I had a bad feeling about the night ahead. Both of us carried piles of straw into the basement, brought some blankets, and prepared beds for ourselves.

dinner, we went to bed in the shelter. Suddenly that night, we were attacked by heavy artillery fire, and everybody from both farms came running into the shelter at once. Two artillery grenades exploded at our farmhouse, one directly between the kitchen and the stables. It killed one of our horses, Max. Everybody was happy that they had left the house and did not get killed, but most of us were also sad and crying about Max's death. I felt very bad, too, but I was glad that I had done something good for him by feeding him extra oats before he died. All of our animals were treated as part of the farm family, and the loss hit home very hard.

One could feel that the end of the war was near. Since the farm village was located in the middle of the second defense line, the daily fighter-bomber and artillery attacks increased dramatically, and we all had the same hope: to survive these last few days without injuries. Just a few days before the Americans took over, my father came back to the farm, making us all feel much safer. Since he had been in World War I and served at the beginning of World War II, he had experience not only in fighting, but also in seeking cover and hiding. The second night after he arrived, everybody spent the night in the shelter and at dawn hell broke loose, lasting the whole morning.

A day or two before our village was taken by the American troops, things became chaotic, and we did not take the two prisoners who worked for us back to their camp. We hid them in the attic of the farm. This was very dangerous. If the local SS has found out, they may well have shot one of my uncles or my father. The night before the U.S. troops arrived, we were again under heavy artillery attacks, and one grenade hit the attic of the farmhouse where our shelter was located. The prisoners were hiding not far from where the artillery grenade exploded. Luckily, neither one of them was hurt, since our farmhouse had three-foot-thick sandstone walls. The prisoners came down to the basement as fast as they could, probably sliding down the stairs. Their faces were ashen. My father and my uncles quickly brought some more piles of straw into the shelter, and covered them with straw in a corner deep inside the shelter.

Starting just before dawn, eight heavy German artillery batteries were brought into defensive position on the hillside just outside the village. My father immediately knew that this could cause a big problem for us. Two of the batteries slid off the road in the hilly terrain and could not be camouflaged in time, nor could they be brought back into fighting position. My father was sure that American observation planes had spotted the heavy guns and that we would be heavily attacked by U.S. fighter bombers and artillery fire after dawn.

I was in the fresh air outside the shelter but very close to one of the entrance doors. Standing next to me, watching the fighter-bombers and observation planes flying overhead, was the son of the woman from across the road. He had been heavily wounded during fighting in Russia and was discharged from the German Army. It was early in the morning and still a bit foggy. We did not think that fighter-bomber attacks were a threat at this time, even though there was now a much greater danger because of the defense artillery units positioned just outside our village.

I stood with my neighbor's son on the upper side of the shelter entrance. The moment that the first bullets from the machine guns of the fighter bombers came flying through the air, and I heard the first bombs explode, I slid from the upper level down the basement stairs on my behind. My friend, the wounded soldier, was running around the corner of the house to reach the lower level entrance to the shelter. Just as he entered the shelter, a bomb exploded across the street and a splinter hit him in the back next to his spine. He fell into the basement and lost consciousness after a few minutes. If I had not taken the shortcut, I also would have been running around the house and might have been wounded or killed. (*I always was lucky, and I am a survivor despite going through hell a couple of times. Even later in my life, through the serious 10-year illness of my German wife and my own cancer at the end of my career, I have had the strength to survive and wait for better times.*)

My father and my uncles used first aid to care for my injured friend, and about an hour later the military Red Cross arrived. They took him for further treatment at a field hospital, located two villages away. Late that evening, all wounded soldiers from the field hospital were evacuated across the Rhine River and taken further into Germany. Our neighbor, in the shelter with us, cried and prayed that her son would survive the ordeal. Her husband was fighting against the Russians on the eastern front, and she didn't know if he was still alive. (*Her prayers for her son were answered. He survived. About six months after the war's end, I saw both of them on their farm, and they gave me a full load of fruit from their fields. I had a bicycle with a two-wheeled wagon attached in back, so I put the fruit in the wagon and cycled for four hours to get it home. Since we still did not have much to eat, that provided a real treat.*)

The attack on the farm village lasted the whole day. Fighter-bombers constantly assaulted us with machine guns, bombs, and artillery fire. We had quite a few civilian and military casualties. On the other side of our shelter was the milk house, a community-owned building where farmers delivered their milk; from there, it was taken to central stations for further distribution in the cities. This milk house had a ramp along its front side that was made of concrete. Under the ramp, five SS soldiers took shelter during bomb attacks. One bomb fell directly on the milk house and only pieces of those soldiers could be found.

In front of our shelter, two heavily wounded soldiers were lying on the ground crying for help. They were no longer able to move by themselves. My father and my uncles crawled out on their bellies and pulled first one, then the other, into our shelter. One had been hit by a bomb splinter that had taken off a big part of his left thigh and buttock. The other was hit by splinters on his arms and legs. My father and uncles gave them first aid. The soldier with the heaviest wounds was still conscious. He held pictures in his hand of his wife and children and cried while saying "I hope I will not die." My father crawled back outside and called to the Red Cross soldiers hiding in corners of homes. He asked them to pick up the two heavily wounded soldiers and take them to the field hospital. For me those were unforgettable scenes, and for a long time I sometimes heard the voices of the soldiers over and over again at night.

While the wounded SS soldiers were in our shelter, the tension mounted, not only because of the outside attacks, but because we still had the French and Russian prisoners hidden under the straw in the corner. Occasionally other SS soldiers from outside would jump into our basement to seek cover, and we'd be on pins and needles until they went back outside. (*Fortunately, when we were freed at the end of the war, these two prisoners were also freed and did not have to go to central Germany to new prison camps. After the war, they visited us on several occasions and thanked us for what we had done to save their lives.*)

In the meantime, most of the roofs from houses and barns had vanished – either from direct hits of bombs and artillery strikes, or from the pressure of exploding bombs. Debris was lying everywhere.

During the early fighter plane and artillery attacks, several SS troop leaders went from house to house to explain that their unit was ordered to defend the village against the Allies, because the village was in the middle of the so-called second defense line. Another reason was the strategic decision to delay the Allies for four to six hours while another German command unit evacuated the field hospital and moved all wounded German soldiers to central Germany. At the same time, Hitler ordered the final defense of Germany, once more, along the Rhine River. This was absolute nonsense, because everyone knew that Germany had already lost the war. The adults could not even understand why the field hospital had to be evacuated. The wounded probably would have been much better off with American military Red Cross units.

Because of the defense order, all civilians were told to immediately leave the village and hide in nearby wooded hillsides and valleys. The SS leaders said these would be much safer places. They also warned that the village might be totally destroyed, and that there would certainly be house-to-house combat, creating a danger for more civilians to be killed.

I saw some of the most terrifying scenes I have ever witnessed in my life when we left the shelter during the ongoing artillery and bomb attacks. We had to make our way through the village twice. Every corner had SS soldiers carrying loaded pistols and machine guns. Then, when we crossed the street, there were parts of human bodies lying around. As we came to the house of a neighbor, a man was lying in the street next to the sidewalk. We looked closer and saw that a part of his head, close to his neck, was gone – probably from splinters from a highly explosive bomb. A group of people from the same shelter was walking with us. Suddenly, a woman broke out of our group and screamed, "My God, this is my son, Ernst!" She kneeled down beside him and sobbed unconsolably. After a few minutes, the soldiers carried her away back to our group which was heading to a hiding place in the woods. She continued to scream and cry, and it was almost impossible for my family to calm her. Her son normally hid in the stables, and he must have come out too late to enter our shelter.

To reach the woods and valleys on the west side of the village as quickly and safely as possible, we had to walk, lie down and cover ourselves, run, and sometimes hide in barns. This running and hiding was very dangerous, because the U.S. fighter-bombers were firing their machine guns at anything that moved. There was also constant artillery fire. My father suddenly pulled my mother and me away from the larger group because he saw four fighter planes coming right for us. He took us by our arms before I even knew it and pulled us into a barn by the side of the road. We lay down flat on the concrete floor until the planes passed and the machine-gun shootingceased. When the attack was over, I looked up and saw blue sky. We had thought that we were protected by a roof, but when we ran into the barn we had not noticed that the roof was gone! Luckily no one was hurt, neither in my family nor in the group of people we were fleeing with. I will never forget the fear in my mother's face. My father had managed to remain relatively calm, and since I was close to him, I stayed pretty calm, too.

Arriving on the periphery of the west side of the village, we found some 8.8 anti-aircraft and anti-tank batteries in position. The commander saw us and screamed, "You cannot stay on this side of the village, not even further down the hillside closer to the woods! The American observation planes have spotted our cannons for sure, and soon we will be under attack from the air and artillery." We had no choice but to turn around and go back through the center of the village to the other side. This was a big ordeal for my mother, who had arthritis and could not walk very well. Thank God, we arrived on the east side of the village without injuries. Shortly before we reached the wooded hillside, my uncles and aunts joined us. When we were passing our farmhouse again, my father ran inside and picked up a small saw, hammer, nails and a small shovel. I had no idea what these were for or why he did this.

When we arrived at the steep wooded hillside, about one kilometer from the village, my father and uncles looked for a big, solid overhanging rock. Many rocks were jutting out of the hillside, and we found two large ones close to each other. Immediately the men went to work. One used the shovel to flatten the ground underneath the rocks. The others cut small logs to use as support beams underneath the rocks. The women collected leaves and put them on the dirt floor to sit and sleep on. If I recall correctly, we arrived at this place about noon or 1 p.m. Our shelter under the rocks was relatively safe. We could not be seen by the U.S. observation and fighter planes.

The U.S. artillery was shooting from south to north, which meant that the artillery shells passed over us before exploding several hundred yards down in the valley. They could not hit us directly. The only danger came from shells that exploded too early, when they hit the treetops. The noise was terrible when they passed overhead on their way to the valley. It was an ugly, wooshing, piping sound. Every time one of them passed over us, we ducked down.

The leaves on the trees were not fully developed yet, and we could see far down into the valley. We observed groups of German soldiers, 10 to 15 in each, walking through the valley in an easterly direction. They left the area without fighting. They were sending messages by Morse Code to other German units. Every time a group walked by, the Allied artillery fire started up. The U.S. observation planes were constantly above us and they probably picked up the radio contacts between the German units. This happened at least four times that afternoon. At night, it was quiet around our place in the woods. We only heard some fairly distant shooting.

In general, we felt quite safe lying under those rocks, mainly because my father was there and we could count on him to be in charge. It was very cold and damp, and we did not have blankets with us, only our coats. After the artillery fire stopped, we heard distant machine-gun fire and occasional single shots from pistols and rifles.

Around 11 p.m., things quieted down. It felt good to have some relief after such a dangerous and fearful day. But we could feel the calm before the impending change. Something was in the air.

At 1 a.m., we heard strange, steady noises. My father said, "Those noises are from heavy trucks and tanks." We listened for about an hour, before my father and uncles decided to take action. They had come to the conclusion that the noises could not come from German Army vehicles because there was no more shooting going on. My father said, "These must be American troops." He asked us all to give him our white handkerchiefs. Some hankies were no longer white, and some were of different colors. I can't remember who among us still had handkerchiefs. He tied them together and bound them on three wooden sticks. He kept one for himself and gave the other two to both my uncles. They then left us for the street, about a kilometer away, where the noises were coming from. The women prayed, for we feared that something bad would happen to the three men. Around 4:30 a.m., they returned and told us the American troops had taken over our little farm village and more GIs were on their way further into Germany.

My father said, "If there are no more counterattacks by the Germans, the war is over for us." Most of us cried and were happy at the same time because we had survived without injuries. My father was advised by the American troops to stay where we were until dawn. If a group of people came out of the woods in the dark, they might be attacked by American soldiers who mistook them for the enemy. This was an easy wait for us. The only comment my mother made was that she hoped her other three boys would survive the war, too.

After dawn, we started our march back. The three men with white flags on sticks walked ahead of us, followed by the women and my cousins, Maria and Agnes, and me. We walked up the steep hill towards the top and crossed some open fields before we reached the village street. There we were stopped by American soldiers who searched us for weapons. We told them, as well as we could in broken English, that we had been ordered by German soldiers to flee into the woods and that we were now on our way back to our homes.

Arriving at the farm, a harsh reality faced us. There were no windows left. Much of the roof of the house was gone; only about a quarter of it remained. The artillery shell that had come through the roof and exploded between the stable and kitchen had killed our horse, Max. He was still lying dead in the stable. What a terrible sight! Flora, the other horse, stood next to him. She had a small injury caused by a splinter, but other than that, she was okay. Plaster from the walls and ceiling lay on the floors and beds, most of the pictures had fallen to the floor, and stools and dishes were scattered everywhere.

The farm had no central heating system. There were wood and coal-fired ovens in the kitchen and living room, but no way to heat the bedrooms. We slept for a few nights without windows, and it became very cold on those late March nights. Even the chimneys had cracks. Although everything looked hopeless and desperate, we still felt happy because we had survived the war and were alive. Nobody went to sleep after the first day of clean up. We all worked through to the next night.

We did not know what to do with Max. There was no hoist to load him onto a wagon and he was too heavy for the men to lift. But we could not stand to see him lying dead much longer, because we had loved him. Also, he had started to decompose. There was only one way to get him out of the stable, and it horrified me. We put chains around his body and had Flora pull him out. We buried him outside of the village in a big hole formed by a bomb, and then covered him with dirt.

When my father first returned to the farm village, before our ordeal, he brought his car and parked it in the barn for safe keeping. When we came back from the woods, we discovered that it had been stolen. We figured that it probably had been taken by the SS soldiers who left our village before the Americans took over.

Despite all the damage, we started to feel relieved, even though it took awhile for us to regain our equilibrium and calm down. The attacks by the fighter bombers and heavy bombers, as well as the artillery attacks, had taken a toll on me. (*To this day, when I hear the fire sirens being tested on a Saturday at noon, I get jitters the moment they start, and I will probably never lose my abhorrence of shrill sounds.*)

21

Post-Liberation: Problems and Pranks, and American GIs Save My Life

About 10 days after the occupation of the western Palatinate area by American troops, my father was asked to return to the factory to be available for questioning. I do not know how they located him at the farm. Since almost no one was still living in the suburb of Ixheim, I joined my father. We felt it was better to leave my mother back at the farm. It was too dangerous for her to come with us, because many Russian prisoners were now free and the danger of rape was imminent.

Over weekends my father and I went back to the farm, sometimes walking, sometimes using our bicycles. We had to time our journeys just right, because there was a curfew. In the city, we were only allowed to be outside for an hour, from noon to 1:00 p.m. We had to time our trips so that we reentered Zweibruecken at 12 noon, to make it back to our house by 1:00 p.m. The curfew was probably imposed because the war had not yet ended and fighting was still going on in Germany, so counterattacks by the German military were still possible.

Most of the time we traveled through the woods and on back roads. It took us about five hours each way. We had to walk our bicycles where the paths through the woods were narrow and hilly. After approximately five weeks we were able to obtain passports, even though we had been cleared earlier, having successfully undergone de-Nazification. This was a relief in case we were caught past the curfew time. Ignaz Roth, the first mayor of Zweibruecken to be appointed by the American military government, gave testimony on behalf of my father during the de-Nazification hearings.

My father's factory was guarded by four American soldiers. They lived in the chairman's and president's rooms in the company office building, two in each room. They slept on their own military field beds. All four soldiers were African Americans, led by a sergeant named Chris. The others were named Mike, Howard, and Lawrence. Those four soldiers probably saved our lives. On weekends at the farm, we still had some food, but during the week at my home in the city we had almost nothing to eat. There was some pork grease and some marmalade, left by the retreating German soldiers, but no bread, no potatoes, nothing else. We were very hungry.

My parents' home, a company-owned house, was directly across the street from the executive offices of my father's factory. Since I was confined to the house most of the day and there was not much to do inside, I was constantly looking out the window. And, because I was always hungry, I probably had a sad look on my face. This may have made the GIs across the street feel pity for me. One of them, Lawrence, came over and asked me to come with him to the company offices where he was staying. They discovered that I spoke a little English, which I had learned at the Helmholz Gymnasium before the U.S. occupation. They liked to have conversations with me because they also had nothing to do and were bored.

The first thing I saw in their room was all kinds of canned food and other edible items that the front troops had available to them. It was not difficult for me to tell them that we literally had nothing to eat anymore and that I was very hungry. I was 13½ years old and in a growth spurt, a time when one has a good appetite and is quite often hungry anyway. The next day, Lawrence came over to my house around 8:00 a.m. to pick me up. When I entered the office, a breakfast with eggs, bread, and many other things had been prepared. I ate one breakfast with Chris and Lawrence in one room, and then a second with Mike and Howard in the other room. After breakfast they brought me back to my house. At noon, Lawrence picked me up again and I had lunch with him and Chris, and afterwards, in the other room with Mike and Howard. This went on for about five weeks. Not only did they feed me, but once in a while they gave me some chocolate and other goodies. They made me feel that I was the most important person in the world. In the evening, when they brought me home after dinner, they put a couple of cans of food in my pockets for my father. He also was very happy and grateful.

At this early stage of the occupation, the soldiers were only allowed to talk to children and not to adults, which was probably the reason they did not invite my father to their rooms to eat meals with them. The good deeds of these American soldiers were the best thing that had happened in my life up to that point, and maybe in my entire life. Not only did we not go hungry, but the food they gave us probably prevented some severe damage to my health. Many German children had major medical problems like tuberculosis. In my neighborhood not more than a block away from our house, two boys, aged 16 and 18, died in early 1956 of tuberculosis. I cannot express in words how thankful my father and I were, and how I still am today, for the goodness and generosity of those American GIs.

During my visits and conversations with them, the soldiers often asked me questions about my family, Germany in general, and about my life during the Hitler regime. I told them that I had been in the Hitler Youth, which was required of everybody who turned 10 years old. I also told them that my father and my family were not Nazis and that my father had been in the passive resistance. I mentioned that my father frequently took me out of the Hitler Youth marches, and they understood that this had been very dangerous for him and for me.

After a while, they started to have fun with me and probably wanted to test me. They wanted to know if the young people trained in the Hitler Youth were really as tough as they remembered from U.S. press releases and rumors. I was a young boy like any other boy in any country, only a little more hardened by the war and the many aircraft and artillery bombardments. Lawrence wanted me to throw hand grenades into the nearby river as he had demonstrated to me. Although I was afraid, I did not show it, and after the third explosion in the river, I started to have a little fun. When a hand grenade detonates under the water, the pressure of the explosion rips the lungs of the fish apart, and the fish die instantly. They immediately float to the surface and drift away. There were not many big fish left, but the few that I could reach from the bank I took home. It wasn't much, but it was another bite to eat.

Lawrence also taught me to shoot with the heavy rifle he always carried with him. We shot at cans placed at a certain distance. His gun was so heavy I almost couldn't hold it straight. It hurt my shoulder each time I shot it, because of its heavy recoil. In general, I did not like the shooting and the fishing with hand grenades, but I did not want to show that to Lawrence and the other soldiers. I did not want to look like a coward, and I did not want to jeopardize the good friendships we had developed. I think now that those four GIs probably saw that I started to sweat when shooting and throwing hand grenades, and they decided to do other things with me.

They asked me to go with them into bunkers on the Siegfried Line. Quite a few were still completely intact, although some had been blown up by U.S. troops. I liked to go with them into the bunkers to look for food left behind by the German troops. They allowed me to take any canned food home.

The four GIs not only fed my father and me, but they also protected us. In our area, many Russian and French prisoners had been freed by American troops. They were stealing everything that was not tied down. Mainly they went to homes where they could see that someone was living, because they were more likely to have things to steal. Not many homes were occupied yet because most had been severely damaged. One day, from across the street I saw five Russian ex-prisoners kicking in our front door and entering our house. I immediately ran to Lawrence and told him. He took his rifle and walked with me to our house. Gesturing strongly, he told the Russians to get out immediately, and they left without taking anything. There wasn't much to take anyway. Lawrence was about 6'5" and weighed more than 200 pounds. When the Russians saw him, his face and his gun, they did not put up any resistance. They probably thought that the Americans who freed them were their friends and they could not quite understand Lawrence's actions. I cannot express often enough my gratitude for the many times the Americans protected us. (*To show my appreciation, I support many organizations like Veterans of Foreign Wars, AMVETS, and others since coming to the United States in 1975.*)

When the time came for the four GIs to move on, they gave me two large wooden boxes with canned food to take home. We hid those boxes under firewood in our barn because of the Russian ex-prisoners and French soldiers. They might have assumed that we had stolen the food from American troops and punished us. The French and the Russians found every way possible to take revenge on Germans, and therefore we had to be very careful. My father and I were very sad when those four American soldiers moved on to different assignments elsewhere in Germany.

By this time, though, a few more Germans had returned to their homes, and new protection was put into effect for us. Because our house was directly across the street from the factory and next to a strategically important intersection, the American Occupation Forces established a checkpoint there. Day and night, two American soldiers checked every German, Russian or French person passing through the intersection. There was concern that some Germans, from a terrorist group called Werewolf, might infiltrate our area and blow up the rest of the bridges. This checkpoint was called Outpost #11, and its field headquarters were located in the village of Eppenbrunn, close to Pirmasens and the French border, about 20 miles away.

All returning Germans had to have temporary passports and documents permitting them to come back to their original dwelling places. They were only allowed to move on after they could identify themselves to the soldiers of Outpost #11 and could prove that their house was still halfway livable, or that it had not been confiscated for use by the American troops. None of the American soldiers at Outpost #11 spoke a word of German, and almost none of the returnees spoke any English. Since I had studied English for two years in the Helmholz Gymnasium and had practiced my English for six weeks with the four American soldiers, I was able to help out and act as a translator between the returning Germans and the American guards. Working as an interpreter naturally yielded a bit of food, chocolate, candies, and other interesting rewards.

The soldiers of Outpost #11 had an armored vehicle at their disposal that looked like a tank with a light gun. On each side there were three wheels the size of a big truck, but it did not have chains, as most tanks do. In early summer, my father and I started to plant in the garden and potato fields. We still owned farmland that my mother had inherited from her parents. Since my mother remained at the farm 10 miles away from us, my father planted the potatoes and I went to the fields to help. The soldiers at Outpost #11 needed me quite often, because the stream of returnees increased daily. They asked if they could pick me up and return me to my father in the field with their armored vehicle when the need arose for me to act as a translator. Our fields were about three miles away, in the suburb of Rimschweiler, and it the round trip did not take long. With a six-wheeled armored vehicle, the soldiers could drive directly to the edge of our fields. It was fun to travel in this vehicle on paved roads. I felt very special sitting with the U.S. soldiers, and I was proud to be needed by them.

Some of my friends were now back from the interiour of Germany, and they were jealous of my connections to the U.S. soldiers and of the chocolate I got from them. Many Germans were still very skeptical about the American soldiers and the occupying forces, and they watched very carefully how they treated German civilians. Quite a few of my friends, however, would hang around my house to get some pieces of the goodies I received from the American soldiers.

Werner Ebersold, a journalist from Zweibruecken wrote a number of books about the time just after World War II. In almost every one of his publications, my family and I are mentioned. This is what he wrote in a little book in 2001:

> Next to the nail factory was the Beller house. We boys liked to knock on the door and call for Walter. If the boy wasn't at home, his mother, a big-hearted woman soothed us with good words and some little sweets. We were happy to wait for a long time. In the

"time of hunger" right after the war, Walter Beller quickly tbecame the primary focus of our interest. He brought us luck. When the hunger almost killed us, he helped to relieve our burden. He found out quickly that, with his knowledge of the English language, he could communicate with the American occupation forces, and he gave us who were even hungrier than he, part of the food that they gave to him.

One time when the American soldiers picked me up in the field, they told me that there might be some danger involved, and they asked my father's permission for me to accompany them. When the German troops had left, they had blown up many bridges, but the first incoming American units were able to prevent the rest from being destroyed. We drove there, but they asked me to hop down from the vehicle a couple of hundred yards away from the bridge. It had been reported to them that the Werewolf unit had installed explosives under the bridge the previous night. The soldiers searched the bridge, but they found no explosives. After a couple of hours, I was safely brought back to the potato field where my father was still working.

As translator, I was able to help many people from neighboring villages return to their homes between the Siegfried Line and the Maginot Line. I could mediate when they did not have proper identification, or when they did not know whether their homes were still intact or were occupied by American troops. For quite a while, I was the main topic of conversation for many returnees. They often asked each other how this young German was connected to the U.S. troops. (*The family of my deceased German wife came back with horses and a wagon, owned by the grandfather, that carried two daughters, five grandchildren, and some of their belongings. Their house was occupied by Americans, but they could prove that an aunt was willing to house them all, so they were cleared after the second attempt. Later, a number of these people came back to thank me for my help, including the soldiers of Outpost #11.*)

Some people who were rejected the first and second time also talked to me also, but usually in a more agitated tone. They blamed the rejection on my involvement and my comments. In truth, it was because they did not have proper permission or their homes had been confiscated and occupied by troops. Since many homes were destroyed or severely damaged during the war, the soldiers at Outpost #11 were probably advised to hold back some people so as to not create additional problems.

By special command, all of the unused ammunition, grenades and bombs that did not explode during attacks, plus all other war materials, were collected and stored in a large field close to our house. For example, there were about 20 rubber tube boats, still in their original packaging. The boats were supposed to be used for crossing rivers and lakes and had been left behind by German troops. Just before Outpost #11 was eliminated, I asked the soldiers if I could have one of those boats. Before and during the war, I had had a canoe that could fold down, and I was very familiar with the local river. The soldiers gave me one of the boats as a good-bye present. They said it was in return for my translation help. I was in Seventh Heaven! I could use the boat on the river by inflating it at the riverside. It was easy to take it there and to bring it home.

While I made friends with American soldiers and had fun being with them, I had quite a negative experience with French soldiers. When the American troops left our area, more and more French troops came to our town. At this time, we did not know the reason why, but we soon found out. Germany had been officially divided into four occupied zones – French, American, English, and Russian – and the French occupied the Palatinate, including my hometown.

One day, while I was floating on the river near my home with some friends, several French soldiers came and confiscated my boat. They assumed that we had stolen it and wanted to punish me. I had a hard time telling them that the boat was given to me by American troops in exchange for my translation services, and I needed my father to help me out with the conversation. He spoke French very well, but the French soldiers took the boat away from me anyway. They started to use it themselves, mainly to fish with hand grenades, in the same way that Lawrence had taught me. It seems that the French soldiers had believed my father's story, though, because two days later they brought the boat back to our house. From that point on, they would pick up the boat two or three times a week when they wanted to go fishing, but they always returned it to us when they were done.

One day after the French borrowed my boat, something terrible happened. A French lieutenant and 10 French soldiers arrived. They had 30 German prisoners with them. The prisoners had to collect ammunition, guns, and other war material to place in the storage field across from my parents' home. The lieutenant and his French soldiers saw the other Frenchmen fishing with my boat. When they were done fishing, the lieutenant ordered them not to give the boat back to me. He kept it and took it to his barracks. Many French people are passionate fishermen. The soldiers who first took my boat probably were fishing during off-duty time. Days later, the lieutenant and his soldiers also started to fish in the river with my boat, while others watched the German prisoners. They were probably bored and were killing time. They kept my boat and I never saw it again. I was very sad and hated them for it.

The French lieutenant usually positioned himself on the bridge over the river, from which he could oversee his own troops and the German prisoners. He did not use the boat, preferring instead to kill the fish by throwing grenades into the river from the bridge. And he played a very dangerous game with the hand grenades. Under normal conditions, a person can activate the ignition of the grenade and keep it in his hand for about four seconds before throwing it. One of the reasons grenades are made this way is to prevent the enemy from picking up a live grenade during a fight and throwing it back. If a soldier keeps it for four seconds after taking off the ignition, it explodes almost exactly at the same time it arrives inside enemy lines. I myself never kept one in my hand. I always threw it away the second that I unscrewed it. We wondered if the lieutenant kept the grenade in his hand for four seconds to impress us boys, or if he was just used to a delayed throw. Nobody knows. The lieutenant activated a hand grenade that detonated sooner than four seconds – and he was still holding it. It exploded in his hand, ripped his chest open, and killed him instantly. He fell backwards into the street. It may have been an older grenade that had been exposed to the rain and snow and was rusted at the ignition. We'll never know. The French lieutenant had survived the long war only to die in this foolish way.

I was standing with six other boys at the edge of the bridge around 35 feet away from him, and we saw every detail of the accident. Even though I had seen many dead people and animals during the war, this officer being ripped apart and his body parts lying around was the ugliest scene I have ever witnessed. I will never forget it. We all ran away from the bridge. I fled to my parents' house, which was only 500 yards away. About 20 minutes later, I went back to the bridge. The officer was just being loaded into an ambulance. There was a lot of confusion among the rest of the French soldiers. Half of the prisoners took advantage of the situation and escaped. It was rumored that they went to German families and asked for civilian clothes so they could flee to their home cities.

After about a week, the French soldiers came back to collect more war debris with the rest of the German prisoners. A few days later, another strange event happened. One of the *Nebelwerfergrenaden*, a newly developed, highly explosive artillery shell that was kept across the street in ammunition storage, started to blow steam. The heat of the sun or some other element must have ignited it. Such shells contained a lot of explosive power and it was normal for six of them to be mounted on one support frame. Alone, the smoking shell would not have been too dangerous, but the whole storage depot held thousands of explosives and bombs. If one exploded, the rest probably would have gone up with it. After the shell started to release smoke and make noise, all the homes around the storage facility were evacuated and all nearby roads were blocked. I went to a hillside about a kilometer away so that I could watch. The French soldiers and the German prisoners quickly went into the bunker located next to my house. My parents did not go into the shelter, but stayed in our basement instead. I was very frightened.

Suddenly, three French soldiers emerged from the bunker and walked towards the storage area. Two of them quickly ran back to the bunker. The third one picked up the large smoking shell. It weighed at least 70 to 80 pounds. The soldier carried the grenade on his shoulder about 500 yards to the riverbank and threw it into the water. I went back to the storage place and I still can remember the grateful faces of the soldiers and prisoners who stood around this brave Frenchman who had risked his life for them.

Another problem I had with the French involved the bicycle I had received from the pastor whose son had died. When we first came back to our house from the farm, I went right to the barn and looked for the bicycles that belonged to my brother and me. Both were still in the same place. I was very happy and wanted to take mine out right away. My father did not let me for two reasons: first, there was the curfew and he was afraid I would miss the time to be home since I had no watch; and second, the French soldiers confiscated and stole everything that was not bolted down.

After a couple of weeks, the curfew time was extended. We were allowed to be outside the house from 8 a.m. to 6 p.m. Until then, my father and I had usually walked every weekend to the farm where my mother was staying with our relatives. Now, we decided to take the bicycles out, and from this time on we went twice a week to the farm. We never took main roads and went as much as possible through wooded areas. We also never traveled through the city on our bicycles, because too many French soldiers and civilians were present. In the suburb of Tschifflik, close to the location of the former castle of Polish King Stanislaus, we had friends. We rode with our bicycles to their house, and we hid them in their barn. From there to our house at the other end of the city was about three and a half kilometers, and we often covered this distance on foot.

One Saturday afternoon, shortly before 6 p.m., when we had to be out of the town because of the curfew, we picked up our bicycles at our friends' house. We rode about 500 yards before four French soldiers suddenly came out of a wooded area and into the street and stopped us. Each of them already had his own bicycle, but they told us our bicycles were being confiscated. They made us ride with them to their downtown barracks. This barracks had been called *Haus der S.A.* (house of S.A.) during the Nazi time, and had served as the headquarters of Hitler's Nazi party. (*To this day, I cannot understand why the French moved into this house, because they hated all Nazis and, at this time, probably all Germans.*)

When we arrived at what were now the French barracks, we were again told that our bicycles were confiscated and that we should get out of the city as quickly as possible, because we were already 20 minutes past the curfew time. What happened then could have cost my father and me our lives. Today, I can see that I made a mistake and took a very big risk. My father, who spoke French fairly well, gave them my brother's bicycle, and it was obvious from his face that he felt badly about doing so. I did not give up my bicycle, however, and I kept holding it while the French soldiers tried to rip it out of my hands. My father stood motionless and watched. This struggle took about five minutes, during which I was pulled – hanging onto my bicycle – at least 15 to 20 yards. I started to scream as loud as I could. By this time, many other French soldiers came to the windows and watched the scene. Two of the French soldiers took their guns and pointed them at me at close range. They said that if I did not release the bicycle, they would shoot me and my father. Since many French civilians had been killed by German soldiers, there was no doubt in my father's mind that they would kill us if I continued to hang on. With a lot of tears and cursing in German, I let go of the bicycle and walked away. I never saw it again. My father, who was a very strong man and had survived World Wars I and II, had tears in his eyes. He put his arm around my shoulders and we walked out of the city. By now it was more than an hour past curfew, and if we had been caught by the American MPs that were still controlling the city, we would have been taken to prison.

This terrible treatment by the French was very hard to take, not only for me but also for my father. All his life, he had considered the French to be his friends, and he had treated the French prisoners left in his charge very well.

My mother felt badly about my bicycle, but more so about my bother's. He was missing in Russia, and she protected everything that belonged him, from his shoes and clothes to his cigarettes. She always hoped that he would come home some day. Emil was her favorite. We had no girls in the family, and he was the son who helped my mother with cleaning every time he was home.

Later, I often saw groups of four French soldiers riding on bicycles and passing my house, but I never saw my own or Emil's bicycle again. I would have identified either one of them immediately. When I saw the soldiers riding past our house, a rage always flared up in me. I would think about what kind of revenge I could take without being caught.

(*Later on, I learned more about France and the French people, and I have to admit that I now like them and enjoy traveling in France. It was easier for me after I learned French in school. After our region became part of the French occupied zone, we had to give up English in school and learn French as our first foreign language. I was able to take English as a second language again at a later date.*)

One day four of French soldiers parked their bicycles at the side of my father's factory and went into the ammunition storage area. A friend of mine and I crawled on our bellies to the bicycles and opened all the valves on the tires, letting the air escape. When the soldiers came back and looked around to see who could have done this, we were long gone. This small revenge was only the first part of my payback.

Post wartime was as exciting to me as the days during the war, except there were no more fighter plane bombings or artillery attacks. About eight months after the devaluation of the Reichsmark and the introduction of the new Deutschmark currency, life started to truly normalize. During the period between the end of the war and this time, though, I had lots of adventures.

Before the depot started to be cleared of leftover ammunition, we played many games that were very dangerous and could have killed us. Most of the time, we crawled into the depot underneath the barbed wire in the back. We stole all kinds of ammunition. First, we liked the little smoke flares, which were relatively harmless. We ignited them, in the same way as hand grenades, and threw them away before they started to hiss. They did not explode, but some gave off yellow or red smoke signals that could be seen from quite a distance, since the smoke went straight up, about 100 feet into the air. Such smoke signals were used during battle, so the artillery would not shoot at their own people or to signal people who had gotten lost during the fight. The smoke smelled bad, and when we came home in the evening, we did not have good explanations for the foul stench on our clothes.

One day, maybe a week or two after my first bicycle-revenge prank, a French soldier parked an old pickup truck next to a small wooden guardhouse at the side of the ammunition storage site. The soldier left his truck unguarded and went inside. Two friends and I hid behind the guardhouse. We had several of the red smoke flares with us. When the soldier came back and started to drive away, we unscrewed their ignitions and tossed them on the back of the truck. The flares normally had a time delay of maybe 4 to 5 seconds before the smoke started to pour out and go straight up. The truck had gone about 200 yards when the smoke signals went off. The vehicle was still moving when the soldier opened the door and jumped out. He was running for cover into the ditch on the left side of the road while his truck got stuck in the ditch on the right side of the road. My friends and I lay low for a few days. We were scared of being found out. But I had my second revenge for the bicycles. (*There are still quite a few of my friends living today who can confirm these stories, and when we are together, we often laugh about them.*)

From the smoke signal devices we went on to using hand grenades, as they were used in the war, and we also fished with them as I had learned from Lawrence and the French soldiers. The next step was our involvement with very heavy artillery shells, like the ones fired off by the 8.8 anti-aircraft batteries. We took the grenade itself out of the cartridge by letting the cartridge fall onto railroad tracks. Then we turned them three times and let them fall to loosen the neck. When the neck of the cartridge was thus widened, we could take off the shell itself. Inside the cartridge were several kinds of high-explosive powders. One kind was in little bags on the bottom of the cartridge and above the ignition device. We put the little white bags on a pile and ignited them. We coaxed some of our friends to stand close by. They lost quite a bit of their hair, and even some of the clothing started to burn. It was an unfair and dangerous game.

The second part of the powder in the cartridges came in long, straw-like sticks, about two feet long, that were hollow inside. When ignited, they slowly burned down, but if you stepped on one end after lighting them, the other end would jump around and fly through the air like a swarm of mad bees. We sometimes ignited 20 or more at a time, and it was a great game to run through those "straws." Sometimes when they flew against our clothes, they burned small holes in them.

Another game was to take shells from the smaller anti-aircraft ammunition cartridges. We did not use what was in the cartridge, we used the contents of the shell itself. We scratched loose the pressed-in powder with a little wire and ignited it. A small blue flame came hissing out and we quickly threw it into the river where it exploded. It had the same effect as hand grenades, but it was a lot more dangerous. (*When I think back today about opening those 8.8 shells on railroad tracks and how we scratched the back of other grenades, I can feel cold shivers down my back. It was war and post-war time, and we were so used to danger, and so young, that we forgot to think about the possible consequences of our actions.*)

One of the games we played brought us big trouble. A worker at my father's company worked in the garden of the president's house, located across from the factory and next to my house. The president's son was two years older than I, and we often played together. We both saw the factory worker digging a hole around a huge chestnut tree. The trunk of the tree was about four feet in diameter. It had been hit by several artillery shells, and it was dying. The man had already cut most of the branches off, but the trunk, 15 feet tall, was still standing with its roots firmly planted in the earth. My friend and I went to this worker and told him that we could make his life much easier. We had the explosive TNT sticks that the German soldiers used to blow up bridges, as well as electrical igniters and the appropriate cables. We had used those explosives before in back of the factory to blow up damaged railroad tracks. Behind the factory, we connected our cables to the central power station, which gave us electricity to ignite the explosives. Since there was always a great deal of noise in our area from mines and ammunition blowing up, our explosions did not get extra attention.

We attached several sticks of TNT to the roots of the tree. This was easy to do, because the factory worker had dug large holes deep into the earth to expose the roots. Then we connected 50 feet of cable to an electrical outlet on the president's porch. (The factory had generators to which a few homes owned by the company were connected. These included the president's villa and my parents' home.) The porch had a stone wall three to four feet high. The rest of the house, above the wall, was wood and windows. We opened all the windows on the porch, since it was only a short distance to the tree. We ducked behind the stone wall and asked the factory worker to duck down with us.

We then turned on the switch at the porch. A huge explosion and big dust cloud followed. Stones were flying everywhere, some as big as a foot in diameter. Windows broke at the company's office and at houses nearby. Luckily, not all the windows had yet been replaced since the war. Stones also flew into the nearby road. Once again, we were lucky that there was little traffic and no one was hurt. Quite a few people heard and felt the explosion and ran into the street. I was in big trouble, and my parents grounded me for several weeks.

It was obvious that we had used way too many TNT sticks, although the tree stump was lying just a few feet away from the roots and the factory worker did not have much work left to do. We later felt very sorry for him when we found out that he was reprimanded and almost fired.

My friends and I were not the only young people playing with dangerous war equipment. A boy from the suburb of Rimschweiler (*with whom I later played soccer*) was heavily wounded when a hand grenade exploded close to him. Fortunately, he was not killed like the French lieutenant on the bridge. Instead, he lost his left forearm and the two middle fingers on his right hand. He also had many small wounds on his body and legs from the exploding grenade. (*Despite those injuries, he was an excellent soccer player. He and I played semi-professional soccer for six and a half years.*)

The large ammunition depot was a big danger. At any time, too much exposure to the heat of the sun could explode the bombs and artillery shells, so the French occupation forces decided to empty the depot. Everyday, for about four weeks, a French-supervised team of German prisoners took bombs and ammunition to a quarry mine about 800 yards away, where they blew them up. Before the detonation, they set off a siren and everybody within a radius of one kilometer had to go into a bomb shelter. Quite often, I did not go into the shelter, but stood at the corner of the house and waited until I saw fireballs and smoke rising. Then I quickly ducked behind the house wall. This was a risky game, and one time I did not get behind the house quickly enough. I was hit by a small iron splinter from a bomb or grenade. It left a scar on my leg that I still have today and caused me tremendous problems with my father.

For a considerable time after the American occupation, there was no school and not much to do. Not many people had returned yet, because fighting was still going on in Germany. People only slowly moved back to their homes, mainly from cities not so far from Zweibruecken or the red zone. One day, just after the curfew hours were expanded to 8 a.m. to 6 p.m., a neighboring family returned with their son. Now I had a playmate. We both were in the same class and had been in the same age group in the Hitler Youth. We both knew the woods and fields in our area very well, as well as the bunkers of the Siegfried Line. Our parents told us over and over not to go far away from our homes. We were to stay only in areas well-known to us that had not been identified as possible mine fields. There was all sorts of ammunition lying around, but we were used to danger from growing up during war time.

First we went to a wooded area called Birkhausen, where we had played many war games during our time in the Hitler Youth. At the foothill of the woods near a horse farm, the Germans had established a defense position that opened into some caves. It was not a regular bunker, built from concrete like Siegfried Line bunkers. Directly in front, the Germans had established several machine-gun positions, and nearby were a number of anti-tank weapons. The bunker was located at a turn in the road, and its gun was directed towards the valley of the suburb Rimschweiler. It also aimed at Muehltal, so soldiers could cover the highest defense area of the Siegfried Line and the location of the command bunker. The American troops must have taken this place and bunker during the time I was living at the farm. It looked like the U.S. troops used flamethrowers to get the Germans out of the caves and shelters. One could see that most of the support structures had large burn marks.

When my friend and I came to this place, we found the damage was not only to the burned wooden structure. The entrance to the caves and outside defense holes had been partly destroyed and closed by mud slides. One could still go inside, but only by bending down. It was quite dangerous. Since we always were looking for food or canned goods left behind by the German soldiers, we crawled into the caves. We did this on three separate occasions. The first time we found a few cans of pea soup, and that was reason enough to return and search for more food. At this time, we also started looking for field telephones that the German soldiers carried with them and used in the Siegfried Line bunkers.

When we went back the third time, we recognized a very bad, sweet and foul odor. It was strongest at the place where the biggest mudslide was. With a small folding military shovel, we moved some dirt to see if there might be some food buried under the dirt. What we found was terrible and scared us to death. First, we saw a boot similar to the type of boot that all German soldiers wore. On closer inspection, we discovered that there was still a leg in the boot. Carefully taking a little more dirt away, we discovered a dead German soldier. We left the place immediately and informed our parents. They told the American military government in Zweibruecken. There was already a special task force, comprised of civilians and established under U.S. supervision, to help with the bodies that were discovered almost daily under the rubble in our town, and in homes that had been destroyed by air and artillery attacks. When the dead soldier that we had stumbled upon was taken out of the debris, the task force also found two of his dead comrades. All three soldiers were, we were told, properly identified by tags hanging on chains around their necks. They were buried at the military cemetery in Zweibruecken. We do not know how the soldiers were killed. It could have happened in a fight with the American troops or they might have been caught in the mudslides while trying to get out of the shelter.

There is more to tell about our food and telephone search excursions. The bunkers of the Siegfried Line were so positioned that if, for example, one were taken by the enemies, or enemies attempted to take it, the bunker was in the fire line of at least two other bunkers that would attempt to protect it. The American troops entering the Siegfried line would take the first row of bunkers, blow them up, and quickly retreat; or they would pass them by in order to take them from behind. Then they moved carefully into the second and third lines. It was assumed that the Germans would try to trick them by leaving the first row of bunkers without defense. When this did not turn out to be the case, the second and third lines of bunkers were not blown up, but were left in their original condition. Therefore, my friends and I were able to explore them.

Equipped with flashlights, we went from bunker to bunker to look for canned food. After a short while, our primary interest was in searching for technical equipment and tools, mainly for field telephone systems that were operated by a hand crank. There was plenty of telephone cable left, which we took home. Three more of our young friends came back with their parents, and they joined us in our activities. The telephones were still in good shape, and using the cables we established our own communication system among the houses of our parents. This was a lot of fun until the French soldiers found out about it. I do not know how it came to their attention, but one day a team of about 10 soldiers came into our area, went from house to house, and confiscated all telephones and cables.

People stole everything that was not nailed down: concrete, tools, cabinets, ovens, water pumps. A black market was developing. We boys collected some rubber air hoses and used pieces from them as soccer balls for many years. This was all we had to play soccer with! The rubber seals from heavy doors were slipped off and used for shoe soles. People who were caught pilfering the bunkers were often given harsh penalties by the French occupation troops.

Shortly before the American troops took over, quite a few German soldiers who were stationed in Siegfried Line bunkers in our area started to wear civilian outfits. They left their military clothes around bunkers in areas where they could change. We carried some of these uniforms home and our parents hid them. Later, when chemicals were available, the military color was dyed to dark blue and we had something to wear. We could not buy clothes for more than a year, and the newly dyed uniforms came in handy. Sometimes when you looked carefully, though, you could tell that there had been other colors in the fabric. Some of the uniforms were used by my father for bartering. For example, he traded a long and beautiful leather military coat with a fur collar (probably an officer's coat) to a French shepherd in exchange for two sheep. The leather coat still was its original color, but the French shepherd did not care. We hired a butcher and for quite a while we had meat to eat.

For us to go from bunker to bunker was not without danger. One day we discovered a wire extending from the earth on one side of a small trench to the other side. It was at the height of our knees. Most of the bunkers were connected with one another outside with *Schützengräben* (trenches). They were used by the soldiers to visit each other, for observation purposes, and for defense during battle. The soldiers could not be seen by airplanes when visiting each other. On one side of the wire, attached to a small pole, was a hand grenade with the ignition already screwed out. The slightest pressure, for example stamping on the wire, would have pulled the ignition out completely and caused the grenade to explode. We could easily have been killed. Luckily none of my friends was ever hurt by such booby traps, set by German troops before they left, hoping to kill Allied soldiers.

Within the bunkers, there were big holes underneath hallways with the covers missing. When using our flashlights, we normally aimed them into the darkness in front of us, not on the floor below us. Fortunately, we discovered the holes and miraculously never fell into them. In Germany we have a saying that "Children and drunks are protected by guardian angels."

There were also mine fields around some of the bunkers. When I think back to our escapades, we were exceedingly lucky that we were not injured or killed. Quite a few German civilians in our region were killed by exploding mines and other traps.

In the summer of 1945, the French announced that they would eliminate the Siegfried Line. But first the mine fields had to be cleared. In the rush of retreating, the Germans had placed mines helter skelter, without specific plans or sketches. Thus, many of the mines were now hard to locate, and the process of finding them became dangerous. It was very hazardous for us boys who continued to play in the fields, considering that 34 mine fields were detected and marked around Zweibruecken.

As I have already reported, our house between the Siegfried and Maginot Lines was not the safest of places, because of its location at the intersection of two roads leading to France and because it was directly across from my father's factory, a favorite target. Our house had been hit by artillery grenades on three different occasions. One went through the roof and the second floor, and the others exploded at the outside walls. We had to replace our windows many times. The grenade that went through the roof and attic created a big hole, so we could see from the attic down into the garage. We fixed the roof, but for a long time we did not fix the floor.

We were constantly in search of food, and this hole from the attic to the garage later proved to be a blessing for my family, neighbors and relatives. The president of my father's company had relatives in Switzerland, and if I remember correctly, he also owned some farmland there. His Swiss relatives sent him two large truckloads of apples, which he was free to distribute to workers from the factory and to others. The apples were stored in a five-foot high pile in our garage, and my father gave the garage key to the president of the company. After many apples had been distributed to workers, a large number were still left in the garage. My father and my brother talked about the apples on several occasions, because the temptation to take some continued to grow. They knew that stealing some of the apples was not right, but they decided to do it anyway. Many neighbor children were going hungry, as well as my elderly aunt and uncle.

Since my father did not have a key to the garage door, he came up with another idea. From the attic he lowered my brother on a heavy rope through the grenade hole and into the garage. My brother had a large basket with him that he filled with apples. My father then raised the basket up to the attic. I was posted outside to watch that the president didn't show up with the key to open the garage door. They took four large baskets of apples. We gave one basket to my aunt and uncle. From the other three, we saved some for ourselves and my mother distributed the rest to hungry neighbor children. I think my parents reasoned that they had stolen the food for a good purpose.

One of the hungry neighbor boys later became a journalist for a local newspaper. He was born into a poor family and was raised by a single mother. Thirty years after the war, and about 20 years after my mother died, he wrote several articles in the local paper featuring my mother and her involvement in feeding hungry neighbor children. Up until nine months before the end of the war, we had more to eat than most of our neighbors because my father continued to barter. When we played soccer on the field across from our house and my mother would call me over to give me an apple and sandwich, she always provided sandwiches for my friends, too. Werner Ebersold, the Zweibruecken journalist reported several times about how good a person my mother had been, and those articles were sent to me in the United States.

Life slowly started to normalize 9 to 12 months after the war, but there remained much turmoil. Only in 1948, when the Reichsmark was changed into the Deutschmark and the Marshall plan came into effect, did our lifestyle truly return to normal. Before long, though, we started to play sports again, and I was drafted into the A-Youth Team of a local sports club. Nobody had more than one pair of shoes, which we wore summer and winter and for playing soccer. When they were soaked from the snow, we had to stay home until they dried out. Some of my friends played soccer with shoes that did not have soles on them, only the upper part of the shoe. They were bound to their feet with wire that wrapped around all sides. I received my first real pair of soccer shoes in 1948, when I moved from the A-Youth Team to the first team, skipping the second and third teams. Shortly afterwards, I played semi-professional soccer and was first paid 10 Marks a week, then 20 Marks. In addition, we received free dinners and beer at the practice sessions held on Tuesdays and Thursdays and at the games on Sunday. The main games were always played on Sundays.

One of my best buddies was the son of the owner of a sausage factory in the suburb of Ixheim. During the war, they produced sausage for the German Army. The Nazis confiscated equipment for the factory in France and brought it back to Germany. This was more sophisticated equipment for the production, smoking and storage of sausage than his own equipment. After the French took over in 1945, they imprisoned my friend's father because he had been a member of the Nazi party, and because he possessed the French factory equipment. After a short time, they freed him and asked him to produce sausages for the French troops occupying the area. He was also asked to prepare meat for their kitchens in the barracks in Zweibruecken. My friend and I were allowed to help in the sausage factory, mainly cleaning the equipment. The French placed a Military Police soldier in the factory during working hours to make sure that no German worker took any sausage or meat. In late 1945, we still did not have much to eat, and we always eyed those sausages hungrily. After a few weeks, the French Military Guard told us that we could have a piece of sausage from those that split open during the cooking process. Often we watched the whole day and none split open. So, when the French guard was not nearby, we would use a fork to split open a sausage. This was not right, but at least we got a nice piece of sausage to eat. It was many years later before we told my parents and my friend's father about this prank.

Everything was up and running again in these postwar days. On Sundays, when no one was working at the factory, the president's son and I took large pieces of lead out of the back of the nail factory. We loaded them into a little hand-pulled wagon. Those lead pieces were used in acid filled pools in which the wire for barbed wire and for nails was cleaned prior to being formed in the machines. It had to be replaced from time to time and was always stored in the factory for a while with the other scrap metal. We brought these heavy lead pieces to a scrap dealer in town and he gave us packages of cigarettes in return. Since we did not smoke, we wanted to use the cigarettes for bartering. We also were afraid that someone in our families would find the cigarettes and we would get in trouble. Therefore, we buried them in the ground near the rosebushes that grew close to my parents' house. We did not notice that next to this spot was a drain spout from the rain gutter. Four weeks later when we wanted to use the cigarettes for bartering, we dug them up and found them completely soaked. We had to throw them away. At this time, one cigarette on the black market could be traded for 20 Marks, or the equivalent of five American dollars (as the exchange ratio was four Marks for every American dollar).

On June 12, 1945, the Allied Control Council ordered in Directive No. 12 that all German defense systems were to be destroyed. On May 10, 1946, the first German mine sweeping command was formed and put to work. It mainly consisted of former soldiers of the Pioneer Units of the German Army, and of volunteers. Soon after the unit was created, it became filled with more people, most of whom were former Nazi party members. Later, some people were drafted by the French against their will. Many of these mine sweepers were wounded while on duty and quite a few were killed.

My best friend's father was the commander of the local mine sweeper unit and he told us all the details. He had been in the Nazi party and was reported to the American Military government. He was a good person and a good family man and father, but he was imprisoned by the occupying forces. To be released early, he enlisted as one of the mine-sweeping commandos. After a short time of working in the mine fields, he was promoted to chief of the local mine-sweeping commandos, which consisted of about 120 people. Because this was a very dangerous job, they received special favors, such as additional food, alcohol, tobacco and cigarettes. All were distributed by my friend's father, and he stored these items in his basement.

My friend and I and several other friends knew about this storage place, and we thought about getting some of the supplies for our barter business. We also wanted cigarettes to smoke, even though at this time none of us smoked. Almost all German men and women who could get their hands on cigarettes or tobacco smoked, because smoking was considered "in" at this time. We had a plan to lower one of us into the basement through a window previously unlocked from inside by us. That person would then hand up tobacco, cigarettes and alcohol to the others. This plan worked very well. The alcohol was in large storage containers and my friend's father could not see if there were a couple of liters missing. It was different with the cigarettes and the tobacco. All the packages were counted and inventoried. What we had to do was first remove a few packages, steam off the seals, take a few cigarettes or some tobacco from each package, and then reseal them and return them to the larger containers. The whole procedure was not easy and it took awhile, but it worked.

One day we heard from my friend's father that a big investigation was going on about cigarettes and tobacco at the original manufacturer's facility. A number of mine-sweepers had discovered that their packages sometimes had several cigarettes missing and that the tobacco packages contained less than the weight stated on the labels. They complained. We stopped our actions. Since we still had some tobacco left, we started to smoke it in an empty chicken house located between my friend's house and garden. One day, six of us were puffing away, so the smoke had nowhere to go but out the small window. My friend's mother saw the smoke and thought that the chicken house was on fire. She caught us smoking, but she didn't tell my friend's father. It was, however, the end of our tobacco smoking.

In the summer of 1946, the practical disarmament of the Siegfried Line around Zweibruecken began. The French ordered local companies to blow up the bunkers and to eliminate the tank traps. By the fall, detonations of bunkers were in full force. Every explosion was announced by the same sirens that had been used during the Allies' air attacks. That brought back horrible memories, and we were deeply affected. Also, whenever we heard those sirens, we had to quickly open our windows so they would not break, although many of the windows still did not have glass in them and were boarded up with wood.

The explosions created much bad blood between the French and the local population. Many large concrete chunks were lying around in the farmers' fields, interfering with crops production. French commandos were driving through acres of land with no regard for the harvest, and houses had cracks in them from all the explosions. Also, the very explosions themselves were demoralizing to the residents, since they were a constant reminder that Germany had lost the war. Finally, it became the policy to completely fill the bunkers with water before setting off the explosives, so that nearby homes would not experience so much damage. It took almost 20 years to completely remove the debris from the shattered bunkers and to restore the farmland.

I would like to mention one last story from the postwar time that took place a few days after the Reichmark was replaced by the Deutschmark. (By this time, one could buy beer and other treats, but we did not have any money because of the 10 to one devaluation of the currency.)

Before 1948, when the currency reform took place, people collected whatever was left by the German military, including empty grenade shells, parts of vehicles, parts of artillery guns and tanks. The 8.8 anti-aircraft battery stationed near my house, however, had foundation parts that were deeply anchored underground. (It was easy to try to cut heavy equipment into parts with welding machines, as long as the parts were located above ground.) In order to reach and dislodge these parts, one had to dig away the dirt and then cut the large, heavy parts into pieces, so they could be lifted and transported without cranes. The parts of the anti aircraft battery that had stood above the earth were long gone.

In 1948, I belonged to a group of 12 guys who were always hanging around bunkers and other war equipment. We wanted to buy beer and treats, but because of the 10 to one devaluation of the currency, we didn't have enough money. Since we needed Deutschmarks, we had the idea to take the steel foundation out of the earth and sell it to the scrap dealer in town. Luckily, one of the guys in our group already had a driver's license and his family owned two old, refurbished working trucks. They also owned the special kind of welding equipment that burned through steel. We cut the foundations into pieces that three of us could lift and transport. We then took all the parts and stored them next to their original location. We had to watch this place all the time, to make sure no one else stole the parts.

When you sold a large amount of scrap metal, you first had to establish the weight of the empty truck at an official weight station. Then, you had to go to that same station again with the truck loaded, and both weights would be officially recorded. The difference between the two weights was the load itself, and for this we would be paid eight German pennies per pound.

When we weighed the empty truck, only the driver and myself went to the weigh station to get the official record. Then we went to the site to load the foundation, and we loaded not only the steel parts, but also the other 10 guys as well. The truck was fully covered and when we returned to the weigh station, the extra people in the back could not be seen. On the way from the weigh station to the scrap dealer, we unloaded all my friends. We did not feel guilty about being paid for the excess weight, because the scrap dealer cheated us and gave us too low of a rate. This was a common practice among scrap dealers after the war. Whenever we meet nowadays, my friends and I still laugh about this story.

Although there was a lot of excitement for us in the postwar era, life in general was almost as bad as the last two years of World War II. There was still starvation, mainly in cities, but also in the countryside. There was crime, a black market, and a great deal of bartering going on. The postwar period was also filled with much disappointment and hope. My family was very sad not to hear anything about my brother who was missing in action in Russia.

(We conducted the search for him until 2001 – first me, and later the family of my other brother, who lived in Germany – hoping to find out something about our missing brother. Was he taken prisoner? How did he die? Where

did he die? Did he have to suffer? My mother carried these questions with her to her grave. My missing brother, who was a lieutenant and the commander of a company, was my mother's pride and joy, and she called him mein Liebling *[my darling boy]. Many years of keeping hope alive ultimately ended in a grave disappointment for my family. My mother would have given anything if she could have seen her son again, or at least could have known how he died and where he was buried.*

There was a better outcome for the family of my now-deceased German wife. Her father was also missing in action in 1943 on the Island of Krim in the Black Sea. He was taken prisoner by the Russians, and they made him work in a coal mine in Siberia. After eight years, in 1951, he returned to Germany, but he weighed only 85 pounds. His weight before the war had been over 200 pounds. His family was very happy that he survived and came home, but he never fully recovered. He died at the age of 57 from cirrhosis of the liver. Most of the prisoners who returned from Russia died at an early age from the same illness. Still, the family was happy to have him at least for a few more years.)

22

Afterthoughts and Conclusion

Living between the lines was the most exciting and dangerous time of my life, and it will stay forever with me. After spending the first 13 and a half years of my life under Hitler's dictatorship, I cannot repeat often enough that I'm grateful to be alive and to now live in a democratic country.

Hitler's total war ended with the total defeat of the German Reich and the unconditional capitulation of the German military. The Nazi Party's politics of suppression and eradication, plus the severity of Hitler's warfare, dominated the thinking during the Allies' conferences. President Roosevelt and Prime Minister Churchill had already formulated and agreed to the goal of an "unconditional surrender" at the Casablanca conference in January 1943. They achieved their goal on May 7, 1945, in Reims, when Colonel General Jodl signed the surrender of the German military in front of the Western Allies. One day later, General Field Marshall Keitel signed in Berlin Karlsberg in front of the Soviets. On May 8, 1945, the Armistice took effect and World War II ended, bringing to a close almost six years of fighting in Europe.

The toll for Germany was 3,250,000 soldiers killed; 3,810,000 civilians dead, mainly from air attacks; and 2,550,000 people missing who were never found. In the last category, 1,550,000 people were from the former German Reich east of the Oder and Neisse Rivers; the other 1,000,000 were of German heritage and living in Russia, Poland, Romania, Yugoslavia, Hungary and Czechoslovakia. The total casulaties represented 10 percent of the population.

Of the 16,000,000 homes standing in Germany at the beginning of the war, 5,000,000 were completely destroyed and 3,500,000 were damaged. The Allies attacked 131 German cities and dropped approximately 1,300,000 bombs. There were 7.5 million people left without homes or apartments. A full 40 percent of the traffic infrastructure was destroyed, as well as 20 percent of all production facilities, and 50 percent of all schools.

Shortly after the capitulation, two-fifths of the Germans were either on their way back to their homes, fleeing from the Russians, or living in East Germany after being chased out of their homes. Throughout occupied Germany, there were millions of lost foreigners walking around aimlessly. This group mainly consisted of former prisoners, people fleeing from the Red Army in the Baltic states, and survivors of the concentration camps.

It is noteworthy that Zweibruecken, without specific war industries, was hit as hard as the cities of Cologne, Hamburg and Dresden. Cologne was struck in one single attack by 1,000 heavy bombers; in Hamburg it was called the Firestorm Attack; and in Dresden it was called the Attack from Hell, with more than 300,000 civilian casualties. The planning of the attacks on German civilian populations was carried out by the English General Arthur "Bomber" Harris. He was a father, yet he killed innocent civilians, and he was decorated for it, too. It is said that he ordered the bombing as revenge for the early German attacks on England. In one of his orders he wrote: "We now must bombard German cities and demoralize the German population." It was also Harris who ordered the so-called "carpet bombardments" of Germany.

The heaviest bombardment of Zweibruecken took place when it was clear that Germany had lost the war, and when Generals Hodges' and Patton's troops were already positioned 25 miles away. Those troops could have entered Germany and my hometown much earlier and taken the Siegfried Line. The order from General Eisenhower to redeploy Patton's and Hodges' troops to support Montgomery and his troops created a delay in their entry into Germany and thus their advance to the defense line. In my hometown, people openly say that the air attacks so late in the war were totally senseless and only ordered by Harris out of revenge.

As I have stated, nobody in my family was a member of Hitler's party or the Political SS. Instead, they were part of the resistance. Nevertheless, it is hard for me to describe how it felt to be German after the war. Even up to the mid-fifties, when I was selling heavy technical equipment in France, Holland, England and Poland, I experienced guilt feelings. I was ashamed about what had happened to the Jewish people, to some Germans, and to people of other nationalities. During the war there was not one iota of tolerance for opposing Hitler's ideas. If my father had spoken out openly against the Nazi Regime, he would have been killed on the spot.

We Germans are not much different from any other people in the Western world. So, it still troubles me at times today that all Germans seem to be branded by the actions of the Nazi Party, which did not represent the majority of the population. Now that 60 years have passed since the end of World War II, the view of German people and German soldiers is a cliché that needs to be set into the proper perspective. Younger German generations, and even some of my own generation, should not be branded by the past anymore.

Many Germans still have some resentment against Great Britain and specifically against Churchill. There is also resentment against those Russian troops that raped many German women and took the last remaining possessions of German survivors. There is very little or almost no resentment against the United States, because the American troops treated the civilian population fairly. After the war, the Germans treated the French with a great deal of caution, but this soon changed, and it is good to see today many friendships in politics, business and the private sphere between German and French people. I can vividly remember traveling in Alsace-Lorraine after the war when I was 15, and nobody spoke German to us, even though every family in this region spoke (*and still speaks*) German at home with their families. When you travel in this region today, everybody answers you in German.

Luckily today, there no longer are border police and army patrols, and no customs and passport checkpoints between France and Germany. Today, major and lasting friendships have developed.

All wounds of the heavy bombardments on my hometown are healed by now. They were actually healed rather quickly after the war, as the following example demonstrates: As described before, the main attack on Zweibruecken on March 14, 1945 was carried out by the Royal Canadian Air Force. It seems somewhat ironic, but after the war, this same Royal Canadian Air Force built and occupied an airbase in Zweibruecken. It never came to serious problems between the German population and the Canadian Airmen. On the contrary, many friendships developed that are intact today.

Several ideas were suggested for preserving the Siegfried Line, but they were rejected by the Allies. People talked about keeping a few bunkers to use as museums, but this was looked upon unfavorably, because they were connected with Hitler and his regime. The French had different feelings about their Maginot Line. Most of the large French fortresses have been maintained and are used as museums. In fact, right across the border from my hometown are two large fortresses that are intact and interesting to visit. One is called Simserhof and the other is Bitche.

I have traveled with my American wife, Cheryl, to places on the first and second defense cordons of the Siegfried Line as well as to the Maginot Line on the French side. We visited the shelter where my family hid the two prisoners during the last days of World War II. We visited Courtroom 600 in Nuremberg, where the Nazi War Crimes Trials took place, and we sat on the benches that journalists had occupied while covering the trials. Together with four American friends and perhaps a dozen other English-speaking visitors, we listened to a presentation in German about the trials. I was able to contribute to the presentation by translating some of it into English. Everyone was deeply touched by how the trials had unfolded and then, after a lengthy process, concluded. It was a chilling experience for all of us to be in that courtroom.

I hope that my children and grandchildren do not have to experience any war. The price my family paid in World War II was very high.

CONCLUSION

Some of the accounts in this book may read somewhat one-sided, because the stories reflect German and European viewpoints of the matter. They may also be seen as heavily critical of American involvement in bombarding civilian areas and helpless civilians.

There is no doubt that the bombardments described in this book were, besides revenge actions by Bomber Harris, conducted for strategic military reasons. First and foremost, the American involvement in World War II bombardments was to free Europe from the evil dictator Adolph Hitler and to give back to people in Germany and Europe their freedom and democracy.

The strategic military reason for the heavy bombardments of my hometown was probably the Siegfried Line. But the defense value was, in my opinion, greatly overestimated by the American Military Intelligence and military command. There also was a desire to interrupt roads and railroads used for supply lines to the Siegfried Line and to the fighting German troops traveling back and forth across the line. Another goal was to curtail or disrupt the movement of German troops. The combination of all those goals probably caused the heavy bombardments by airplanes and the artillery attacks.

Were the U.S. Intelligence reports old and out-of-date, or were the updates of those reports purposely overlooked? The fact was that there was no more strong and coordinated resistance. When the U.S. troops reached the Siegfried Line, there was some heavy fighting, but nothing like the resistance and intensity that had been originally expected by the American Intelligence.

One could probably argue forever about the value and motives of such air and artillery attacks. Were they really necessary in those final weeks and months of World War II, when the German resistance was completely broken and it was only a matter of a short time before the unconditional capitulation? Or were they the result of a deep-seated, century-old hatred by the British against

Germany, enforced by Churchill and Bomber Harris, who – stoked by a desire for revenge for German air attacks on England – ordered the bombardments?

There is also a bright side for the Germans and Europeans, which was the result of an initiative by the United States. It was the United States, not England or France, that developed strategies to rebuild Europe, to build a strong front against Communism, and to integrate Germany into the Western Alliance on a democratic basis. Yes, it was the United States, at this time governed by great statesmen with great foresights, great capabilities, and the willpower to communicate their ideas to new elected governments, specifically in Germany. Two of those leaders were the former Secretary of State Dean Acheson and General Marshall. The lesson they have taught us is that the greatest export of the United States to the rest of the world has been and always will be the incredible freedoms people enjoy and cherish in this great land. Acheson exported his ideas to Germany, and he found a great supporter and friend in the first German Chancellor, Konrad Adenauer, one of the founders of the *Christliche Demokratische Union* - CDU (Christian Democratic Union).*

First there was a necessity to establish a base for a long-lasting freedom in Europe with an integration of Germany, beginning with the western part and later with the eastern part as well, under German unification. Furthermore, it was necessary to build a front against Communism. Again with foresight, U.S. statesmen accomplished this, creating a diplomatic base involving a defeated Germany, alongside France and England.

The new German *Bundestag* (parliament) elected Acheson's friend Konrad Adenauer as Chancellor of the Federal Republic of Germany by a one-vote margin on September 15, 1949. He beat out Kurt Schumacher of the *Soziale Partei Deutschland* - *SPD* (German Social-Democratic Party). Schumacher was an outspoken critic of

---

* *The discussion of Adenauer and Acheson's relationship is based on "ACHESON: The Secretary of State Who Created the American World" by James Chase, Copyright © 1998 by Swain Enterprises, by permission of Simon & Schuster Adult Publishing Group.*

a divided Germany. He wanted a unified nation that would pursue a "third way" between communism and capitalism. Although hesupported social democracy, he often spoke glowingly of German nationalism, far removed from ties to the capitalist West; including a close relationship with France.

I was a party member of the SPD for a long time, but I could never support this part of the party and Schumacher's course.

Contrary to Schumacher, Adenauer believed that the establishing of harmonious relations with France was essential and that only through political and economic integration with the west could Germany rise from the ashes of defeat. Lifting the restriction on Germany's industrial production would lower unemployment. Only a stong economy would engender the necessary respect and support for the new government and pave the way for democracy. After Hitler's demgoguery, Adenauer distrusted the German tendency to be swayed by nationalistic romanticism. Thus, he wanted to anchor Germany to the West, rather than pursue unification with the East.

At their first meeting, Adenauer sketched out for Acheson his vision for Germany. He pointed out that Germany was in some ways the opposite of the United States. While U.S. rivers run north to south, German rivers flow from south to north, bringing civilization and Christianity to the Rhineland. In Adenauer's judgment, a largely Catholic Germany was the safest for Europe. (Adenauer was a devout Catholic; his opponent Schumacher, from Prussia, was a confirmed atheist.) Germans, Adenauer told Acheson, would benefit leaving their purely national concerns behind by embracing a larger perspective. If Germany were to be reunified some day, it would best happen in the context of joining its European neighbors within a larger, pan-Atlantic alliance. Such an arrangement would best support and strengthen Germany's liberal traditions.

Adenauer's words paralleled much of Acheson's own thinking about the future security of Europe. While Acheson liked Adenauer (in time, they became good friends), he found Schumacher's attitude and point of view distasteful and dangerous. He warned Schumacher in no uncertain terms against trying to play the western Allies and the Russians off against one another.

It took a tremendous amount of political action and maneuvering by Acheson to achieve European unity and Germany's integration with the west. He acted brilliantly, and he stressed French leadership during the process.

To establish a front in Europe against communism, in addition to the political base, a solid economic foundation had to be built. This was certainly accomplished through the Marshall Plan, which was the foremost tool for creating economic recovery and freedom in Europe. What started politically in the late 1940s and '50s, and continued economically with the Marshall Plan, was the base for the normalization and transformation of Europe.

Perhaps the most graphic example for this transformation is a place in Berlin known as CheckPoint Charlie. It was a grim checkpoint in the middle of the Berlin Wall. I stood at the place where American and Russian tanks pointed their guns at each other, only 200 yards apart. Now, this once forbidden zone is the site of a new, upscale plaza and an office tower with a festive sign that reads in English "For information, see our Website: www.Checkpoint-Charlie.com." It has been more than 15 years now since the Berlin Wall came down, and during that time, a new stage of economic prosperity has been set, the likes of which Europe has never seen.

It has been a long and painful adjustment, but now all of the fundamentals are in place. What started slowly is now in full force all over Europe. Why? It is simple. It is now recognized that there is no other choice. European countries are now tied together with one currency, the Euro. This means that the economies are tied together also. They are no longer just competing with each other in a small European microcosm, with government monopolies, domineering labor unions, and separate cultures and economies. Europe has come through the painful process of realizing that the world is too small for that now. In order to compete on a global scale, Europe realized that it had to start doing what America began in the late 1970s and in the 1980s: become more efficient in world trade and world leadership. Again, the seeds for all this were planted by the United States.

In the early 1950s, I participated as a student in an essay contest initiated and supported by the *Europäische Wirtschaftsgemeinschaft* (EWG, European Economic Community) about the Marshall Plan. At the time, I read much about the plan the positive consequences it had for Germany and Europe. The European community has almost totally forgotten the American generosity, and many Americans do not even know about it or remember it.

The Marshall Plan, authorized by the Truman Policy, pumped billions of dollars into discouraged countries. Germany, Japan, and to a lesser extent, Britain, France and Italy were lifted out of the debris of war by the Americans who poured money in and forgave billions of dollars in debts. Today, none of these countries is even paying the interest on its remaining debts to the United States.

Despite the memory of the heavy bombardments of and casualties in my hometown, I would like to conclude with a big "Thank You" for the generosity of the American people and government. It would be greatly appreciated if, from time to time, some reminders with thank-you notes for those good deeds would come from European newspapers and statesmen.

Appendix A

Zweibruecken's History, Including the Regiment Royal Deux Ponts and Its Role in the U.S. Fight for Independence

Much has been written and published about historic Germany, both in text and pictures. But who in the United States (or throughout the world) has heard of Zweibruecken? The exception would be the GIs stationed in the region after World War II, and maybe a few people who have not forgotten the 1945 New York Times articles and pictures depicting U.S. troops storming the Siegfried Line and capturing the city.

Zweibruecken was once the residence of dukes and has its own castle, located in the center of the city. This resident castle, designed by the Swedish architect Jonas Sundahl, has been completely restored to its original form after the extensive damage it suffered during World War II. Now the office of the state's Supreme Court, it is the largest baroque building in the Palatinate. Heavy bombardments and destruction did not leave much of the other historic buildings. A modern city grew out of the ruins, with many new schools and important government institutions. The city is now at the center of the Saar/Palatinate border region.

With roots reaching far back in history, the living symbols of the city are horses and roses. In former times, the city had its own breed of horse, the *Zweibrücker*, and today it houses the so-called Trakener breed from East Germany in horse farms owned by the state. Zweibruecken has Europe's largest rose garden, one of the largest in the world, with more than 80,000 roses, including more than 2,000 varieties. The garden also has many other local and exotic plants.

Zweibruecken has more than 600 years of history connected very closely to Germany and to bordering France. This chapter will describe some of that amazing history, as well as provide an overview of ancient and pre-historic times in the countryside surrounding the my hometown and its environs.

The valley basin where the city of Zweibruecken is currently located, and where the Hornbach River and the Schwarzbach River come together to form the new Blies River, was all uninhabitable swampland in prehistoric times. The people who lived in the area more than 5,000 years ago were mainly hunters and gatherers.

The original denizens were followed by the Celts of the late Bronze Age, about 2,500 years ago. The Celts were farmers and practiced animal husbendry. They also were good craftsmen, working with gold, silver, bronze, and later on, iron. Much later, they also used wheels. Graves, stone walls, megaliths and other important findings prove the existence of a sophisticated culture and dense population.

About 2000 years ago, Romans arrived in the area to the west of the Rhine River, and the Celts cohabited with them on friendly terms. The Romans wrote and spoke Latin, while the larger Celt population used its original language. A cross-cultural exchange developed. In the nearby village of Schwarzenacker, the prevalent Celtic EPONA cult was also accepted by the Romans. In 400 years of Roman domination, a highly developed culture and civilization was established, one whose level would only be matched 1,000 years later.

In the fourth and fifth centuries A.D., several waves of Germanic tribes came into the area from the north and the east, across the Rhine River. They destroyed and conquered the Roman Celtic culture. Then they continued to migrate southward. Only the Francs would develop the land again after they settled here in the sixth and seventh centuries.

The neighboring city of Hornbach harbored a monastery founded by the Monk Benedictinus, who was later declared a saint. (*It is still intact today and houses a hotel and restaurant.*) This is where Christianity was introduced and practiced in the region. Eventually Roman thinking returned through Irish and Germanic priests and monks. The monks not only acted as priests, but also were the academic leaders and teachers of the population. They founded churches, farms and villages. They supported agriculture, crafts, art and science. They also organized the first modern states and administrative systems.

In this epoch, the suburb Ixheim (my birth place) was founded by the Benedictine Monastery and made into an administrative center. For more than 400 years, Hornbach remained the center and driving force of the western Palatinate and Saar regions. A small town also developed around the Hornbach Monastery. (*Even today one can find remnants of the monastery around Zweibruecken, as well as documents on the foundation of the city.*)

Not only did the abbots from the Hornbach Monastery, together with the dukes of Saarbruecken, protect the monastery and the citadel of Zweibruecken, but they felt it was their duty to also protect the economic interests of the territory. As mentioned before, the citadel of Zweibruecken was built near the Schwarzbach River in the middle of the 12th century.

When the settlement was started at the confluence of the Hornbach and Schwarzbach Rivers, the territory was owned by the Monastery of Hornbach. In a wider sense, the land at this time was still part of the Holy Roman Empire of the Middle Ages. Based on political problems lasting centuries, the emplire was close to ruin, and therefore the border region was an endangered zone. Wars, changes of ownership, and destruction were rampant, and the physical effects were evident. The deep and complex historical intertwining of the French and German cultures is more noticeable in Zweibruecken than in any other Palatinate city.

Original Settlement

To construct a large building or to build a whole town today would require a tremendous amount of planning, architectural work, legal and government permitting, etc. To build a water castle (castle surrounded by a moat) was strictly and simply a military decision.

The water castle was built on the salt street (along the salt route from France to eastern Europe) leading from Dieuze in Lorraine to the Rhine River. The way into this water castle was over two bridges, which gave the name "Zweybrucken" to the castle and to the quickly developing settlement that grew up around it: two bridges (English), Zwei Bruecken (German), Geminis Pontis or Bipons (Latin), due pontis – deux ponts (French).

A duke from Saarbruecken started to reside in the citadel in 1182, and he called himself "Duke von Zweibruecken."

During the same era, one of the last and biggest battles on German soil occurred. On July 2, 1298, King Adolf von Nassau fought against King Albrecht of Austria for the combined German crown. Duke Walram I from Zweibruecken and Duke Eberhardt from Bitche and Zweibruecken participated on the side of King Albrecht. The battle was lost by King Adolf von Nassau, resulting in the loss of both his crown and his life.

Kaiser Karl IV bestowed city status to Zweibruecken on the 16th of April, 1352. The ducal line in Zweibruecken became extinct in 1394 with the death of the childless Duke Eberhardt. At this time, the castle and the land were sold to the *Kurfuerst of the Pfalz* (Elector of Palatinate) from the Wittelsbacher line.

The German king's son Stefan inherited the former duchy of Zweibruecken. He combined it with the inheritance of his wife, the Comtesse von Veldenz, and created the new dukedom of Palatinate/Zweibruecken, which reached from the Mosel River to Alsace-Lorraine, close to the Swiss border. Stefan was very intelligent and loved peace. He put his whole effort into the consolidation of his various lands and made Zweibruecken the capital and his residence city. His son Duke Ludwig der Schwarze (The Black) governed from 1444 to 1489, but he was the opposite of his father. As it was fashionable at the time, he hired mercenaries and paid them to settle his differences with other leaders. The mercenary warriors no longer fought for honor only, as knights had. Instead, they sold their body and soul for the bloody business of war, in the hope of amassing material wealth.

In July 1470, due to carelessness on the part of the soldiers on guard, the city caught on fire. Approximately one third of all houses, most with wooden framework and straw roofs, sunk in gravel and ashes.

Duke Wolfgang of Palatinate/Zweibruecken, in 1569, assembled an army of 7,646 cavalry and 8,446 footmen, plus artillery and workers, to build defense systems to help the French Huguenots in LaRochelle. With this army he covered 1,500 kilometers in little more than four months. After winning the last battle against the Duke of Aumale, Duke Wolfgang died unexpectedly on June 11, 1569, in Nessun. The campaign and final encounter still elicit admiration today as good examples of military logistics and tactics.

His sons and successors – Dukes Johann I, who governed from 1569 to 1604, and Johann II, who governed from 1604 to 1635 – expanded the militia system further. To make weapons, they needed craftsmen, mainly blacksmiths, who were called into the cities and enrolled under a firm employment system. In 1618, Duke Johann II called into Zweibruecken the architect Adam Stapf, who had a reputation for building fortresses. He ordered him to fortify the castle and modernize it, because the war, later called the Thirty Years War, was close at hand.

At first, the population of Zweibruecken saw the Thirty Years War only from a distance. The hour of destiny came in 1635. The duke and his family left Zweibruecken and went to Metz. The city, under the command of Rheinhold von Rosen, was well-prepared and equipped, and supported by a large unit of Swedish soldiers. The army of the German emperor arrived in June 1635, encircled Zweibruecken, and demanded the surrender of the city. The troops of the Kaiser eventually moved away, knowing that reinforcement troops from Sweden were on their way. Von Rosen joined with the Swedish troops and Zweibruecken now was protected by an additional French unit. When the emperor's troops returned in October 1635 and again demanded surrender, the French colonel did not want to fight and negotiated to leave the city without a battle. The defenseless city was plundered and left as a pile of rubble. Close to 30 years after the treaty of Westphalia in 1648, the Unification Wars and the War of Succession for Palatinate (also called *Orleanischer Krieg*) brought death and destruction again. During this time, Zweibruecken was occupied by the French, whose goal was to extend the French border all the way to the Rhine River.

At the end of the Thirty Years War, a big change in the way armies were organized took place. It was the creation of local stationary units, so-called garrisons, that were kept in place during peacetime. This development began in France. The French war ministers, together with the Minister of Finance and Construction, built a chain of fortresses along the border where the troops were located. The effectiveness of this French system was copied by many other countries.

As a political power, the dukedom of Palatinate/Zweibruecken was relatively unimportant, but because of its location along the French-German border, it had strategic value. It was chosen as a place of deployment for the armies of French King Louis XIV (1643-1715). In 1676, large-scale destruction began throughout Europe, from Holland to Switzerland. In the process, Zweibruecken was completely burned down.

After the Thirty Years War, the Palatinate/Zweibruecken line of dukes died out. The land was inherited by the line of Kleeburg, which came by marriage to the throne of Sweden. Based on the reunification provisions of The Treaty of Metz, France, in 1680, the city of Zweibruecken, as well as the entire dukedom, became occupied by France. Until 1693, it was administered by the French from the city of Homburg. Only after the Peace Treaty of Rijswijk in 1697 did France waive its rights to Zweibruecken and the dukedom, and King Karl VII got his land back. Karl VII, who built his army based on the example of the French, now initiated drafting soldiers again in Zweibruecken. The legal heir at this time was

King Karl XI of Sweden, who was born a Wittelsbacher, a sideline of the Zweibruecken dynasty. The following 20 years were spent under ownership of the King of Sweden and administered by his Swedish governors. Stability returned to the region, creating a base for economic growth that lasted into the 18th century.

From the rubble of the 17th century, a new city emerged. A new city hall was built from 1699 to 1702. With funds from Sweden, the Lutheran church was built from 1708 to 1711 and named after King Karl XII. King Karl also built the so-called *"Landsitz Tschifflik"* (country villa) with beautiful gardens. This villa was constructed for his friend, the Polish King Stanislas Lesczinsky, who lived in exile in the *Westrich*, the western Palatinate.

In the Swedish Reich archive in Stockholm, many details can be found about the army in Zweibruecken. One battalion with two companies was stationed in Zweibruecken. This small unit stayed out of the War of Spanish Succession, but it could not prevent troops from other countries from moving back and forth through the territory. The Swedish troops saw action only once, when a special command from August the Strong of Saxony tried to capture the Polish King Stanislas and bring him back to Saxony as a prisoner in August 1717. At this time, the Polish King lived in Zweibruecken, where a pleasure castle called *Fasanerie* had been built for him. (*Part of the Fasanerie still exists today. It is now a first class hotel with a restaurant; my wife and I stay there when we visit Zweibruecken.*)

The local successor of Karl XII, Duke Gustaf Samuel Leopold, built a new baroque castle in Zweibruecken with many parks and pleasure gardens. He made Zweibruecken a new and blossoming metropolis for high society on the west side of the Rhine River.

The following excerpt from the 1785 diary of Johann Heinrich Merck, regarding the residence of the dukes' court of Palatinate/Zweibruecken, gives an indication of what castle life was like:

> Every evening the duke had a conference with Madame von Esebeck to hear about the spies' activities. [*Today there is still a Von Esebeck Street in Zweibruecken.*] Next to the apartment where the Dukes stayed is a big hall, and at the end of the hall is another big room where the cavaliers and the ladies stayed. No living soul was ever allowed to enter the big hall without being announced.

A chef was sent back into the storage house to pick up a brace of pheasants, because he planned to cook stuffed pheasants on the stove. Three months earlier, the duke had forbidden the chef from making stuffed pheasants. The good chef thought the honor of the good art of cooking required stuffing pheasants. He wanted to make them especially good because guests were in the house.

A Moor was punished with 50 strokes because he wanted to close the door of the carriage and align the step into the carriage before the carriage was at the normal running speed. In the whole castle, there were 50 Moorish servants, most of them allowed to carry weapons.

None of the servants was ever allowed to sing or whistle in the castle. A maid that took care of overcoats and hats was singing a little song in her room. The castle guard who was standing on the floor opened the door and said 'Please stop, in God's name, the singing,' because he knew if the singing were to be discovered, he as a guard would be severely punished.

Such was the life in the castle. (*How different than the problems we have to deal with today!*)

Zweibruecken and its dukes had military garrisons most of the time. The city grew into a more political and economic center of the Palatinate under the rule of Duke Christian IV (1740-1775) and his well-organized government. His interests were more in art and science than in the military. Concerned with security, though, and to receive promised payoffs, he probably decided to lean towards France. He started the Regiment Royal Deux Ponts and gave it fully into the service of France.

Regiment Royal Deux Ponts

This Regiment Royal Deux Ponts was formally founded by the Duke of Zweibruecken on April 1, 1757. For Americans, the most interesting part may be the connection of this regiment, recruited entirely in and around Zweibruecken, to the American War of Independence. The regiment fought in the decisive battle around Yorktown, Virginia, between October 14-19, 1781. It also fought

at Williamsburg. The following history describes the development
and activities of the Regiment Royal Deux Ponts.

France was governed by kings in the 18th century, and those
kings exercised their power to put pressure on the smaller dynasties bordering their territories. These dynasties had no choice other
than to seek the favor of their powerful French neighbors. The
French bestowed upon them many honors and subsidized them
with money, because they had the same excessive tastes as their
wealthier neighbor. Once in a while, the heads of these dynasties
needed to be reminded that money also had to be given to their
poor and needy populations.

France, on the other hand, needed soldiers to fulfill its goals.
The soldiers were recruited mostly from the states of their
German friends. The military units were founded as royal French
regiments, and the soldiers were paid much higher salaries than
they had received from the Germans. At this time several such
regiments existed, including Royal Allemand, Royal Nassau, Royal
Baviere, Royal Hesse-Darmstadt, and Royal Deux Ponts. In 1763,
in a history book belonging to a Catholic church in the small city
of Kusel (close to Zweibruecken), the Regiment Royal Deux Ponts
was called the French Legion from Zweibruecken. One could say
that the regiment was France's first Foreign Legion.

Herzog Christian IV, Duke of Zweibruecken, enjoyed his
friendship with France. Every year he spent many months in Paris,
having the time of his life. In his absence, his dukedom was governed by a team of three high-ranking government officials. While
in Paris, he developed a close friendship with King Louis XIV of
France, and the king's influential mistress, Madame Pompadour,
became his mistress.

On March 30, 1751, the French king and Duke Christian IV
signed an official agreement to pay the Duke 40,000 florins for
his efforts to start a battalion of 1,000 infantry soldiers. The king
agreed to pay all expenses for the battalion and promised that the
unit would not be called upon to fight against the German emperor. Louis kept his word. In 1756, the money was doubled, to address Duke Christian IV's feelings of embarassment for constantly

asking the French government for more money. While the Duke considered it bribery money, King Louis XIV did not. The king declared the increase to be necessary to strengthen the union and keep freedom in the empire.

The agreement of April 7, 1756, which led to the founding of the Regiment Royal Deux Ponts, had two parts: one public, and one secret addendum. The Duke of Zweibruecken and the French king also signed an alliance that later became the foundation for the freedom of Westphalia. The alliance spelled out that the troops of Zweibruecken could not be used to fight against the king of France and his allies. The secret appendix stated that the Duke of Zweibruecken would get 80,000 florins a year for eight years, his reward for raising an army of 2,000 soldiers. And it was agreed that the French government would pay for the army.

Duke Christian started his task immediately. (Austria and Prussia were already actively recruiting their own soldiers.) In September 1756, the enlisting of soldiers was in full operation. That same month, Duke Christian announced that the recruiters he had situated in every part of the country would pay premiums for every person who enlisted. The approach worked, and by October 31 of that year, there were 1,000 soldiers under contract. At the end of 1756, the number had grown to 1,600 soldiers, and in February 1757 it reached the goal of 2,000 soldiers. The French were not prepared for such quick action, so payments were late and the Duke's own money was dwindling. The hiring premiums, food and uniforms alone cost him a fortune, and the French did not pay when expected. The situation in Zweibruecken became critical, until the payments came through the Strasburg bank, Herrmann and Dietrich, and brought relief.

In the meantime, Baron von Closen, a very capable troop commander, shaped the soldiers into an orderly unit. Von Closen was asked to talk to other German border dynasties to help recruit more soldiers. It was not known why Duke Christian asked him to do this. Rumors had it that, if Von Closen was successful in his recruiting, the Duke could have asked the French king for more money. Letters from Marshall Belleisle to Duke Christian, written January 5, 1758, stating that they did not want more soldiers, are in the archives. Belleisle mentioned that King Louis XV might be interested in the Duke's proposal to add a fourth battalion. When Louis XV was contacted, he requested that the new battalion be ready to march by May 1, 1758.

Over the objections of the Catholic church, specifically the Archbishop of Trier, the Duke of Zweibruecken continued with his plans to build a fourth battalion. The official day for the inauguration of the Regiment Royal Deux Ponts, in its complete formation, was set for April 1, 1757. The French 99th Infantry Regiment, which today carries on the tradition of the Regiment Royal Deux Ponts, was also inaugurated in 1757. The documents stating that the 99th Infantry Regiment was formed in Strasburg are wrong. It was assembled around Zweibruecken. Only Zweibruecken had enough reputation and publicity at this time and owned enough buildings to house that many soldiers.

At first, the Regiment Royal Deux Ponts was referred to as the "New Regiment." On February 7, 1757, the first commander of the regiment, Baron von Closen, sent a memorandum to the duke in Zweibruecken and proudly reported that the regiment had reached 2,000 soldiers and was completely equipped. It was ready to march by April 15, 1757. He further wrote that it was to the credit of the Duke that only excellent officers and first-rate soldiers were recruited.

The first known time that the official name of Regiment Royal Deux Ponts was used involved a register in a church book in the city of Homburg, when a Jewish soldier in service of the regiment was baptized, on May 7, 1757. From this point on, the unit was publicly referred to as the Regiment Royal Deux Ponts. Now the regiment officially entered into French service.

But what would happen when a peace treaty was signed and the regiment was no longer needed? The Duke of Zweibruecken could not maintain such a regiment by himself. Closen was worried about what would happen to his proud officers. Duke Christian acknowledged the baron's concerns and started to negotiate new terms with Louis XIV. They eventually signed an agreement that granted support for those "Zweibruecken-born children," as he called them, for many decades to come.

The recruiting of soldiers was quite a process and much has been written about it. The procedures stated that recruiters were not allowed to hit or kick anyone in order to get him to join up. Although recruiters were allowed to drink a "measure" of wine with possible recruits, they could not sign anyone up who was under the influence of alcohol. If it took longer than drinking one liter of wine to enroll a someone, the recruiter did not have to pay for the second liter. No bar owner was to give more than half a liter of wine to any person unless that person paid for it. Everything after the first half liter had to be paid for in advance. Prostitutes were often brought into the bars where recruiters operated. In the 50th edition of the Zweibruecken newspaper, an advertisement on December 15, 1757, read as follows:

> The beautiful youths ready to serve his majesty the King of France in the honorable Regiment Royal Deux Ponts can sign up with Major von Gersdorf. They will receive a cash bonus, beautiful uniforms and other equipment. Persons with German language background will have the opportunity to learn to speak French. Dance teachers, writing instructors, and sports teachers are available for free. Summer camps and visits to the King's house near Compiegne are also available. Pension money is offered, and housing in the *Invaliedenhaus* (Veterans' Home) is possible after retirement. Those who speak French and German will receive preferred treatment with promotions.

In the same newspaper, an article stated that anyone who brought a good-looking person with a shoe size of 5.2 or above to the recruiter would receive a payment of 20 livres. That shoe size was equivalent to a Paris foot. A minimum height of 1.67 centimeters and an age not exceeding 36 years was mandatory for all recruits. The people had to have good teeth and not be bald. People suffering from any sickness would not be accepted. The procedures also said that no one could be forced against his will to fight in a war. Rumors had it that other methods of enforcement were also used. Many criminals ended up joining the regiment.

There was a report from a Colonel Marx about some of the companies receiving bad weapons from a warehouse in Zweibruecken. Yet, another report from Duke Christian stated that there was no weapons warehouse in Zweibruecken. Some assumed that all the weapons had come directly from the king's armory in Paris. It is not possible to find out who delivered the weapons to the regiment.

Duke Christian reportedly complained that his soldiers and officers did not receive the same honor as was given to other regiments. Duke Christian also complained about the lack of honor in a letter to his mistress, Madame Pompadour, and he asked her to support him by talking to the French King. She wrote back that she would give her full support to the duke, which was accomplished.

During the Seven Years War, the regiment brought some of its wounded soldiers back home to a specially established hospital in Zweibruecken, located in the Ixheimer *Strasse* (street), very close to the suburb Ixheim. Even though the battles took place far away from Zweibruecken, many heavily wounded soldiers were brought back to their hometown. Quite a number of deaths were recorded in the three church books of Zweibruecken; the entries noted that the soldiers were buried with military honors.

The Hubertusburg declaration of freedom ended the first war in February 1763. It also stopped the fighting activities of the Regiment Royal Deux Ponts, which was brought back to French territory, to the city of Diedenhofen where it had first been stationed. Then, by request of Duke Christian IV, the regiment returned to its original location in Zweibruecken. The duke granted vacations to the soldiers and ordered farmers to provide them with horses. He also ordered that the officers and soldiers be paid during their stay around Zweibruecken and during their vacations. It was decided that if they stayed on vacation for longer than four weeks, their pay would be reduced to half the normal amount. The regiment stayed in Zweibruecken during peaceful times until 1765. It was then moved to the cities of Strasburg, Schlettstadt, Sedan and Mexieres. War training camps at Compiegne sur Oise were used to keep the soldiers ready for future wars, and were looked upon as a place for a welcome change from the normal routine of a soldier's life.

After the death of Duke Christian IV, important changes occurred. Karl II signed an agreement on June 3, 1776, in the first year of his rule, that contained the future provisions for the Regiment Royal Deux Ponts. It was negotiated by Counsel Wilhelm von Beer, born in Alsace-Lorraine, and by Claudius Peter Maximilian, the French representative for the dynasty in Zweibruecken. This agreement, as many others, also had a public and a secret section. It was very much influenced by Karl II and his opinion about the incorporation of the successor of the dynasty of Zweibruecken into the *Kurfuerstentum* (electorate) of Bavaria. The duke wanted to continue to be strongly connected with the French king in the same way as the elector of Bavaria, and he promised to have the Regiment Royal Deux Ponts in French services for all time. The regiment had been only a support unit to the French before. Article I of the agreement described the regiment as a national Zweibruecken regiment in service of and paid by the French. As a special gift, the regiment could keep the title Royal Deux Ponts, and it would still belong to the Duke of Zweibruecken. (This was written in Article II of the contract.)

The commander of the regiment could only be appointed by the French king, as written in Article V. Article VI said that the soldiers had to be of a German-speaking background. The officers could be recommended by the duke, but only confirmed by the French king. Two-thirds of the regiment could come from German speaking parents and one-third could be of German Lorraine and French Alsatian heritage. People could be recruited in Germany and in the German-speaking parts of France. The soldiers from both countries would be evenly divided in their designated companies. If another battalion had to be added, it would have to be done by the duke. Article XII declared that the duke had the right to also use the regiment to defend his own territory. However, the duke was not allowed to fight against the king and his allies. As an explanation to Article XII, a secret provision was attached.

In 1780, the fanfares of war blew a second time for the Regiment Royal Deux Ponts. This time it was not for the usual French wars in Europe. Instead, Louis XVI offered his troops to participate in an overseas expedition to support the War of Independence for the American colonies. The French supported the North Americans because of their old resentment and hatred of the English and because of England's aggressive expansion activities to gain more colonies. Quite a few German principalities also delivered troops to the English, for tremendous amounts of money. This contributed to the sympathy the French felt for the independence movement in America.

Before I continue with the history of the Regiment Royal Deux Ponts, the history of Yorktown, the final battle of the American Revolutionary War, might be of interest. The following is reprinted with permission from Colonial National Historical Park, "The Story behind the Scenery", KC Publications:

> Nicholas Martiau, a French Protestant, was one of the early settlers on the banks of the York River. He was granted the land upon which the town of York would be built almost 70 years later. Yorktown's excellent harbor and river crossing were recognized as great assets, and the city was designated as one of a series of tobacco ports throughout coastal Virginia. The new community's location adjacent to the rich tobacco lands of the York River basin, combined with easy access to the government at Williamsburg, attracted a number of capable and ambitious men. They arrived with the experience and capital necessary to move directly into large business ventures.

> Fifty acres were surveyed into lots that were quickly sold to persons interested in investing or settling in the new community. Buyers of lots were required to build upon them within a short time. Soon it was discovered that the original survey did not include the waterfront. The legislature later resolved this embarrassing situation by purchasing the waterfront land and designating it as a commons.

> Yorktown's political leaders helped lead the resistance against what they considered the British government's tyranny. The situation degenerated to such a degree that the Royal Governor, Lord Dunmore, seized the colony's ammunition supply in Williamsburg and placed it upon the British naval ship Forwey, anchored at Yorktown. The action so outraged the citizens that the Governor decided to flee to the ship. The Forwey's commander threatened to bombard Yorktown if anyone attempted to prevent its escape. Governor Dunmore boarded the ship and sailed away, and with him went the last vestiges of royal government in Virginia.

War with Britain was imminent, and the newly formed state government repaired the badly deteriorated fortifications and stationed troops at Yorktown. The hostilities severely disrupted the town's way of life, prompting citizens to move their families and businesses farther inland. Poorly supplied and badly disciplined troops caused considerable damage to unoccupied properties.

While peacetime commerce declined, commerce in support of the war kept the port and its citizens very busy. In 1780, British troops under Brigadier General Benedict Arnold began to raid up and down the James River. General George Washington countered by sending the Marquis de Lafayette to resist the British. Events elsewhere were pointing towards a major confrontation in Virginia. General Henry Clinton led British troops into the south, convinced that there lay an opportunity for success that had eluded him in the north. He believed that the colonists would rally to the crown if given a chance.

Within a few months, Clinton captured Charleston, thereby adding South Carolina to the area already under British control (which included Georgia). He then returned to New York, leaving Lord Charles Cornwallis in charge. Cornwallis moved aggressively to subdue the region. The patriots, already disheartened by the loss of Charleston, were devastated by the defeat of their troops at Camden, South Carolina, under General Horatio Gates, American victor at Saratoga, New York.

With Washington's appointment of General Nathaniel Green to command in the south in late 1780, American fortunes immediately began to improve. Green orchestrated a successful campaign that culminated in the bloody and bitterly fought battle of Guilford Courthouse in North Carolina.

When American and French troops stormed the earthen battlements of the British in Yorktown on October 14, the Regiment Royal Deux Ponts had a decisive role in winning the battle.

Generals Lafayette and Rochambeau had moved several French regiments to America in order to support the fight for independence. Although another report refers to the date of April 4, most research verifies that in February 1780 the Regiment Royal Deux Ponts boarded ships in the port of Brest in northern France. Their mission was a mystery. Neither officers nor soldiers knew their destination, which General Lafayette purposely kept a secret. Two brothers, who were dukes from Forbach, were on the ship. They were Christian and Wilhelm von Zweibruecken, both born in Zweibruecken and both holding the title of Duke of Zweibruecken. They were sons of Duke Christian IV, and they were the highest officers in the Regiment Royal Deux Ponts. When they visited General Rochambeau on June 3, 1780, on the frigate Duc de Bourgogne, he revealed to them the secret destination of America. Five days later he made an official announcement to all his troops, conveying the command of the King of France that they should sail to America. Although the Americans appreciated French help, they did not welcome the troops with open arms. One soldier's diary read: "A frosty reception was given to the French troops in America, and many soldiers regretted coming here."

This did not deter the two brothers from Zweibruecken, who were officers. They fought bravely in America and were both highly commended for their actions. They were most recognized for their actions around Yorktown during the siege and storming of the British battlements. This description is from one of the official regiment reports:

> On October 14, the Regiment Royal Deux Ponts stormed the British fortresses with the greatest courage. The highest merit of the day belongs to the young officer, Wilhelm von Zweibruecken, at this time a colonel in the regiment.

The French chronicler of the Regiment Royal Deux Ponts wrote the following:

> To the Colonel and Duke of Forbach belongs the glory of being the first soldier to step on the entrenchment of the enemy. When he arrived at the top, he gave his hand to a grenadier to help him to also get on top. The grenadier was hit by a bullet and dropped dead. In a cool manner, the duke helped a second grenadier to the top. During this brave action, he was hit by a flying stone and was lightly wounded.

Duke Wilhelm was given permission to sail back to France very soon after the battle. It was a personal honor given to him by the American Congress. Congress also gave him several flags that were captured from the army of Lord Cornwallis, so that Duke Wilhelm could give them to the King of France.

Wilhelm, the brave son of Christian IV, received a French medal and was promoted to a French Dragoon regiment for his success in the Battle of Yorktown. His brother Christian happily wrote to his mother (who lived in the castle of Zweibruecken) about the great success of his younger brother.

Regrettably, in the Battle of Yorktown, Germans fought against Germans. One unit of mercenaries from Ansbach-Bayreuth was fighting with the British. In a diary, one German soldier fighting for Britain wrote:

> On October 14, around 8:00 in the evening, the beleaguered attacked from the left wing and stormed towards us. They also stormed the 9th and 10th battlements. The bigger defenses were stormed and taken by the grenadiers and chevaliers from the Regiment Royal Deux Ponts under the command of Colonel Wilhelm von Zweibruecken, who was wounded in this attack. Also attacking with him in his troop contingent were soldiers from a French regiment. The attackers had very heavy casualties. The smaller enforcement was attacked by American troops. We all had to march past the Duke von Forbach (Duke Wilhelm von Zweibruecken) into a camp for prisoners of war. Our flags were rolled up when we marched past the duke. The Duke von Forbach was a great warrior and a gentleman. He was the first to return to Europe. He reported about the Battle of Yorktown and our defeat to the Markgraf von Ansbach-Bayreuth, the man who sold us to the British for a lot of money.

In 1783, the rest of the troops from the Régiment Royal Deux Ponts returned to Europe.

Zweibruecken's History Continued

The last governing Duke, Karl II August (1775-1795), did not share his predecessor's desire to build Zweibruecken into a metropolitan center. During his rule, Zweibruecken lost its economic base. Political forces again determined the destiny of the city. Coalition Wars following the French Revolution caused a third destructive plundering of the city. Duke Karl II fled to Mannheim in February 1793. The dukedom and the city government were eliminated and all the government workers left the country. Zweibruecken lost its central governing position, as the small state Palatinate/Zweibruecken was ended.

Until 1797, the occupied territory was governed by the French. The peace treaty of Campio Formio (October 17-18, 1797) delivered the whole territory west of the Rhine River to France. By administrative decree, completely new territories were created. The peace treaty of Luneville (February 9, 1801) confirmed the annexation by the French government. Four states were created in the area of today's Palatinate and Hessen, causing the elimination of 44 different territories and dukedoms. Zweibruecken was the capitol of one of those four states. By the end of the 18th century, the growing city had exploded beyond the city walls and spread over the whole valley basin.

Zweibruecken was integrated into France by the agreement of "Campo Formio and Luneville," 1797-1801. At that time, under the regime of Napoleon I, Zweibruecken did not have any strategic importance as a garrison. But Napoleon positively intervened several times into the destiny of Zweibruecken. He ordered that all the confiscated horses from Zweibruecken be brought back and that a horse-breeding farm be established. It is interesting to note that Napoleon I owned and rode a horse of the Zweibruecken breed. Napoleon saved the castle from destruction after it was burned down by the revolutionary troops. He return ownership of the castle to the city and ordered that it be rebuilt as a Catholic church.

After the Peace Treaty of Paris and the Congress of Vienna, the Palatinate was returned to Bavaria, and once again became a garrison city from 1816 on.

After the Napoleonic era, Zweibruecken was part of the Austrian/Bavarian administration, which took back all lost areas. The city was again declared capital of the state. On April 14, 1816, Bavaria and Austria signed a new treaty in Munich. By this time the former Palatinate/Zweibruecken territories were annexed by the state of Bavaria and ruled by the king.

The first Bavarian king, Maximilian, who came to the throne with the help of Napoleon, now allowed the installation of a new administration in the city of Zweibruecken. The king permitted former French government workers to be hired back. A certain dependency on Napoleon continued. King Maximilian I was also the commander of the Regiment Royal d'Alsace, which was a German regiment at this time but reported to the French government. This was one of the reasons that a smooth transition from a French to a German administration was possible, even though the Napoleonic wars caused many deaths in the local population. Despite his close relations to Zweibruecken and his command of the Regiment Royal d'Alsace, the king ultimately did not make Zweibruecken into the capital of this new state. Rather, he chose the city of Speyer.

When King Maximilian I visited the new province for the first time in June 1816, people celebrated his visit. They were very happy to hear that he would not change the laws or the liberal institutions established by the French. King Maximilian I promised to transfer the appellate court of the new country to Zweibruecken. From this time on, the city and politics were influenced by lawyers and judges (*which is still the case today*).

The Bavarians did not like the freedom allowed in this region, however, and they wanted to change it. The Bavarian administrators in Munich tried very hard to eliminate rights and move more towards a dictatorship.

Zweibruecken became a brief center of opposition against the Bavarian government. The judges of the Zweibruecker Court of Appeals took action. They followed the law strictly, despite tremendous pressure from Bavaria. People from Zweibruecken could publish some of their opinions under the judges' protection. With newspapers owned by local citizens, they could start to spread republican and democratic ideas. The local populace was strongly supported by Christian Dingler, who founded the first machine factory in the Palatinate and built the first printing presses, leading to the founding of the Fatherland and Press Club. This club represented the first organized opposition in Germany, since radical university clubs were forbidden. The club members were also the advance-fighters for democracy and a republic in Germany. With lightning speed, this organization spread over all of Germany, and even people from Paris joined.

The organization and preparation for the Hambach Fest began with the support of the press club. Unfortunately, it was soon declared illegal, just like the university organizations preceding it. In May 1832, about 30,000 people demonstrated for individual rights and democracy in the neighboring cities of Neustadt and Hambach. (Thirty thousand people at this time in history was a tremendous number for a public assembly.) Since newspapers were forbidden, the leaders of the movement for democracy distributed flyers, which had been printed in Zweibruecken. The first democratic assembly on German soil was an important precedent, a call to action for a united Germany under democratic rules. The symbol for this was the colors black, red and gold, which were shown the first time during the mass assembly in Hambach. In the vanguard of the revolution of 1848-1849, this was the most remarkable of all demonstrations in Germany, no matter which political party one ascribed to.

Heinrich Heine said once, "Zweibruecken should be very proud for the contribution the city and its people gave to the foundation of the democracy." He further said, "Zweibruecken is the Bethlehem where young Europe lay in its cradle."

Many people from Zweibruecken were persecuted by the Army of Bavaria. More than half the Bavarian Army had moved into Palatinate, and fights broke out in Zweibruecken. The leaders of Zweibruecken continued their fight for democracy while they were in exile.

Over time, tensions were reduced. Even though the Palatinate had been part of Bavaria since 1816, there were still many customs barriers, and considerable duties had to be paid. Zweibruecken was finally unified with all states after the treaty was signed by all German states on January 1, 1834. For Zweibruecken, still located in a buffer zone between France and Germany, major economic growth followed. It was influenced by the nearby Saar area, which was Germany's second largest center of coal mining and steel production. Many people moved into the city where they found work. (This positive development for Zweibruecken was drastically interrupted by World Wars I and II.)

Zweibruecken's leadership in ideas and actions in the struggle for democracy continued. Although the movement failed in 1849 and 1933, it finally came to fruition in today's German Republic. That the town harbored rebellious elements pushing for democracy paid off in the Revolution of 1848-1849. Several people from Zweibruecken returned from exile and were elected to the Parliament of the Frankfurter Paulskirche. When the Bavarian king did not accept the constitution voted for in Frankfurt, events turned revolutionary. In an assembly on May 2, 1849, in which the City Council from Zweibruecken participated, a decision was made to force the Bavarian king to accept the newly developed democratic constitution. The City Council of Zweibruecken decided on May 8, 1849, to accept the new democratic constitution as law.

They also decided to borrow 3,000 Gulden to increase the defense by a so-called People's Militia. It already had more than 400 stone fire rifles in 1848 (as reported in the archives). On May 17, 1848, a government for Palatinate was established. Shortly afterwards, the Prussians entered Palatinate and brought down the new government, despite several big battles with heavy casualties. On June 16, a large Bavarian military unit entered Palatinate and took over the government. The resistance capitulated. Just before they entered, the Bavarian king declared war against the democrats in Palatinate. The revolution failed.

After defeat of the opposition, specifically in 1849, citizens started to honor the Bavarian government. The establishment of a Bavarian garrison in Zweibruecken probably contributed to their change of heart.

A Bavarian battalion of chevaliers was then permanently stationed in Zweibruecken. Between 1850 and 1866, the state of Palatinate was integrated into Bavaria. Many people were prosecuted and about 700 had to defend themselves in court. After years of negotiations, the new King Ludwig II granted a general pardon. At this time, borders came down between German states, and starting around 1871, Zweibruecken began to become heavily industrialized. The industrialization had started earlier; in 1827, the Dinglerwerke was founded. (*I started my industrial career at the Dinglerwerke A.G. and until my retirement, I survived three mergers and takeovers there. Wilhelm Bauer, the inventor of submarines, was employed in this same company for a while.*)

In the second half of the 19th century, Zweibruecken's industry consisted of machine shops, printing companies, breweries, tobacco and cigar factories, flour mills, tanneries and rug manufacturers.

The American railroad king, Heinrich Hilgard, lived during his young years in Zweibruecken. In the United States, he was the builder and owner of the Northern Pacific Railroad. On several occasions, he donated large sums of money to Zweibruecken, including funds to build an orphanage. Today, there is still a street in Zweibruecken named after him.

After World War I, Zweibruecken was again occupied by French troops until 1930, when France gave the whole territory west of the Rhine River back to Germany. Alsace-Lorraine returned to France after World War I, and the Saar region was autonomous for 15 years. Consequently, Zweibruecken again became a border town. When the border to the Saar region was closed, Zweibruecken's economy was hit very hard. Only after the return of the Saar area to Germany in 1935 was the city able to overcome the crippling provisions of the Treaty of Versailles.

For Zweibruecken, World War II ended on March 20, 1945, after the occupation by American troops. From this time on, the city was part of the new administrative areas of Trier, Koblenz, Rhein-Hessen and Saarland. In July 1945, under the order of the Allied Control Administration, the American government transferred this new territory to a French administration. By April 1946, the French replaced the military government in this area with a civil government. The reconstruction of factories and buildings proceeded very slowly in the French-occupied zone of Germany. Not only was there a lack of available building materials and equipment, but also the French confiscated and transported many modern machines and equipment to France. An enormous change took place when the Marshall Plan came into effect. It brought not only

Germany, but also many other countries, back on their feet.

Soon after Zweibruecken was occupied by American troops, French engineering teams came into town with military personnel. They visited Dinglerwerke A.G., which had built compressors and steam engines, boilers, structural steel for dams and locks, and quite a few other products. Starting in 1934, the company also was involved in building large wind tunnels for aircraft and automotive testing. (*This division reported to me from 1966 to the time of my immigration to the United States in 1975. We built most of the new test equipment for German government-owned research centers, as well as for the automotive industry, including Volkswagen, Ford Germany and Opel Germany, owned by General Motors.*)

The French engineers confiscated everything that was of value. At Dinglerwerke, they marked most of the newer lathes, boring mills and other equipment for transport to French facilities. After they had left, some German workers removed the tags from quite a few of the machines, and marked older machines in their place. When construction crews came from France to remove the equipment, they did not know about this deception and just took what was marked.

A part of the story also concerns the largest wind tunnel under construction at the end of World War II, the so-called Herman Goering Wind Tunnel, to be built and operated in the Oetztal Mountains. It was in its final stage of construction under the leadership of engineers from Dinglerwerke. The French took every little piece from this wind tunnel and reassembled it in Modane in the French Alps. Construction workers from Dinglerwerke were required to rebuild the tunnel in France. Some of the crews were still on our payroll and reported to me in the mid-sixties. (*In this wind tunnel, after it was operational, the French Mirage fighter plane was tested as well as models for the Concorde. The test section of the wind tunnel was of a size that allowed a lengthwise half of a Mirage to be tested. This wind tunnel has two test sections, each weighing 600 metric tons. The fan was totally designed and built by my company and has a diameter of 47 feet, with two counter-turning rotors. The fan is driven by two Pelton turbines, part of a hydropower station, and the fan motor has 120,000 h.p.*)

When the crews started to assemble the wind tunnel in Modane, the large drive shaft between the motor and the fan was missing. The shaft could not be found for nearly two years. When it was finally located, it turned up in a U.S. NASA research center near San Francisco. Before the French had become involved in marking and taking German machines, the American Corps of Engineers had taken the shaft from the forge. It was thought to be part of a new weapons system and was brought to the United States for inspection. It was returned in time for the French ONERA to finish the wind tunnel in Modane and get it into operation.

Today Zweibruecken has about 43,000 inhabitants and hosts approximately 5,000 U.S. and German soldiers. Its airport has a large runway that accommodates jumbo jets as well as fighter planes. The airport was built by the Royal Canadian Air Force, ironically the same air force that destroyed most of the city of Zweibruecken during the war. Later, until it was privatized, the airport was operated for several years by the U.S. Air Force.

Over the years, Zweibruecken developed into a tourist city. Its rose garden alone has more than 130,000 visitors yearly. Other visitors come because of the city's beautiful location. Many people enjoy going through the local libraries, to research the historical background with cultural highlights from past and present, while others visit the city for its horse races and dirt bike races.

I am proud to display a picture of a soldier of the Regiment Royal Deux Ponts, as well as a watercolor painting of my hometown, in the office of my Florida home. A sister city partnership and friendship exists today between the cities of Zweibruecken and Yorktown. This collaboration is also in effect between Zweibruecken and Boulogne-sur-Mer in France. While I still lived in Germany, I was twice elected as a city councilman; I served for seven years, and I was involved in those collaborative partnership decisions.

Appendix B

The Maginot Line and the Citadel of Bitche

My home was "between the lines," east in front of the Maginot Line and west in front of the Siegfried Line. A dangerous place in wartime. My home was also only two miles away from the famous Adolph Hitler bunker of the Siegfried Line and only thirteen miles east of the French fortresses at Bitche and Simserhof.

Since 1927, France had been planning a defense system to protect the French eastern border, reaching from Basel, Switzerland, in the south up to the Ardennes in the north. The belt of fortresses built under Louis XIV stirred thoughts of an extended defense line that would provide even more security for France. A final government decision to build the Maginot Line was made on January 4, 1930, which was finished in 1938.

The fortresses – tremendous in size and quite plentiful – were grouped together under the name of "Maginot Line," in honor of the French War Minister Andre Maginot (1877-1932). The French government was convinced that this defense system could never be defeated. Some of the fortresses even bore the words: *On ne passe pas* (No one can ever pass here.) Unfortunately, the system could not keep pace with the sophisticated technical developments of armaments and with modern tactical warfare.

About 20 kilometers south of my hometown, just inside the French border in the beautiful province of Alsace-Lorraine, stands the citadel of Bitche, which was one of the major fortresses of the

Maginot Line. Although an important part of the overall defense system, it had been built 200 years earlier and later became enclosed within the defense corridor. German troops advanced past this fortress at a fast pace, never bothering to attack it. When the German army overran France, the soldiers defending the Bitche fortress had little food left and found themselves with no choice but to surrender. Afterwards, there were ironic comments about this brave French commander and his troops that were not able to contribute to the defense of their country during the war.

Many Americans under the command of the Generals Patton and Hodges fought in this area during World War II. Some survivors of the war, their children and grandchildren visit this region each year. I personally met people from Hodges' units in Bitche and had interesting conversations with them.

Contrary to those of the Siegfried Line, the French fortresses of the Maginot Line are still in their original positions. They were mothballed, while the fortresses of the Siegfried Line were destroyed by Allied order. This is perfectly fine, in my opinion, but for quite a few Germans it left a somewhat bitter taste, as they feel that either all the fortresses of both lines of defense should have been eliminated, or all should have been mothballed. The Siegfried Line had already, close to the end of World War II, lost its original strategic importance, and it was almost worthless against attacks of the 7th U.S. Army, which was equipped with modern weapons and was supported by superior air strikes.

Before I go into further detail regarding the fortress of Bitche, it might be of interest to note that the city of Bitche has two golf courses, one 18-hole and one 9-hole. These French golf courses are frequented by Germans, and several of my German friends and business partners belong to them. Every time I visit my hometown, I play golf there, smack in the middle of the Maginot Line.

Sometimes during my visits I have American friends and business associates traveling with me who are also invited to play golf at Bitche. Whenever we play there, I am asked by my American friends about the concrete blocks located on the course that are now surrounded by small trees and bushes, and we interrupt our game to look at them. They are bunkers remaining from the Maginot Line, and they remind me of wartime. Everyone is amazed that they are still there.

The golf courses themselved are quite nice, but in comparison to American country clubs, they are subpar: their greens are like our fairways and their fairways are like our first and second roughs. My friends are also amazed that they have to stop playing for a few minutes whenever a shepherd walks his sheep across a fairway. The location of Bitche and the golf course is deep in the countryside, and from a landscape point of view, it is very beautiful. On a clear and sunny day, one can see from the hills of the golf course all the way to the Vosges Mountains in Alsace.

I would imagine that a few GIs from the 7th Army still remember Lorraine and the area around Bitche. The 7th Army was camped there for quite some time before General Eisenhower allowed Patton's Army to enter Germany and capture the Siegfried Line around my hometown. These GIs and their children and grandchildren may be interested to read about this area of Bitche in Lorraine where fighting took place.

The Citadel of Bitche is not to be compared with other castles or ruins in this part of Europe. It is a fortress built long before the Maginot Line, and it has long enjoyed its exclusive military character. Nevertheless, the last copper plaque of the citadel is still marked *château* or castle. It has worn this designation since its origin and the beginning of the Franco-Prussian War (1870-1871). The following description of the building of the fortress and Bitche's history, regrettably, has details only as far back as the eleventh century, as documents are missing before this time.

The citadel of Bitche, the city, and its chateau are nestled in the northern Vosges Mountains. Although the summits barely reach 6,000 feet, they create an effective shield for the foothills to the east. The fortress itself is carved out of the rock and includes a massive cistern, above which is built a chapel. Large openings were carved out of the rock walls so weapons could be fired, and when the fortress came under attack, soldiers sought protection in underground shelters.

Duke Albrecht of Lorraine was probably the founder of the dynasty around Bitche, starting in the year 1044. One of his successors, Simon I, founded the abbey of Sturzelbronn in 1135 and was later buried there, only 20 kilometers from Zweibruecken.

In 1176, *Lothringen* (Lorraine) was not yet unified. At the time of the marriage between Agnes, Countess of Bitche, and Count Eberhard of Zweibruecken, several territories were exchanged and formed into a more compact, united principality. The land exchanges were later ratified in a legal agreement. Count Eberhard of Zweibruecken built a castle on the rock of Bitche, and it was officially declared the seat of the administration of the duchy of Zweibruecken. The castle at this time was protected by six large round towers. The Bitche dynasty belonged to the Count of Zweibruecken for about three years.

During the 30 Years War, the Swedes conquered the Bitche dynasty. They burned down the villages of Kaltenhausen and Rohr, which were located in the foothills of the castle. A year later, the castle was defeated by Cardinal Richelieu, whose troops were commanded by Marshall d'Humieres. The garrison of the castle capitulated after a 12-day seige. Thereafter, the castle was occupied at various times by the French, the Lorraines, the Swedes and the German Kaiser.

In 1680, Louis XIV took over Bitche. His annexation was confirmed by Chambre Royale of Metz in 1683. The castle of Bitche, owned by the Count of Zweibruecken, was at this time completely destroyed and lying in rubble. Louis XIV was informed by his military staff of Bitche's strategic importance, and the king began the building of the citadel. The work was done by the engineer Vauban, who finished the reconstruction in 1683. The work was accomplished by local business people who later settled around the citadel. Thus the city of Bitche grew.

The peace treaty of Vienna promoted Stanislaus Lesczinski, the former King of Poland and father-in-law of the French King Louis XV, to Duke of Lorraine. After Lesczinski's death, Lorraine was finally integrated into France. The duchy of Lorraine ceased to exist, and with it the duchy of Bitche.

Louis XV, who had practically already taken over Lorraine by March 21, 1737, ordered a marble plaque to be placed above the entrance of the restored fortress with the following text:

> Louis XV, the honorable, victorious and peace-loving king of France, ordered the rebuilding of this fortress to block the way of his enemies towards the Vosges and Lorraine, so that the border of Alsace may be defended and that the fortress may also protect the soldiers living in the foothills of the fortress: Anno 1754.

It took about 13 years to rebuild the fortress.

Several American friends, my wife and I visited the fortress of Bitche. It is not easy to describe. Although it was partially destroyed around 1870 and again in 1945, most of the underground systems are still intact and can be viewed by the public. The little church that is still standing there was built in 1683. It was restored twice and now serves as a museum. Observation towers and powder-storage units were added in the eighteenth century.

The fortress consists of three parts. Within the massive central rock is the biggest cistern. Above this is the chapel. Walls for artillery guns can still be seen, with large openings carved into the rock for firing the weapons. Before 1870, when artillery guns were not yet so sophisticated, the cannons were located outside, on top of the fortress. During attacks by enemies, soldiers found protection in the underground shelters. Everything essential was installed underground: water fountains, a bakery, a hospital, bedrooms for the soldiers, a cafeteria and kitchens, stables for the animals, and storage for ammunition, weapons, spare parts, etc. All the buildings on the plateau were designed to house about 1,000 people.

Despite some humidity, the air inside the fortress is fresh and does not contain mold. One could stay underground for a long time without suffering health problems. The main concern at that time was the adequate supply of material and food during attacks. In general, the citadel can be compared to a large battleship that can defend itself against attackers from every angle.

During World War I, Bitche suffered no damage. In 1918, the residents of Bitche greeted the French troops with excitement after they defeated Germany. From 1939 to 1945, the people of Bitche were evacuated to the departments of Charente, while the Germans defended the city and surrounding areas. At the end of the fighting, three-fourths of the houses were completely destroyed by the artillery of the 100th Division of General Patton. The city was freed again on March 16, 1945.

While the fortress of Bitche was part of the Maginot Line, its design was not typical of that defense system. Twenty kilometers east of Bitche, the fortress of Simserhof represents a more modern and typical version of Maginot Line defense design.

A typical large fortress like Simserhof consisted of casemates, cupolas, turrets, underground rail, power plants, munitions storage, and barracks. Casemates contained loopholes for infantry arms, or embrasures for artillery. Where artillery fired from an embrasure, rather than from a roof turret, it was said to be "in casemate." Casemates mainly provided flanking fire in a 45-degree horizontal arc. The facade was protected against artillery ordnance by an overhang on the enemy side. A deep ditch protected the embrasures and loopholes from explosive attacks and assured that the debris from the shelling did not obstruct the field of fire. There were machine-gun casemates, 75 mm casemates with two to three guns each (and occasionally more). There were also casemates for 135 mm bomb throwers and 81 mm mortars.

Fixed cupolas were domes made of molded steel, pierced by loopholes, and sealed in the concrete roof of the casemate. The majority, called GFM cupolas, were used for signaling or for riflemen. They permitted surveillance and observation with periscopes and diascopes, the defense of the top of casemates and the rear area, and the firing of flare guns. It was customary for each block to have an observation cupola. Finally, there were small ventilation cupolas called mushrooms.

Artillery turrets were built in one piece and were extremely elaborate. Each turret structure was about three stories high. Protruding from the roof of the concrete block was a round, low-angled dome about 4 feet in diameter. This was surrounded by a steel collar, which provided further protection and was fixed into the concrete. Turrets revolved 360 degrees and rose up or down to a height of one foot above the roof surface of the block. If the turret was raised, an observer could see two horizontal holes about 2 feet apart, half-way up the outer surface. These were the gun barrels and there were two guns per turret. Underneath the steel dome was the firing chamber. The armament itself was encased in a special steel dome to protect the gunners and the guns underneath.

A 75 mm firing chamber was just barely high enough for a man to stand and wide enough to reach out and touch both sides of the circular walls. Most of the space was taken up by the two guns, which sat on carriages. Shells were sent up to the guns from below by a hoist. The shell was then loaded into the breech and fired. Once it was fired, the shell was ejected from the breech and fell into a container connected to a tube, where it was finally ejected onto the floor at the bottom of the block, at the tunnel level.

The machinery that operated the turret was below the firing chamber. The turret was controlled either electrically or manually, using a series of wheels and levers. From this level the turret could be raised or lowered, and pointed in a specific direction, and the guns could be raised or lowered to the correct firing angle. Just below the firing chamber floor, at head height and fixed to the circular outer wall, was a metal band about 3 inches wide and etched with numbers that indicated zero to 360 degrees. This served as the direction finder. A small pointer attached to the turret would spin on the inside of this band and would be turned until the turret was facing in the proper direction.

Simserhof had two entrances, one for the troops and one for munitions. These were located to the rear of the combat blocks, deep in a wooded ravine on the reverse slope of the hill. The soldier's entrance was actually only used for ventilation purposes. All other movement came through the munitions entrance. Each entrance was well protected by anti-tank weapons and anti-tank cannons pointed at the access road.

Entering through the munitions entrance, one encounters a long concrete gallery that could accommodate a truck. The exterior was protected by a ditch approximately 12 feet deep, which ran along the facade of the outer wall. A bridge ran across the ditch to the entryway. Firing chambers on the left and right of the entryway guarded the entrance and the approaches. From the outside, the only thing that showed was gun embrasures and the barrel of the anti-tank cannon or machine gun. The interior entryway had several defensive features: an iron gate, a ditch covered by a rolling bridge that could be retracted into a chamber on the other side of the interior wall, leaving a large ditch over which a vehicle could not pass. Armored doors a foot thick and interior blockhouses sited on the entrance, about 35 mm back. Beyond the first blockhouse, the concrete was replaced with masonry, as the natural protection of the earth was sufficient at this depth.

Beyond the entrance gallery, the main gallery was equipped with an electrified train track. To the left, the main gallery branched off to the troops' entrance. This part of the fort was known as the *caserne* (barracks), and it contained the infirmary with showers for poison gas decontamination, sleeping chambers, lavatories, police station, kitchens and storerooms. This area also housed the heart of the fort, the electric powerhouse, as well as the gas neutralization chambers. All of this was 35 meters underground.

Electrical current from the powerhouse was needed for heating and lighting, ventilation, elevators, turrets, radio stations, electric kitchens and munitions ramps. The current normally came from the rear of the fort, from the national grid; it was connected by underground cables to a nearby concrete-protected transformer station, from where it traveled via high-tension cables to the fort. A generating station inside the fortress provided power in case of rupture from the outside. It consisted of four electrogenerator groups of Sulzer diesel motors, each 290 horsepower and 250 kilowatts. They were powered by diesel fuel stored in six reservoirs that would last two to three months, plus a reservoir for lubricant. Chambers adjacent to the powerhouse held eight reservoirs with a total of 400 cubic meters of fresh water, auxiliary generators to assure lighting in the powerhouse, ventilators and pumps for fresh air, transformers to power the substations in the combat blocks, and a substation to power the train tracks with continuous current.

The fort was provided with a ventilation and gas protection system in case of a World War I-style gas attack. In such an attack, ventilators would cause air overpressure to blow the air out of the fort. Ventilators also cleaned the air of gunpowder smoke and the exhaust from diesel engines. To prevent total depletion of the air supply, air would be pumped from the outside, through round air filters about the size of a washing machine.

After the left branch to the *caserne*, the gallery continued to the combat blocks and the command post, the brain of the fortress. The gallery widened at certain places to permit two trains to pass each other. The front part of the fort was protected by a second armored door and by mines on each side of the gallery that could be detonated to close off the tunnel. In this manner, if the enemy penetrated past the entrance defenses into the galleries, the tunnel leading to the combat blocks could be destroyed, preventing the enemy from reaching the nerve center of the fort, and at the same time allowing the combat blocks to continue fighting. Past the second armored door, the gallery branched off to the different combat blocks. The length of the gallery from Simserhof's entrance to the furthest combat blocks was 2.2 kilometers.

Simserhof could fire three tons of artillery shells per minute. An elaborate transportation system was necessary to keep the guns replenished. Because of the destruction of the magazine of Liege's Fort Longin in August 1914, the designers decided to maintain three types of munitions storage areas rather than one central magazine. The main storage area, known as M1, was by the munitions entrance. It had seven chambers, each 5 by 25 meters, which were isolated from the troops' entrance and the *caserne* area. At the foot of each combat block, 20 meters below ground, was M2 with stores enough for two days of battle. In the block itself, near the weapons, was M3. For one 75 mm cannon, M1 held 3,000 shells, M2 held 2,800, and M3 held 600. They were transported by locomotives of 5.5 tons along the 600-volt railways. Simserhof had four Vetra locomotives and 57 wagonettes, commonly called the *metro*.

Shells were transported in a movable container, called a chassis, from the munitions depots on a 60 cm railway system. A chassis was a metal box that held around one hundred 75 mm shells in racks and was the size of a small refrigerator. The train from the depot entered the munitions entrance and traveled along the gallery to a location known as *la gare* (the train station). There the chassis was moved to another wagonette pulled by a small locomotive and was transported to M1 or to the combat blocks' M2 magazines. Chains connected to pulleys on overhead rails were hooked to the top of the chassis, which was hoisted out of the wagonette and pushed by hand along the rails into M2. To replenish the gun, the chassis was again pushed along a rail and transferred to a rail in the roof of the elevator leading up to the combat block. The elevator rose to the gun level, the door was opened, and the chassis moved onto rails in the ceiling of the surface block to the M3 storage area near the base of the gun.

Telephone communication throughout the fort was handled by a switchboard located in the command post near the combat blocks and connected to the outside system by underground cable. All the combat blocks were connected to each other and to the command post, to the storage depots behind the lines, and to reinforcements, as well as to all observation posts. This system allowed the guns to fire just three minutes after an observer spotted a target. The fort was equipped with a transmitter-receiver and an outside antenna in case the telephone service was cut.

In time of war, the garrison was manned by 812 men: 27 officers, 97 NCOs, 107 corporals, and 587 soldiers, plus 161 engineers. Beds were available for those who were off duty. The fortress was set up like a ship, where the number of beds was less than the number of occupants. In Simserhof there were 509 beds for 812 men. There was plenty of water, as well as chemicals for the toilets. Although conditions were hardly luxurious, they were better than in the trenches or the forts of Verdun and Liege.

Operations inside the forts were an exact science. Three fortresses were linked to form an artillery group under the control of a sub-sector artillery commander. This would enable one fort to support the other and allowed massive battery fire to be easily coordinated.

The French justified the defense value (and probably the high expenses to build the Maginot Line) with the words: "If you entrench yourself behind strong fortifications, you compel the enemy to seek a solution elsewhere." This is exactly what happened. The German attackers went around those fortresses, through Belgium, and won the Blitzkreig in 1940. In my opinion, neither the Maginot Line nor the Siegfried Line ever had the strategic value promoted by the military staff and planners. The biggest value in both the French and German border regions was the enormous economic impact created by the construction of the two defense lines, especially at a time when both countries had to come out of recession and overcome high unemployment rates.

Appendix C

Arms Build-up Post World War I

Many people believe that the rearmament after World War I started because Hitler built up the German air force again. My research shows a different picture:

Air Force 1934	No. of airplanes
France	2800
England	2400
Russia	1700
U.S.A.	3100
Italy	1500
Poland	1000
Czechoslovakia	600
Germany	0

While the German Air Force ordered its first four-engine bomber, the HE177, in 1938, the British War Ministry had already built the Sterling and Halifax in 1936.

The U.S.A. began designing the B17 (Flying Fortress), which later flew many attacks against Germany, as early as 1934.

The specifications for a second strategic bomber with four engines, the B24, were released in January 1939. Like the B17, it was supposed to have a distance range of 2,500 kilometers, so that it could leave England and reach Germany. At the time, the Germans commented, "What do the Americans want to do with bombers capable of flying such distances in their own country?"

The third U.S. bomber was the B29. A request was made for a plane that could fly from the U.S.A. to Europe. Some Europeans say that this is the proof that Roosevelt was willing to enter the war long before the Japanese attack on Pearl Harbor. The model of this plane was constructed in 1938, the specifications followed in November 1939, and the test flight occurred in 1942. This plane was not used against the Germans, but it was used against the Japanese. The plane did not quite achieve the performance levels specified and requested by the Air Force. Two B29s dropped the two nuclear bombs on Japan.

On April 11, 1941 (the exact day of Hitler's declaration of war against the United States), the U.S. Air Force released a new specification for another bomber, a plane that could fly from the U.S.A. to Europe and back. This was in case one could not use England anymore, which was at this time the aircraft carrier of the Allies. The plane should be able to fly 12,000 kilometers and carry 45 tons of bombs. The result was the B36 with six engines. The first one was built in August 1936, and larger production started in 1938.

One plane that came under heavy criticism was the B24, because it was given the name "Liberator." In Germany, where American humor was not appreciated, it was said one needed a lot of cynicism to baptize a heavy-duty bomber with that name.

From a German viewpoint, just as tasteless was the name for the B29: "Peacemaker." How can a bomber attacking helpless civilians be called Peacemaker? The bombs on Hiroshima and Nagasaki came from a Peacemaker. Everything has two sides and viewpoints.

The bombardments and killing of innocent civilians and the destruction of irreplaceable cultural buildings and monuments by "Liberators" and "Peacemakers" took place despite President Roosevelt's request to all nations involved in the Allied air war, which were all under the command of "Bomber" Harris and reporting directly to Churchill. Roosevelt's request, early in the war, had the following text:

To all governments involved in the air war, it is expected that they publish a resolution that the troops under no circumstances are bombarding civilian targets and population and un-armed cities; under the condition that this request is also answered by the enemies.

Hitler answered that he would totally comply. Did he?

There was considerably more harsh and detailed criticism in the United States and in England against the air war. One I would like to mention is from the British officer and military writer Lidell Hart, in an article published on April 14, 1946:

In addition, it was the unbearable burden from the Treaty of Versailles that drove the Germans into an irreversible reversion to fight for returning lost properties and which ended in an orgy of reciprocal destruction. This is not yet all that is to be criticized. For example the British sea blockade triggered a German blockade by their submarines. There was the start of our bombardments on the German industry beginning in 1940 that triggered counterattacks by the Germans on London and Coventry. It was Hitler who in 1935 and 1936 pressed for a world treaty to only bomb military targets, and it was we who turned down such limitations.

Appendix D

Details of the Final and Devastating Air Attacks on Zweibruecken, March 14, 1945

(*The following is based on information found in historical archives in England.*)

What was going on in England in preparation for the March 14, 1945 attack?

That night's attack on Zweibruecken and Homburg was part of the "order of priorities," which meant that the sequence was adjusted to current circumstances. Valid at this time was the target schedule from January 31, 1945, which had the following priorities:

First priority: hydro-electric factories involved in the production of aircraft material.

Second priority: attacks on Berlin, Leipzig, Dresden, and other cities in Eastern Germany, to interrupt the retrieval of German troops and to interrupt supply lines.

Also, attacks on roads and railroads anyplace, to interrupt supply lines, mainly in the western part of Germany. Attacks on airports where German fighter planes were still stationed.

The crews of the airplanes flying the attack on March 14 were informed of these priorities. From the above list, only the third priority could be applied to Zweibruecken. On March 14, there was no longer any reason to destroy such a beautiful and historical town, close to the French border and no longer occupied by German forces.

In the debriefing, the crews of the bomber squadrons talked about those alleged goals. Members of four planes said they saw big explosions followed by big fires. They talked about hitting places or railroad cars containing ammunition. There were no such targets anymore in Zweibruecken or its surroundings. Even the valves of the gas pipes had been shut down, but there might have been some gas left in the pipes. What the crewmen saw were probably explosions of the remaining traces of gas and its burning afterwards. The observer of the Lancaster PA 269 from the 427'th Squadron spoke about several freight yards, which he saw in the flares of the light bombs. What he saw was probably the racetrack and and the fairgrounds, as well as the inner city. None of these places had been used for military purposes for almost 10 years. The official summary of the debriefing reads: "Railroad and streets/intersections were blocked and therefore closed for troops and supplies." This report from the 6th Bomber Group was incorrect and probably submitted as a cover-up for the real reason – Bomber Chief Harris' determination to bomb the German population until it was tired of war.

The attacks had been originally carried out by the Royal Air Force at night and by the U.S. Air Force during the day. This was no longer the case in March 1945, because the Allied Air Forces were by then completely in control of the air above Germany. The same squadrons attacking Zweibruecken and returning after midnight to attack the city of Castrop Rauxel in Western Germany the next afternoon were ample proof.

The confidential reports from the Sherman Air Defense Command, which talk about March 14, give a very thorough overview; morning, afternoon and evening reports were condensed into one account. In the southwest area the following attacks took place:

4:50 p.m. - 6:25 p.m. Continuously incoming fighter planes and fighter bombers; about 140 planes flying between 1,500 to 6,000 meter altitude, between Honnef and Saarlautern until Dillenburg, Frankfurt (radius about 150 kilometers).

7:45 p.m. - 9:00 p.m. Incoming 450 - 500 4-engine planes from Luxembourg into the area Saarbruecken/Homburg, about 150 - 200 planes changing course towards Kaiserslautern.

8:10 p.m. - 9:15 p.m. Incoming 40 - 50 Mosquitos flying at 6,000 meter altitude near Trier towards Frankfurt/Mainz/Wiesbaden.

8:27 p.m. - 8:40 p.m. High-explosive and firebombs dropping on Wiesbaden, mainly on suburbs.

8:40 p.m. - 9:56 p.m. Incoming 10 - 15 long-distance night fighter airplanes at about 3,000 - 5,000 meter altitude between Ahrweiler and Metz.

10:20 p.m. - 10:45 p.m. Return flights of about 300 - 400 4-engine bombers and Mosquitos flying at about 2,000 - 2,500 meter altitude from attacks on the city of Schweinfurt.

A follow-up announcement was added:

7:45 p.m. Registration of a mid-size English squadron with about 200 planes of the 5th B.G. with Mosquito protection over Metz, France, flying southeast course. Incoming to German soil by Strasbourg, flying east course, later north course to attack Leuna and Luetzgendorf around 10:00 - 10:20 p.m. at an altitude of 3,500 - 5,000 meters.

8:19 p.m. Heavy bombardment of Homburg. City about 80 percent destroyed.

8:19 p.m. **Attack on the city of Zweibruecken by about 200 - 300 4-engine planes. Approximately 800 - 1000 high-explosive bombs. City totally destroyed.**

8:27 - 8:40 p.m. 600 - 800 firebombs on Wiesbaden's southwest suburbs.

This is only the report about the southwest attacks in an area of a of 120-kilometer radius. It shows what was going on in this small part of Germany, a fraction of all the activities on one single day over all of Germany.

In the actual attack on Zweibruecken, the following squadrons were involved:

8th B.G. (PFF) Staff		Huntington	
105	4 Mosquitos	Bourn	RAF
109	4 Mosquitos	Little Staughton	RAF
405	12 Lancasters	Grandsen Lodge	RCAF
608	3 Mosquitos	Downham Market	RAF
635	11 Lancasters	Downham Market	RAF

6th B.G. (MF) Staff		Allerton (All RCAF)
419	15 Lancasters	Middleton St. George
424	12 Lancasters	Skipton-on-Swale
427	12 Lancasters	Leeming
428	15 Lancasters	Middleton St. George
431	14 Lancasters	Croft
433	15 Lancasters	Skipton-on-Swale
434	14 Lancasters	Croft
408	14 Halifax	Linton
415	14 Halifax	East Moor
420	14 Halifax	Tholthorpe
425	14 Halifax	Tholthorpe
426	14 Halifax	Linton
429	14 Halifax	Leeming
432	14 Halifax	East Moor

Details of the amounts of bombs dropped:

11 Mosquitos PPF	2.7 tons H.E.	1.3 tons I.B.
23 Lancaster PFF	49.1 tons H.E.	10.9 tons I.B.
97 Lancaster MF	451.8 tons H.E.	10.9 tons I.B.
94 Halifax MF	286.2 tons H.E.	
3 Halifax MF	9.1 tons H.E. (early return)	
1 Halifax MF	3.0 tons H.E. (no bmbs over goal)	
Total	**801.9 tons H.E.**	**12.2 tons I.B.**

The kind and number of bombs dropped that evening on Zweibruecken:

4000 lb.	HCNI Tritonal	93
4000 lb.	HCNI Minol	4
1000 lb.	MC	59
1000 lb.	MC 65	36
500 lb.	GP	112
500 lb.	ANM 64 (USA)	1,888
500 lb.	MC TD 025 (BR)	432
500 lb.	ANM 58 SAP (USA)	225
250 lb.	GP BR TI	112
250 lb	MC	96
Flares	White CP No 3	136
1000	Red TI	9
1000	Green TI	11
250	Green TI	30

In total 3087 high explosive bombs!

Bombs not dropped on Zweibruecken (dropped in the Channel or by return):

500 lb.	ANM64 (USA)	46
500 lb.	MC TD 025 (BR)	19
500 lb.	ANM 58 SAP 025 (USA)	2
1000	Red TI	1
1000	Green TI	1

In total 67 high explosive bombs.

Appendix E

Outline of Activities Leading up to the Beginning of World War II – July 31 to September 2, 1939

Many Germans are of the opinion that Hitler tried to avert war with Poland up to the last moment and that unreasonable demands by Poland, backed by England and France, are the real cause of the Second World War. Most historians, however, believe that Hitler's last minute diplomatic efforts were merely a cover for his decision to invade Poland, which he had made weeks, if not months, earlier.

Below is a list of the flurry of diplomatic events that preceded the beginning of the invasion of Poland, which plunged the world into war.

July 31

Polish restrictions against merchandise from the German city of Danzig.
Britain begins the largest land and sea maneuvers in twenty years.
Departure of a British military mission to Moscow, ordered by Chamberlain in the Lower House of Parliament.

August 4 - 8

Increasing German-Polish customs disputes.

August 5

Official Polish protest against self-government in Danzig.

August 7

Rejection of the Polish note from August 5, 1939 by the Senate of Danzig, with the words "provocation, intolerable."
The Polish newspaper, "Czas," threatens shooting and bombardment of Danzig.

August 10

Soviet announcement for a very detailed discussion about the current political situation with the German Reich; immediately accepted by Hitler.
The National Assembly of Danzig meets in an emergency session with the decision to support the German Reich and Hitler and to be reunited with Germany; general decision to oppose Polish political maneuvering.

August 11

Arrest of eight German travelers in the transit train through the corridor by Polish police.
Arrival of an English/French military mission team in Moscow.
Restart of English/Japanese negotiations in Tokyo.

August 14

Molotov declaration to the German Ambassador in Moscow, Graf von Schulenburg: just before the Ribbentrop visit in Moscow, the Soviet Union believes the honesty of the German intentions.
197 deserters from the Polish Army come across the border into the the German Reich.

August 15

Winston Churchill visits the Maginot Line accompanied by the French Generalissimus Gamelin.

August 16

The Hungarian Foreign Minister Graf Csaky visits Germany officially. He states that 76,535 people, mainly of German heritage, had fled Poland since the beginning of August.
Cclosing of the border of Upper Silesia by Polish authorities.
Arrest of members of the German Volksgruppe in Upper Silesia.

August 17

Closing of the borders by Polish authorities against the
Protectorate Boehmen-Maehreh and against Slovakia.
Flight maneuvers and exercises of 190 heavy French bombers over
Great Britain.

August 18

Establishment of a SS Home Defense Unit in Danzig to support
local police.

August 19

Building of Polish fortresses at the Jablunka Pass. Deportation of
all Germans in a 30 kilometer zone.
The Hungarian Foreign Minister meets with Mussolini.

August 20

Personal memorandum from Hitler to Stalin.
Finalization of the German war preparations against Poland.

August 22

Speech by Hitler to all of the highest ranking generals: Overview
of the political situation and military consequences thereof.
Announcement of the German/Soviet non-aggression pact.

August 23

German Foreign Minister von Rippentrop visits Moscow (comments that it was a very positive meeting, almost like with own
party members). Signature of German/Soviet non-aggression pact.
A secret protocol determines how to split Poland between these
two nations.
British Ambassador Sir Neville Henderson meets Hitler at the
Obersalzberg.
Confiscation of a Polish railroad car loaded with ammunition and
war material by the Danzig police.
Continuous Polish war preparations and reinforcement of defense
walls at Upper Silesia.

August 24

Draft of further military reserve units in Poland.
Shutdown of all German newspapers in Poland.
British Lower Parliament meeting with Chamberlain's speech about
the political situation. Vote on empowerment by 457 to 4 votes.

August 25

Ratification of the British-Polish Assistance Treaty.
13:30 Ambassador Henderson meets Hitler.
14:30 Ambassador Attolica from Italy visits the Reichskanzlei.
15:02 Order from Hitler eliminating the "Fall Weiss" attack against Poland; date set for August 26, 1939, 5:45 a.m. for beginning of the Secret Mobilization in Germany.
17:00 News of ratification of the British-Polish Assistance Treaty reaches Berlin.
17:30 Reception of the French Ambassadeur Coulondre by Hitler.
18:00 Italian Ambassador Attolica delivers notice of Mussolini: Italy is not ready for a war.
18:10 Hitler stops attack order against Poland.
18:15 The German Navy ship Schleswig Holstein enters the harbor of Danzig.
Killing of 27 deserters, most of German heritage, by Polish police.
Message from U.S. President Roosevelt to different presidents of several European countries to keep peace.

August 26

Start of food stamps, stamps for clothes, soap, shoes, coal, etc.
German guarantees neutrality of Belgium, Denmark, Holland, Luxembourg and Switzerland.
Swedish businessman Birger Dalerus, as confidante of Hermann Goering, visits the British Foreign Minister Lord Halifax for peace talks.
Daladier declaration that France honors its obligations to Poland.
1.5 million German soldiers in ready position.

August 26-30

Detailed German-British negotiations at all levels, with Hitler's goal to keep England out of the conflict.

August 26-27

Exchange of letters between Hitler and Daladier with the German request that Danzig and the corridor must be given back to Germany.

August 27

Second Dalerus visit with Halifax and Chamberlain.
Hitler's speech to the senators in the Ambassador Room of the Reichskanzlei.

Italy begins to draft those born between 1902 and 1910.
Declaration of the Czechoslovakian President Dr. Tiso:
Czechoslovakia will stand side-by-side with Germany.
France signs paper with a credit of 480 million francs to Poland to
buy war materials.
By this date, already 5,000 English military personnel have entered
France.

August 28

Hitler honors many WW I veterans at the 25th Anniversary of the
Battle of Tannenberg.
Britain and France guarantee neutrality for Belgium.
Mobilization of Army and Navy in Holland.
Complete closing of the French-German Rhineland border by
French authorities.
Presentation of a note to Hitler by Ambassador Henderson with
an offer to mediate in the German-Polish conflict.

August 29

Hitler repeats his request to Poland. Declaration of readiness for
direct negotiations between Poland and Germany. Italy tries to
mediate.

August 30

Constitution of a German team on minister level for defense of
the German Reich.
14:30 Total mobilization in Poland.

August 31

Mediation negotiations by Mussolini in London, Paris and Berlin.
Polish Ambassador Lipki with Rippentrop. The Polish government
had forbidden him from direct negotiations without full consent
from Warsaw.
Henderson, Oglilvie-Forbes and Dalarus meet with Goerring.
Hitler declares via radio his proposal to Poland is withdrawn. The
reason given was that no Polish negotiator or mediator was ready.
12:40 Renewal of Hitler's attack order to the Army to start on
September 1, 1939 at 5:45 a.m.

August 31-September 1

Germany feigns attack on the radio station Gleiwitz, with German soldiers in Polish uniforms.

September 1

5:45 a.m. Beginning of war against Poland and the beginning of World War II.
Hitler's speech to the German Army.
10:00 Hitler's speech to the German Parliament with the remarks "Starting at 5:45 a.m. we are returning fire."
21:30 Coulondre with Rippentrop.
22:00 Henderson with Rippentrop.

September 2

10:00 Again mediation proposal by Musslini.
Ultimatum from Henderson and Coulondre with a time limit, and the declaration of war by Great Britain and France against Germany after the expiration of time limit.

The Germans see and accept as a single big lie the feigned attack on the radio station Gleiwitz, where the Nazis used prisoners and soldiers in Polish uniforms. Hitler used this as a last pretext for starting the invasion of Poland.

It is said that Hitler did not need such a masquerade, the Poles had delivered plenty of reasons before that. The Polish provocations were tolerated and supported by the British and the French, backed by a commitment from the United States to support the war by supplying weapons.

Was there therefore some American involvement from the beginning? According to the diary of the U.S. War Minister Forrestal, on December 12, 1945, the former U.S. Ambassador in London Joseph Kennedy said during a meeting, "Neither the Polish nor the British would have made Poland the reason for war, if the support from Washington had not been in the background."

Acknowledgements

Over the years, many people have been generous with their time and expertise to helped me bring this project to completion. I want to express my gratitude to all of them.

In particular, I want to thank my two editors, Susan Hicks and Chris Angermann, whose advice, help with translations, and attention to detail proved invaluable.

Helmuth Lauer, a German historian and curator of the *Heimatliches Foto-Archiv Zweibrücken* in Germany, was kind enought to make available his extensive research, gathered in German and English archives, regarding the Allied bombardment of Zweibruecken. His many contributions and support are much appreciated.

I further want to express my thanks for permission to use material from:

"Colonial, National Historical Park: The Story behind the Scenery," by James N. Haskett, KC Publication, Inc., Las Vegas, for background information on Yorktown, South Carolina.

"Knight's Cross: A Life of Field Marshall Erwin Rommel" by David Frazer, HarperCollins Publishers, 1993.

"ACHESON: The Secretary of State Who Created the American World," by James Chase. Copyright © 1998 by Swain Enterprises, by permission of Simon & Schuster Adult Publishing Group.

"Joachim Peiper 1915-1976," Biblio Verlag GmbH, Bissendorf, Germany.